Advance Prais(*and Rig..... .... Role*

"When you're starting off in this industry, the people who you interact with in the beginning are so important. John Frank Levey saw something in me and gave me the chance early in my career to succeed. Myself and so many others in Hollywood appreciate John and celebrate his accomplishments throughout the years."
-Jessica Chastain, Academy Award-winning actor (first professional job, *ER*)

"To be blunt, the audition is the worst part of acting...greater minds than mine have searched for a better way to get the right actor for the role, and no one has come up with a solution. We can only thank the Lord for wonderful casting directors like John Frank Levey."
-William H. Macy, Emmy and SAG Award-winning actor (*ER*, *Shameless*)

"John Frank Levey not only has an eye for talent, but he also loves talent. Not everyone has both, and most people have neither."
-Rob Lowe, Emmy-nominated and SAG Award-winning actor (*The West Wing*)

"*Right for the Role* is fantastic. Thoughtful, illuminating and just plain fun."
-Lydia Woodward, Emmy-winning writer and producer (*China Beach*, *ER*)

"*ER*'s success was an incredibly diverse ensemble—offering proof of concept for inclusive casting every Thursday night. John Frank Levey was largely responsible for that. He certainly changed my life."
-Noah Wyle, Emmy-nominated and SAG-award winning actor (*ER*)

"One of the things that made me feel so comfortable on *The West Wing* was the fact that all of my castmates had come from very strong NY theatre backgrounds. We had shared experiences that allowed us to bond very quickly. Acting is a team sport and John stacked the bench deep!"
-Allison Janney, Emmy, SAG and Academy Award-winning actor (*The West Wing*)

"It's rare and invaluable to walk into an audition in LA and know, without a shred of doubt, that casting is one hundred percent on your side. It makes you a better actor. That's what John Frank Levey brings and I couldn't be more grateful for it."
-Noel Fisher, actor (*Shameless*)

"The auditioning process is unlike any other job interview… and the environment John creates in the room is an actor's dream. Put simply, my collaborations with John have made me a better artist."
-Shawn Hatosy, actor (*ER, Southland, Animal Kingdom*)

"John's casting sessions offer an abundance of choices, and he keeps the often hair-splitting deliberations that follow auditions focused, sensitive and fun."
-Carol Flint, Emmy-winning writer and producer (*China Beach, ER, The West Wing*)

"Working with John was a master class in the craft of casting, and in the creative joy and passion one can find in collaborating with artists."
-Jinny Howe, former EVP and Head of Television, John Wells Productions (*ER, Southland, Animal Kingdom, Shameless*)

"A true craftsman in this industry, John has always handled his career with such an earnest passion that is truly palpable, whether in the casting room or at a table read on set. I feel so incredibly honored to have had the opportunity to kickstart my career working alongside John as a mentor, colleague, and friend."
-Jacob Weary, actor (*Animal Kingdom*)

"When you work with someone who loves their job, they tend to be relentless in the best possible way. They leave no stone unturned—and that's John."
-Cheo Hodari Coker, NAACP Image Award-winning writer and producer (*Southland*)

"John's innate understanding of script analysis and character description, and then matching that with the right actor is John's singular talent."
-Marg Helgenberger, SAG and Emmy Award-winning actor (*China Beach*)

"The real stars of our industry are casting directors like John. They don't only launch careers but also set us up to be a part of beautiful, unfolding stories."
-Lucy Liu, Emmy-nominated and SAG Award-winning actor (*ER, Southland*)

"John is the type of casting director that truly roots for actors. When you walk into a room with him, you really feel how much he wants you to win."
-Eriq La Salle, Emmy-nominated, SAG-Award winning and NAACP Image Award-winning actor (*ER*)

"John has played a pivotal role, both personally and professionally, in my career. I can't tell you how fortunate I feel to have him as an advocate, and to have had the opportunity to get to know him over the years."
-Dichen Lachman, actor (*Shameless, Animal Kingdom*)

"John Frank Levey is one of the most admired casting directors in our business. I am in awe of his talent, his taste, his generosity and his friendship."
-Anthony "Tony" Sepulveda, Senior VP, Casting, Warner Bros. TV

"I love *Right for the Role* so much—the words are unusual, thoughtful and brilliantly descriptive."
-Mindy Kanaskie, associate producer (*The West Wing*)

"Casting is destiny. We live and die by it. Our visions would never come to life without the right actor for each part. I can't think of a better insight into the magic behind the truth of filmmaking than the lessons in *Right for the Role*."
-William Broyles, Jr., Academy Award-nominated screenwriter and co-creator of *China Beach*

"John is an incredible person and I have learned so much from him throughout the years. Not just how to make a good cast deal, but how to be an honorable human being while doing your best to live life to the fullest."
-Ned Haspel, COO, John Wells Productions

"John is such a soulful human that he just falls in love with the human spirit. You can feel his love for the art form."
-Mariska Hargitay, Emmy Award-winning actor (*ER*)

"Because of John, I got my SAG card, my big break, and am in the second decade of a dream career built on the foundation of his passion, belief and guidance. He is truly one of the greats."
-Josh Gad, actor (first professional job, *ER*)

"John and his team are by far the best casting team I have ever worked with, and I will look forward to every opportunity to work with him again."
-David Nutter, Emmy Award-winning director (*ER, The West Wing, Shameless*)

"John Frank Levey loves actors and does everything he can to make us feel safe and empowered."
-Tim Bagley, actor (*ER, Southland, Shameless*)

"John gave me my first job, and I remember his creativity, generosity, specificity and persistence so clearly many years later. I wouldn't have a career if it weren't for him, and I am forever grateful!"
-Jane Levy, actor (*Shameless*)

Acknowledgments

Thanks to:

Trudi Roth, without whom this would be nothing.
Shari Shaw, for introducing me to Trudi.
Karen, for giving me a second chance at love.
John Wells, for providing me with the opportunity for
meaningful work.
My children, Oliver and Joanna, for not caring
about my
success and loving me as their dad.
Kim Wong, Tawni Tamietti, Melanie Burgess, Cheryl
Kloner, Kevin Scott and Patricia Noland, for making
me better than I could ever be without their dedication
and hard work.
Gary Marsh of Breakdown Services, Ltd., for intro-
ducing me to the first casting directors I ever met and
for allowing
us to use the breakdowns in this book.
Barb Held of the Television Academy, for providing
me with transcripts of my Emmy acceptance speeches.
All the actors who made me look good.
All the writers and directors who I got to collaborate
with.
All the viewers for caring and watching.

ISBN: 978-1-956955-41-5 (ebook)

ISBN: 979-8-9852253-8-9 (paperback)

ISBN: 979-8-9852253-7-2 (hardcover)

RIGHT
FOR THE
ROLE

**BREAKDOWNS, BREAKUPS
AND BREAKTHROUGHS
FROM 35 YEARS OF
CASTING ICONIC
TV SHOWS
INCLUDING *ER*,
THE WEST WING,
SHAMELESS AND MORE**

JOHN FRANK LEVEY
AS TOLD TO TRUDI ROTH

LEGACY
launch pad
PUBLISHING

Contents

Foreword

BY JOHN WELLS

What makes a good casting director? Organizational skills, negotiating prowess, fortitude.

What makes a great casting director? Exceptional taste, integrity, patience, thoughtfulness, an understanding of narrative and text, compassion, joy at discovery, incredible people skills to handle all the lunatic writers and directors stomping through your office, and a love of acting and of actors.

John Frank Levey is a great casting director.

I was fortunate to meet John on only my second job as a writer for television. We both came from the theatre and quickly found that we had a common philosophy in casting—the best actor should always get the part. John is a ferocious advocate for actors and the craft of acting. For the importance of training and attention to professionalism. John believes in acting as alchemy but also as a product of hard work, preparation, and intelligence.

Over the three and a half decades that we've worked together, John has introduced me to thousands of actors he believed in (literally thousands—we cast over five thousand actors on *ER* alone). He fought for them, supported them, encouraged them. Acting is often raw talent and intuition, but

it's never *only* raw talent and intuition. Of equal importance
are listening and training, movement and voice, scene analysis
and the ability to be alive in a scene. John nourishes these
qualities in actors, drawing the best out of actors in auditions
and helping them to succeed. Calming nerves, correcting bad
habits, encouraging and then encouraging even more.
Demanding each actor's best.

Dozens of times, John has called me overflowing with
excitement about an actor he's just met, an audition he can't
wait to share or someone I absolutely have to meet. And he's
never been wrong. Never once. The actor wasn't always right
for the part, but damn, they could always really *act*. We
laughed together endless times in the casting room and wiped
away tears together when actors have absolutely killed in a
scene. We've witnessed true genius and good actors absolutely
tanking. We've been transported by incredible performances
and remarkable talents in bland rooms with terrible lighting.
But always, the actors John brought into those rooms
belonged there. And that is a true gift.

As you read this book and look for insights into acting and
the casting process, understand that John Frank Levey is a
maestro, a savant. Like a musician with perfect pitch, John can
hear the talent underneath a terrible audition and with a swift
comment or adjustment bring out the best in an actor so they
can show their talents. He speaks a language that we don't all
speak, and he translates that language into performance and
something transcendent.

He has been my collaborator and trusted guide to talent
for over a thousand hours of produced television. He's earned
numerous Emmys and industry awards, all richly deserved.
But most remarkably, John has always loved and believed in
the actors he's championed. Every single one of them.

John cares deeply about the craft of acting. He nurtures talent and understands the incredible courage it takes to become an actor. He has much to say: listen. I always have and I'm much the better for it.

John Wells
Los Angeles
November 11, 2021

Introduction

I come from a family of writers. I have never been one (until now). And my father, Stan Levey, a *New York Times* reporter, was famous for boiling down the written word into three simple steps:

Tell them what you're gonna tell them.

Tell them.

Tell them what you told them.

So the first thing you should know is that when I came to Los Angeles, California from New York State in 1973, a newlywed 26-year-old, I didn't know there was such a thing as a casting director.

And then, through some happy accidents, it became not just a job, but a career where I could seek (and find!) community and a greater understanding of myself.

As it turns out, I was right for the role.

So, this is a professional memoir that gives you a behind-the-scenes view of casting groundbreaking shows, including *China Beach, ER, Third Watch, The West Wing, Southland, Animal Kingdom* and *Shameless.* Of course, I'll touch upon others, but we'll go deeper into this handful of iconic series. Likewise, I'll describe some of my personal journey toward living honestly, but fear not: there's just enough there to be of interest and offer perhaps a touch of inspiration without falling into a self-important Hollywood tale.

I hope so, anyway.

Most importantly, like the statues in my home from the Television Academy (Emmy Awards) and the Casting Society of America (Artios Awards), this book is a testament to my successful collaboration with a community of talented people. I have had the unique experience of being part of a shift in American storytelling, where the shows we watch on TV reflect raw, brutal, funny, sexy, eccentric, irrepressible and uniquely American reality.

I'm not talking about "reality TV"—I'm talking about fictional shows driven by characters who are so real they become family to us.

When Dr. Mark Greene, played magnificently by Anthony Edwards, died on *ER*, it hit me almost as hard as either of my parents' deaths. Similarly, Leo McGarry's passing on *The West Wing* was like a punch to the gut—so much worse because his death was compounded by the loss of the wonderful John Spencer, the actor who played him. If you had to pick a person's arms to die in 10,000 miles away from home, I'd venture that a nurse like *China Beach*'s Colleen McMurphy, played with enormous compassion and girl-next-door charm by Dana Delany, would be it.

And on the other end of the spectrum, it's not hard to fall in love with Fiona Gallagher, vividly portrayed on *Shameless* by Emmy Rossum as wise beyond her years but still fun to party with. Or even her dad Frank, who, though arguably the worst father on the planet, is somehow a guy you'd want to have a beer with. (That's all thanks to Bill Macy, who brings his real essence as a lovely, decent, generous human being to an otherwise horrible man.) You can't help but worry about *Animal Kingdom*'s Andrew "Pope" Cody, played poignantly and terrifyingly by Shawn Hatosy, because you know the degree to which he's troubled will have repercussions. And the nuanced way Michael Cudlitz played police officer John Cooper on *South-land*—yearning for love and acceptance yet felt he didn't deserve it—was so relatable to me. I loved that character because he led me to explore that compelling dichotomy and my own sense of masculinity, especially having been raised by a strong and complicated mother.

All of these characters and shows are complex, which is why I believe they resonate with us, hook us and earn a space in our hearts and minds. Notice there's a distinction between *complex* and *complicated*.

Complicated is when you take all the colors in the world, put them together and end up with mud.

Complexity gives everything its distinct color and uses each hue to add depth and meaning without mucking things up.

We all bring our own complexities to bear in life and art, so before we tackle the series I've had the honor to collaborate on, I'd like to give you a bit of my background. Instead of hundreds of pages that only my mother might have read, we'll do this with a handful of casting breakdowns and a few vignettes that would perhaps be a part of a pilot episode.

In my life, I've played many roles: Innocent kid. Enabling son. Estranged son. Nervous new parent. Workaholic. Dedicated family man. Divorcée. Company man. Long-term partner. Entrepreneur. And now, of all surprising things, author.

All of this has shaped my casting process, and as the book progresses, you'll see how it all fits. That's the funny thing about writing a memoir: life doesn't have a narrative, but we sure do like trying to shape a message, a flow and a moral to the story.

One more note:

There is no claim from me that it is *the* truth. This is a subjective account.

It's just how I stored the events of my life and career.

I did that without a plan. I did that, like so much of my life, by accident. Here's my attempt to share with you my recollections from the start.

[JOHNNY LEVEY, BABY OF THE FAMILY]

(6 to 10 years old)

This skinny, young child doesn't know a thing about anything—and that's a blessing. His parents, Stanley and Sylvia, are serious people—not exactly well matched, but in the 1950s, divorce isn't an option.

To break up the family tension, Johnny discovers humor. The first time he found out that he was funny was at breakfast when he got his brother Robbie to spit milk out of his nose. From then on, Johnny was always a crack-up or chasing the other kind of "crack" he loves—the crack of a baseball bat hitting a ball.

I was born in 1947, a notorious year in baseball and America. Jackie Robinson joined the Brooklyn Dodgers. I lived in the Bronx, and the Yankees did too. The Giants played across the river in Manhattan. I'd never been to Brooklyn; it was like a different planet.

My family was ahead of its time, or rather, my mother, Sylvia, was an academician and a scientist. She was also apparently a member of the Communist Party, albeit briefly. My father, Stanley, was undoubtedly a liberal Democrat but a conservative person. In those days, being a newspaperman was fancy.

I have an older brother, Robert (Robbie as a boy, Bob as a grown man), who's just under two years ahead of me. The best times we had when we were boys were summers when our family went to Martha's Vineyard. *New York Times* intellectuals were a big contingent who summered on the Vineyard: the husbands typically arrived Thursday night on the last ferry and left Monday morning on the first ferry to go back to the City to work. And the moms and the kids were on the island for six weeks.

Pure bliss.

When Robbie and I were young boys, Mom would deposit us on the beach in Menemsha with a dollar bill tucked into the little pockets inside of our swimsuits. We'd play on the beach for hours, collecting driftwood and dozens of shells. At lunchtime, we'd walk up to Poole's Fish Market, slap down the buck Mom had given us, and buy a dozen raw clams and a Coke. Just before sunset, Mom would pick us up and take us home, and we'd busy ourselves building mobiles with our seaside treasures and a bit of nylon fishing wire until supper— bluefish, striped bass or lobster when we were feeling flush.

When I got into my teens, the highlight of the season (for me at least) was playing softball against our father. Once I even remember hitting the ball over my father's head. These games were the only times I remember him watching me play ball, even though I played on teams through high school.

At any rate, he wasn't the person who imbued me with my love of baseball.

As my parents both worked full-time, my brother and I needed someone to watch over us. They hired a woman named Millie Crawford, who came from one of the Carolinas (wherever the hell that was). Millie lived in Harlem (wherever the hell that was). As a kid, all I cared about was the place she took me to, which was the incredible world of Dodger baseball. She'd even been to Brooklyn to see them play—wow!

We listened to Dodger games on the radio as Millie did her work, mainly in the kitchen. She talked about the game and especially about Jackie Robinson. She told me about her experiences being Black in America—though I didn't understand it politically, I understood it emotionally.

By the time I was 10, I had my all-time favorite player picked out: Hank Aaron of the Milwaukee Braves. Hammerin' Hank was a champ, and he beat the dreaded Yankees in the '57 World Series. That made me a Braves fan. I didn't love the Dodgers again until they (and I) both made our home in Los Angeles.

These were among my happiest childhood memories.

───

[TEEN JOHNNY]

(14 to 18 years old)

A high school freshman in 1961—the year his mother called "the upside-down year"—Johnny reacts to his family's implosion by spending more time with friends and developing the skill of playing the fool.

Outwardly he seems confident, strong, and secure, ready to fight for

everyone else's rights. But the truth is, inside, he's fractured; The Miracles'
"Tracks of My Tears" is the theme song for this budding optimistic cynic.

As a child of divorce, I experienced the confusion and pain of being left behind. My father was off on his new life in Manhattan with his new wife. Robbie, on his journey to be "Bob," would soon follow as he went off to the University of Chicago to study journalism.

This left Mom and 14-year-old me in the "family" home. The breakup badly damaged her self-worth, and while I did try mightily, I was not the answer. I promised myself then and there that if I were to marry, I'd make it work somehow.

Ultimately, that was a vow I was unable to keep. (More on that later.)

Spending time and energy trying to figure out what happened to my parents' marriage (or eventually my own) was a futile but irresistible exercise. So, like all good clowns who cry on the inside, I did my damndest to laugh on the outside.

This wasn't difficult in my "ethical culture" school, the Fieldston School, which I attended from kindergarten through 12th grade. Just minutes from the house, it was an excellent education that taught my classmates and me a great deal about how to think and how to be part of the world. While there were plenty of good times, a pair of memorable moments stand out in my mind, not least of all because they were two of the most defining historical events of our times. Both took place when I was 16 years old in 1963.

The first was at the tail end of summer in August. I had an older cousin whom I adored, Judy Heintz, a politically passionate, warm and risk-taking young woman. She was part of the Congress of Racial Equality (CORE). At her urging, we got on a bus in Manhattan to travel to Washington, DC to attend a demonstration. As I recall, we sang "We Shall Over-come" repeatedly all night long. I'm sure the people sitting near me were horrified because the song "Johnny One Note" was written for me.

Finally, as dawn began to break, we arrived. We made our way to just outside the Lincoln Memorial, right by the pond, and were among the first people there. As a theatre lover, I quickly assessed our seats from a stage perspective: a perfect location. We were in the down right corner—the equivalent of orchestra seats—sitting on a bucolic grassy patch. Thrilled to be at the now-famous March on Washington, I managed to stay awake for several speeches.

And then, as my story goes, just as Dr. Martin Luther King Jr. spoke about having a dream, so too was I having a dream. I slept through the whole iconic speech.

Later that year, on a fateful day in November just before Thanksgiving, I twisted my ankle during basketball practice. The coach sent me downstairs to get it taped, and while I was sitting there, the report came through a crackling transistor radio that President Kennedy, an early hero who taught us all the word "charisma," had been shot.

In a daze, I limped back upstairs to the gym and inter-rupted a drill to tell my teammates and coaches the awful news. Because I was adept at playing the fool, I recall being pelted with basketballs and perhaps a sneaker or two.

Nobody believed me, although devastatingly, it was true.

By the time I was a high school senior (1965), my class-mates and I were more than ready to leave all the events of our high school behind, along with our childhoods. The last few weeks of school, a handful of wealthy Fieldston dads gave their offices over to us teens for some sort of pseudo-business internships. While I was itching to try something new, I knew deep down that corporate life would never be for me. I decided to try out for the senior play to get out of it, figuring I might get a small part and a chance to hang out with the girl I was interested in.

As luck would have it, I got the lead, and she didn't get

any part. So, I didn't get what I was really after—her—but I did discover that I enjoyed acting. Then again, it's not like I didn't know how to put on a façade to keep my audience entertained—elevating my mom's spirits was part of my daily repertoire.

The lucky/not-so-lucky streak continued, as the play we selected, *Camino Real* by Tennessee Williams, turned out to be unacceptable and inappropriate. If you're not familiar with the play, it's pretty surreal. A key plot point entailed having my character, Kilroy, hooking up with a gypsy's daughter. Magically, her virginity was always restored at a monthly fiesta.

A while into rehearsals, the school principal dropped by and, within minutes, put the kibosh on the play. As progressive as Fieldston was, sex was too controversial. War, on the other hand, was just fine. We ended up quickly switching gears to a production of a French play by Jean Giraudoux, translated into English by Christopher Fry, called *Tiger at the Gates*. It's all about fake news, derailing protestors and warmongering. (Rings sadly true over a half-century later.)

Why? was frequently on our lips during those turbulent times. The answer, my friend, is blowing in the wind, as Bob Dylan warbled.

Learning that life lesson at such a young age, whether related to fighting racial inequity, comprehending a familial breakup, or losing a hero like JFK, may well be the one good thing to come from anguish, disillusion, injustice and loss.

All one can do is continue moving forward and recognize that doors burst open and slam shut all the time. Often simultaneously. By the time I left the Bronx, I understood the contradictions of life quite well. And now I had a collection of masks to hide behind—it would be years before I learned how to be comfortable revealing myself.

[COLLEGE BOY/20-SOMETHING JOHNNY]

(18 to 25 years old)

This long-haired hippie lives for what college is all about in the mid-late 1960s: community. A psychology major with a concentration in theatre, he's conflicted—while his friends are dedicated to the picket line, his true devotion is to the theatre. One community feeds his conscience; the other his creativity.

Johnny does his best to balance both; after all, equality, justice and peace are part of all the stories being told at that time. (The most interesting ones, anyway.) Without realizing it, the dramatic tension settles into his soul, making him permanently a product of the '60s, drawn to people and situations that prioritize cooperation and collaboration alongside creativity, where stories are told with meaning and heart, absurdity and humor.

In what had become a pattern in my life, my arrival at the University of Rochester was purely accidental. I wanted to go to California for college, to San Francisco State University. But my father was worried about the political climate in 1965, and he knew that I was big on attending demonstrations. So Dad told me he wouldn't pay for San Francisco State, and instead, because both he and my mother were Rochester alums, they pulled some strings to get me in. I don't remember even applying, but lo and behold, I was accepted to join the class of 1969.

When I headed up to Rochester for summer orientation, I met a girl called Betsy Swift, who helped me continue my serendipitous journey. She looked like the luscious, sweet, braided maiden that graced Vermont Maid maple syrup labels. I was instantly lovestruck.

Or at least lust-struck.

"What are you going to study, Johnny?" Betsy asked after

mentioning that she was considering becoming a theatre major.

And while I thought, "*You would be a good thing to study,*" I heard myself say out loud, "I'm going to be an actor."

Did I have any real interest in acting? Despite my short-lived star turn in high school, not really. I was just trying on a mask in that accidental effort to define myself and to woo a girl. If I had any chance of studying what I was really interested in, I figured I'd better go to the extracurricular acting meeting my first week at school. That way, the next time I saw her, there would be some truth to what I told her.

Back to the dumb luck files, Betsy never showed. A couple of years later, I heard she'd traveled to Africa and sent back a ton of ganja to her friends—which made me wish we had stayed in touch beyond that fateful freshman orientation. But thanks to her, I ended up being involved in theatre for all four years at Rochester. And I became part of a small, tightly knit band of friends who created a theatre major at the college and also founded a summer theatre.

More thick irony in my college years: my father banned me from going to California because of my demonstration inclinations, but Rochester was no different. We didn't finish a single year because, being student activists, we were on strike by February or March. It felt like I was perpetually at a sit-in or a demonstration, although I was one of only a few of my friends who went to class—because class meant rehearsal for plays.

I also enjoyed studying psychology. And that's worked out well because my understanding of human nature is one of my key attributes, I think.

Altogether, my years in Rochester solidified my outlook as an optimistic cynic. Faith is hard to hold on to—in people, ideas and institutions—but disillusioning experiences tend to stick. That said, it's my experience that even the most crushing disappointments have an upside. The transitions and

changes that have filled me with dread, fear and anxiety
turned out to be opportunities where I've made great friends.
At the University of Rochester, I had a spectacular four years
that included a profoundly satisfying communal living
situation.

The inscription on the cover of the University's 1969
"Interpres" yearbook did an excellent job of describing the
transformation my classmates and I underwent. It read:

"My face is a kaleidoscopic image in a process of
absorbing and casting away...growing and changing and
becoming."

That process of becoming is ultimately a lifelong
endeavor; however, those early years in the mid-to-late '60s for
me were especially dynamic and formative.

Upon graduation, I extended my upstate New York run
for a few more years, living with my friends in a community,
first in the dairy country outside of Rochester, and later in the
Catskills. I worked for Strong Memorial Hospital's suicide
prevention service and also taught continuing education
classes in acting.

An interesting juxtaposition.

I actually have vivid memories of playing poker with
psychiatrists and other doctors who took me for just another
dazed and confused hippie. In this case, wearing a mask
worked out great; it was the ultimate poker face. I won nearly
all of the time.

As part of my weekend routine, I would frequently tag
along with friends who were in the band North to the Red
Creek Inn in Henrietta—a great local joint with steamed
clams and draft beer on the menu where they played regularly.
North was good enough to go big, but on their way to
achieving fame and fortune, a gig playing the Playboy Club in
New Jersey led to their downfall. (But that's a story for another
memoir.)

It was there that I met Blaine McLaughlin, who was

bartending and, in her spare time, attending the Rochester Institute of Technology after graduating from Northwestern.

She was beautiful.

I was persistent.

She was…dating the owner of the Red Creek Inn.

I was charming and flirty and not stalking or disgusting (if memory serves me).

Eventually, she relented, and Blaine and I had many wonderful adventures together. The most memorable was going to visit my mom in Nairobi, Kenya. When I went to college, despite all of my mother's extraordinary accomplishments—which included being among the first women to get a PhD from Columbia in one of the hard sciences—Mom was a bit lost. She didn't want to be alone in that house of horrors where she had been left by first my father, then Bob, and ultimately me.

So, she decided to change her life by applying for a Fulbright Fellowship. Mom got it after being carefully investigated because, as I've mentioned, she had been a leftist in the '40s when my brother and I were babies.

How do I know her application was scrutinized?

Because despite my mind-altering proclivities at the time, my sixth sense about being followed proved true—it wasn't just pot-induced paranoia. After about a day and a half of feeling like I was being watched, a straight-looking guy followed me into the bathroom at the University of Rochester auditorium. I suspected it was because of my involvement with Students for a Democratic Society (SDS), but not so. He took up residence at the urinal next to me and started asking me questions about my mom's "affiliations."

Suffice to say I was uncomfortable talking about my mom in general and certainly not while urinating. I'm pretty sure he got nothing out of me.

Luckily she passed her background check and was sent to Addis Ababa in Ethiopia to teach. She became so embedded in the African community that after her three-year stint in Addis Ababa, she went to Nairobi and stayed for another six years.

Blaine and I traveled to visit her in Africa by way of London, Amsterdam and Sweden and had a sensational trip. I remember vividly being on the beach in Tanzania and walking around a mile out into glorious water that got no deeper than our waists.

All of that and more is to simply say, how could we not fall in love? I don't remember asking Blaine to marry me, but I know that she said yes.

The newlyweds

Back in upstate New York, we were both a bit adrift "professionally." I worked a few random handyman jobs in the Catskills (I had no skills) before we decided to tie the knot. The drive from our Catskills mountain house to Washington, DC to get hitched at my brother's house was full of signs that the time to move on was imminent.

As it often does in the Northeast, it had rained or maybe snowed, warmed a bit and then froze again.

The trees were all covered in ice, and the whole world sparkled.

The promise of a shiny new life.

We were married in Bob's living room by a judge who was later implicated in the Watergate scandal. We stood before him and realized that we had forgotten either the flowers or the rings after smoking a joint upstairs—maybe both.

Our hippie antics did not amuse our families. I remember looking at the sea in front of us, grandmothers sitting side by side. Jews (mine) and Catholics (hers). Northerners and Southerners. (Ditto.) Although it was my grandmother on my mother's side who was overheard by someone saying, "at least she's white."

Which made me even more ready to get on with our new life.

That said, I always look back fondly and gratefully on my formative years in Rochester.

It was there, deeply steeped in the values of the '60s, that the seeds of becoming a successful casting director started to take root. I learned that I love to be part of a team, and settling into my role and doing it as well as I could was the most incredible feeling.

When you're part of a working community, nobody's scanning your face to see if you're showing up truthfully or not. Because if you're in flow and progress is being made, the fact is, you are.

[YOUNG MARRIED JOHNNY]

(26 to 32 years old)

This guy with a new wife is ready for a new life. As luck would have it, they land in Los Angeles. Johnny sports a fresh haircut and decides to try on a new identity in Hollywood. The thing is, he didn't know enough about himself yet to know what mask he should try on. All he did know was whatever the next move was, it was all about feeding his soul, not selling it.

The theme song for this phase was really about one great line from The Band's "The W.S. Walcott Medicine Show" about preferring to die happy to being immortal.

Moving to California was a great decision. As usual, it was kind of an accident, a twist of fate that helped make some unconscious desire materialize in the present. It wasn't like Blaine and I sat down to write a list of pros and cons. No way! We were loose and free, easy and honestly, naïve. We sent a handful of letters (remember them?) to friends in Chicago, San Francisco and Los Angeles and agreed that whoever responded first, we'd crash at their place.

LA was the lucky winner (or maybe we were).

We left our car at Blaine's parents' place in southern Ohio and took a bus to Chicago to get on a train headed west.

More signs: a tornado tore through Blaine's folks' neighborhood and toppled a tree onto our car. But who needs a car in LA?

At any rate, we splurged on a sleeper car, being newlyweds and all, using the cash gifts we got from the wedding—all $100 bills. Whenever we had to pay for a meal on the train we had to use a C-note. The porters started calling me "fistful of dollars" after a Clint Eastwood movie that was popular at the time.

The signs continued. Something happened to the train in Bakersfield, and we were ushered into a small plane and flown into LAX. All we really knew about California was what Mama Cass told us: we'd be safe and warm if we were in LA.

Bullshit.

So much for the ideal that the Mamas and the Papas and Albert Hammond sold us about how it never rains in Southern California.

It was fucking pouring.

We somehow got to Santa Monica to our friends' place. It proceeded to come down like crazy for four or five days.

Good thing we didn't believe in signs because shortly after that, we experienced our first earthquake. Eventually, the rain and the earth-shaking stopped; we found our own place and began to settle in.

Of course, initially, I thought I wanted to be an actor.

I was cute enough.

I was funny.

I was creative.

I had some charisma.

And I didn't know who the hell I was. (Photos: Steven Schwartz)

I was hiding and pretending. Actors have their experiences and their imagination out of which they create characters. If they are hiding and pretending, they can never do anything else.

Ironically, my first job in LA was selling crystal balls. Not for predicting the future—the psychedelic kind that refracted light and projected rainbows, cool! Actually, I would've enjoyed the predictive kind at that phase of my life, as I didn't have a clue where I was headed.

I wasn't the only one. Shortly after we arrived, my new father-in-law asked me clumsily if "there was *any* hope for my future."

I assured him I thought there was, although inside I wasn't the least bit certain.

My second job was at an acting school I attended shortly after I arrived in LA, called the Academy of Stage and Cinema Arts (ASCA). Three guys were running the place: Bob Ellenstein, an actor who enjoyed some success in film television and the theatre; David Alexander, a director with considerable success in television; and Michael Dewell, the business director. Bob and David taught, and Michael kept the whole ship afloat.

At ASCA, I took a scene study class with Bob, did some acting work, taught a teen acting class, and directed other students' scenes. I also did odd jobs like mopping the space and cleaning the bathrooms, which provided me with a scholarship and a bit of pocket change.

The job was fun and demanding, and it created a sense of family. Bob often had us over to his house for potluck provided mainly by his wife, Lois. It made Los Angeles finally feel comfortable and welcoming.

About six months into my stint at ASCA, Michael invited Blaine and me to dinner. He lived in Benedict Canyon in a lovely home with a pool and lavish gardens. For East Coast kids like us, it was quite splendid.

Michael's wife was Nina Foch, a genuine movie star in her day who had previously been married to James Lipton of *Inside the Actors Studio*. When we met her, she was a very well-known acting teacher in LA with a reputation for serious toughness.

We were seated at the dining room table, awkwardly trying to make pleasant conversation. I remember thinking how small, thin and angular Michael looked compared to Nina. She had a few years on him, and she seemed regal.

At some point, Nina said something that Blaine found odd, so my wife blurted out, "Give me a break, Nina."

Nina flipped.

"Give you a break? You spoiled children in your generation have had nothing but breaks. You don't know the first thing about earning what you get!"

That was just the beginning of an aggressive and unpleasant tirade that continued for what seemed like forever. Blaine could be pretty reserved and shy, but not under that attack.

She ordered me, "Let's go home," and we left unceremoniously in the middle of the meal.

I remember that we laughed in the car before we drove back to our apartment in Santa Monica. I worried that it might impact my job, but I was also quite taken by Blaine's bravery.

No one ever spoke of it again.

That was the first time (and certainly not the last) that I witnessed celebrity-driven entitlement on display. I took it as both a warning signal and an education.

As time progressed, I realized that my calling wasn't on screen but somewhere behind the scenes. Also, I needed to shift gears and start making a good living because I was about to step into the most important role of my life: Dad.

At the time, Blaine and I were living in a cute place behind a duplex. One side had our new friends, Kenny and

Susie, and the other was occupied by the owner's nephew, a former child actor.

Show business and flowers were blooming everywhere.

Susie got pregnant in the fall of 1975, and Blaine was pregnant five weeks later. Kenny said, "It's in the water," and I tried to tell him that wasn't how women got pregnant.

I was never sure what he believed.

My mom came to visit right after we found out that Blaine was pregnant. There were already strain-induced fissures in their relationship, so I think it gave us all a touch of morning sickness. At any rate, Mom was delighted by the news of her impending grandma status and famously said, "This changes everything."

An understatement.

Oliver Leo Levey was born on July 26, 1976. It was a glorious event, although Blaine was exhausted; it had been a long and difficult delivery. Of course, this was long before cell phones. When I went back to a friend's place to make calls to tell family and friends, I couldn't reach anyone.

With a new baby, I knew I needed a more stable work situation. And so, I inadvertently landed somewhere that ultimately would become a part of my life and career: Breakdown Services.

Gary Marsh, a shrewd businessman and lovely guy, launched the brilliant business of providing character descriptions from new projects to talent managers and agents in 1971. I joined Gary's team in 1977 as a field rep who would go around to casting directors at studio offices to see if they had scripts they needed breakdowns for.

I loved being a part of the action and knowing what was coming next.

I met many casting people in my travels, of course, but nothing registered (yet) that this might be a career move for me.

What I do remember are some fun, colorful and wacky experiences, from being chased by a female casting director hungry to cast someone in the role of a lover (I ended up playing a heartbreaker instead) to late-night visits to actor collectives who were illegally getting breakdowns without paying for them. This was my first time playing "the heavy," which came in handy later in my professional life.

As the '70s drew to a close, I still was trying on masks. However, there was a truthfulness that shone through.

I've always been straightforward, regardless of whether it's been poorly or wonderfully received. I've been faithful to my word about who I am and what I want. And I think people know what to expect from me. I don't think I'm terribly surprising.

In some ways, I'm predictable, or better yet, consistent.

Life, however, isn't any of those things. The next phase proved to be a true challenge, personally and professionally.

But now that you've discovered a bit about me, you can also see what goes into becoming a casting director. It's not a solo gig at all—it's a group effort. There is strength in the collective, made even more durable by talented leaders like my longtime boss, John Wells, for example. Success is sowed in a field of inclusivity and collaboration.

So while some casting directors have an encyclopedic knowledge of who played what role and use that intelligence as a blueprint for their work, I'm not that way.

As a product of the '60s, I'm a "vibist."

I know what you are when I'm sitting in a room with you. I get you, and I get a sense of where to put you. From my summers as a boy on Martha's Vineyard making mobiles out of driftwood and shells, I understand aesthetic balance. When you've got a fiery, passionate, wild-child George Clooney in one corner, you have to balance him out with a level-headed, pragmatic Anthony Edwards in the other.

My bottom-line advice to actors, aspiring casting directors and everyone in between is simply this: Keep figuring out who you are so you can be yourself with honesty and delight, humor and absurdity.

ONE

The Training Ground

THE THEATRE

[THEATRE DIRECTOR JOHN LEVEY]

(32 to 38 years old)

This 30-something is beginning to step into his adult self as John, no longer Johnny. While all his dreams are coming true with a directing fellowship at the Mark Taper Forum, home of LA's famed Center Theatre Group, his worst nightmares are also coming to fruition as his nearly four-year-old son battles leukemia.

If there's a song playing on the radio in John's reef blue Karmann Ghia on the way to the Taper, it's Judy Collins crooning the Joni Mitchell classic "Both Sides Now."

From childhood, I have always loved the theatre. My introduction to it, like so many other seismic shifts in my life, came courtesy of a painful experience. On the heels of her divorce and the implosion of our family, my mother began taking me into Manhattan to see off-Broadway plays.

At the time, I was appropriately lost, as most 14-year-old boys are; I hadn't found anything that lit my fuse or got me interested, well, in anything. As was typical of Mom, the shows she selected for us were inappropriate beyond belief—in a great way. She took me to plays that I had no business seeing, that I didn't understand, and that I had to react to intuitively.

So, we spent a lot of time seeing off-off-Broadway shows in Greenwich Village, like Samuel Beckett's absurdist, one-person play *Krapp's Last Tape*, where a 69-year-old man reflects on his life using a recurring banana motif that represents unfulfilled goals. (I'm sure at the time, I thought the banana stood for something else.) We also soaked in ennui and angst watching Edward Albee's *The Zoo Story* (which I later directed and acted in during college).

Not all of our theatre-going involved avant-garde works— I remember loving *Guys and Dolls*, for example. And I had a life-changing moment seeing Richard Burton's *Hamlet* at the Lunt-Fontanne Theatre in the early summer of 1964. Not that it had anything to do with the action on the stage...

We had great seats, a few rows back on the aisle in the orchestra section. At the end of the curtain call, just as the lights came down on stage, a woman in the first row stood up and started to walk up the aisle. She reached my row just as the lights began to come back up.

It was Elizabeth Taylor. Her violet eyes (not to mention other things that came in pairs that a teenage boy couldn't help but notice) were quite spectacularly alluring. It was clear she was escaping early so she wouldn't detract from her newly wedded husband in his moment of glory. And as a result, I had a moment of glory from my first brush with a bona-fide superstar.

Later, as I was finishing high school, we caught *America Hurrah* by Jean-Claude van Itallie, described as "an early expression of the burgeoning American counterculture." In the end, the actors decimated everything on the stage, which I thought was fantastic.

Destruction seemed like a positive action at the time.

But perhaps the most memorable performance to me was one that had nothing to do with megawatt actors, mind-blowing absurdity or high-profile plays. It hit close to home because it was a moment of heart-stopping failure, redeemed by a magnificent performance by a nine-year-old Black actress. I only wish I remembered her name and that of the show, which was a series of short plays.

At any rate, her piece was about race relations and school desegregation in Mississippi. Keep in mind that while segregation legally ended in 1954 with the landmark case *Brown v. The Board of Education*, it wasn't until 1970 that Mississippi was forced by federal authorities to suspend their 95-year-old "separate but equal" school system.

So in the mid-'60s, it was a hot-button topic, loaded with meaning and importance.

In the midst of an impassioned monologue about her experience integrating in a Mississippi elementary school, the young actress lost her lines.

The quiet stretched for what seemed like an eternity as she rummaged her mind, searching for what she was supposed to say.

Finally, without breaking character at all, she strongly said, *"line."*

A stage manager whispered two or three words to her from off stage, and miraculously, it all fell back in.

Hallelujah.

I remember thinking this must be what religious people experience in mosques, temples and churches. The physical theatre delivered transcendence unlike anywhere else for me. The experience of watching people reveal themselves through storytelling felt sacred.

Sitting in a dark theatre, I discovered what would become the thrust of my life: my interest in human beings and human nature. I always want to know what happened and why.

The stories that evolve from the simplest acts are the ones that fascinate me most. I think it's partially because my family was dramatic and also because plays showed me that everyone is subject to the absurdities of life.

This is why I created a theatre major with my peers in college. It led me to take memorable summer jobs, first at home in New York City, and later, as a founding member of a summer theatre group in Rochester.

One of my favorite theatre jobs was running sound and lights for an off-Broadway psychedelic production of *A Midsummer Night's Dream* at the Theatre de Lys on Christopher Street in the summer of 1967. (Today, it's known as the Lucille Lortel Theatre.)

This was not a Richard Burton Shakespearean production; as I recall, Titania, queen of the fairies, was played by a 6'4" transvestite. And the sprite Puck had a strobe light in his jockstrap that started to blink every time Titania came on stage. It was creative and memorable, and it starred wonderful actors, including Gloria Foster, Alvin Epstein and a teenage Susan Anton.

By my junior year, our summer theatre was in full swing, and I was directing multiple productions, about 20 or so plays throughout my time in Rochester. Finally, a cross-country trip with a van full of friends—my first trip to California—broke my summertime streak and ended my initial run as a director.

A few years later, when Blaine and I fortuitously settled in Los Angeles, I, of course, had a return to directing on my mind. But my ambitions were put on the backburner as I worked for ASCA and Breakdown Services to support my young family.

Ironically, it was hippies who brought me back to the theatre in late 1979. Several friends of mine were part of a company called the New Artef Players, dedicated to exploring the complexities of modern Jewish life. One member of the ensemble brought a play to my attention called *The Night of the 20th* by Israeli playwright Joshua Sobol.

The piece was about a group of Eastern European youths who formed an early kibbutz in what was to become Israel. Of course, the play was in Hebrew, which I neither read nor spoke, so I had to get it translated—and I loved it. It was a fantastic expression of the counterculture, all about these kids ditching the politics and social and sexual repression of their parents' generation and culture to form their own identity.

This search for identity hit home for me. After all, I was doing the same—developing into my own person, leading a life that felt honest and real.

With Blaine's blessing, I took on *Night of the 20th* as a side project. The show played at a space right across from the flagship Tower Records on the Sunset Strip. Getting the gig alone was a stroke of incredible luck, and it quickly got even better.

One of the actors in the show, Jeremy Lawrence, was the partner of the Mark Taper Forum's director of audience development: a lovely guy called Robert (Bob) Schlosser. Jeremy kept telling Bob how great he thought the show was and that I was doing a good job at directing. Bob came to a dress rehearsal and agreed. When the show opened, he brought Taper's artistic director, Gordon Davidson, and producer/director/actor Jules Irving to see it.

Fortuitous connections were opening unimaginable doors once again.

This brings us to the spring of 1980, the most dramatic time of my life. Two life-changing things happened at once when Blaine, Oli and I were in Washington, DC for my brother Bob's wedding.

Somehow Gordon Davidson got my brother's phone number and called to offer me an NEA directing fellowship. I accepted it on the spot, both thrilled and terrified.

My mixed reaction had nothing to do with the opportunity, and, of course, everything to do with it.

Oli was limping and very pale. He tried to keep up all day with his slightly older cousins.

He couldn't.

My mom had spent a lot of her professional life around cancer research. She took one look at Oli and told us she suspected he had some form of cancer.

When we got back to LA, we went straight to the pediatrician. We huddled in his office while Oli played in the area for kids.

The doctor looked at us with serious eyes and said, "What do you know about leukemia?"

The answer was nothing—nothing at all.

The truth was I thought it meant that he would die. My mother's words when she learned of the pregnancy came flying back at me: "This changes everything."

And it did.

A father's job is to protect his children, and I couldn't help but feel that I had failed.

Feeling hopeless and helpless, I threw myself into the opportunity at the Taper. There was some cruel irony at work there, too: the woman who wrote grants missed the NEA's deadline, so the original fellowship fell through. Thankfully, Gordon decided to create a special fellowship for me paid from the Taper budget, which gave me hope and a purpose.

The more I got into my work and life at the Taper, the more Blaine dedicated her life to Oli, the less connection we had.

This sounds very black and white, and, of course, it wasn't. I went to almost all of Oli's appointments at the UCLA Children's Hospital, so it wasn't as if I was totally unavailable. When he had to get a spinal tap, he sat on my lap with his arms around my neck, belly to belly.

Oli was brave and miserable.

Who wouldn't be?

Finally, he went into remission—not too long after diagnosis. But the treatments continued for quite some time after. And they were, in many ways, more pernicious than the disease itself.

I give all credit to Blaine for quite literally willing Oli back to health. She spent years down on her hands and knees, tending to his every need and infusing him with the life force of her maternal love. I was grateful to have her in a single-minded pursuit of our son's full recovery.

And at the time, Blaine was proud of the work I was getting to do in my life, so we weren't totally fractured.

Yet.

My role at the Taper was busy and varied. One of the things I did most was help develop new plays. The usual suspects included someone from the literary department who would be the dramaturg, the playwright, the actors collected by a casting director and me.

We would rehearse each play for three or four days. Finally, there would be a presentation to the Taper's staff of these new plays, some of which would get chosen to be developed further.

This particular aspect of my job, in many ways, was a great training ground for a career in casting. Working on those new plays, I gained tremendous insight into the writer's perspective. The rest of what I did at the Taper helped me better understand a director's perspective. And the intensive work with actors (both at the Taper and previously) helped me develop and refine my approach to communicating with them.

All of these skills, in my opinion, are enormously important to be successful as a casting director. So, once again, life was beginning to move me in a new direction, unbeknownst to me.

Because, of course, at the time, I believed my trajectory was to create productions for the stage. I helped produce the Taper's literary cabaret at the Itchy Foot, a restaurant down the street from the theatre. And I directed a couple of devel-

opmental productions as part of a new play festival at the
Taper's second stage, Taper, Too—*Cakewalk* and *Estonia You
Fall*, which starred two actors who later became icons in the
field, John Astin (perhaps best known as Gomez Addams from
The Addams Family TV show) and Dennis Dugan (both a
talented actor and director, who has notably directed several
Adam Sandler films, including *Happy Gilmore*.)

Once, I remember walking into the theatre after
rehearsing *Cakewalk* all day. It was pitch black, just the outlines
of the seats visible. In that intimate moment, I thought, "Look
out, Johnny, your dreams all came true." To share that feeling
with my wife and mom on opening night was the icing on the
cake.

But perhaps the most incredible opportunity during my
three-year stint at the Taper was to act as the assistant to
whoever was directing the main stage production. And I was
extremely fortunate to work with some accomplished directors, actors, writers and producers.

During the 1982–1983 season, I assisted Douglas Turner
Ward with the West Coast premiere of *A Soldier's Story*, which
starred a young Denzel Washington. Douglas was the co-
founder of New York's trailblazing off-Broadway theatre
group, the Negro Ensemble Company. I remember picking
him up from the airport, where he was the last person off the
plane and dressed in jeans and a t-shirt. I was expecting a
fancy NYC theatre director in a suit, so I almost missed him.
We didn't get off to the best start, but my coffee-fetching abili-
ties made up for my initial faux pas.

Working on that play was meaningful to me for several
reasons, but most of all because I became very close friends
with the incredibly talented Larry Riley, who played CJ
Memphis (both in the theatrical production and later in the
film based on the play). He won an Obie and a Clarence
Derwent Award for his work in the off-Broadway production
of *A Soldier's Story*.

Larry and I clicked on many levels aside from our love of the theatre. In *A Soldier's Story*, he played centerfielder for the troop's baseball team, and he also was a blues musician who played guitar and sang during the show. He brought honesty to those aspects of his character because baseball and the blues were his passion, too. (And mine as well.) He was a wonderful guy with so much energy who went on to play the first Black series regular, Frank Williams, in *Knots Landing*.

I remember Larry used to camp out in Venice on his days off, and he'd say to me, "Damn, John, these women are riding by on their roller skates in almost no clothes. I'm in real trouble!"

That turned out to be prophetic. A few years later, Larry died of complications related to AIDS, which he attributed to his womanizing ways. Losing him brought home the devastation of that pandemic to me in a very personal way.

Back to the Taper and the next project I worked on: the West Coast premiere of Jules Pfeiffer's play *Grown Ups*. While working with director John Madden (who later directed the Oscar-winning film *Shakespeare in Love*) was professionally exciting, it was some personal milestones that made this production memorable.

Oli was doing much better—a piece of his "artwork" hung on the refrigerator on the *Grown Ups* set, which was thrilling. It felt life-affirming and hopeful. The show itself is somewhat the opposite, about an acrimonious Jewish family who really can't get along. Cheryl Giannini, a wonderful New York stage actress who originated the role on Broadway, played the depressed wife, Louise. And the smart-alecky nine-year-old daughter, Edie, was played by an endearing Jennifer Dundas. The three of us, along with Jennifer's mother and Oli, spent a memorable day at Disneyland.

This lighthearted interlude was helpful, as my next Taper assignment was assisting the American premiere of the Kafka classic *Metamorphosis*, adapted and directed by British playwright, author, actor, and most of all, *enfant terrible,* Steven Berkoff.

The latter was a role he had cultivated with care, but it seemed to me that he was way too old to maintain. Steven was around 45 at the time—funny what my perspective of what "old" was.

His intensity was amazing. It always felt to me like he wore his bravado like a tight black t-shirt.

Steven had starred in the show in London, and now he was directing Brad Davis in the surrealistic piece about a bland little bureaucratic man who transforms himself into an insect. The set was a giant jungle gym made of metal piping. When the insect emerged, the actor crawled, climbed and skittered high into the maze of metal.

It was exhilarating and innovative theatre and unlike anything the Taper audience had ever seen. Some loved it and others, not so much.

I sat on the steps next to Steven, high up in the center section, poised to take notes as he barked them at me.

Not even halfway through, subscription patrons began fleeing in droves.

Steven responded—not in a stage whisper—"Go home to your fucking swimming pools, you bunch of fucking cunts!"

I tried to get him to quiet down, but it wasn't possible. In fact, it was part of the show in a way.

I was the one who needed to quiet down and let it be.

Brad Davis was fantastic. His physicality in the role was mesmerizing. And yet, he was a troubled genius.

I had met him previously when he returned from shooting *Midnight Express,* a great film purportedly based on a true story of an American kid imprisoned in a brutal Turkish prison for trying to smuggle hashish out of the country. The one evening I spent in Brad's company, it was clear he was wild.

Years later, Brad's and casting director Susan Bluestein's daughter attended the same school as my daughter, Joanna.

Their daughter appeared quite unhappy to me; I speculated it was because her father had recently passed away.

Cut to many years later when I was casting an episode of *Shameless.* An amazing thing happened.

We were looking for a transgender actor to play a love interest for Ian, the second brother on the show and an out gay character. I saw a parade of young men who had been born female and made the brave decision to right that wrong.

One of them was Brad and Susan's child.

It became clear as we chatted that he was a happy, well-adjusted young man. I happened to have a framed poster from Berkoff's *Metamorphosis* on the wall in my office that featured a distorted image of Brad's face.

After I pointed it out to the young actor, he walked over to the poster and placed his fingertips on his father's image.

"Hey, dad, I'm okay," he said quietly.

I'll never forget that moment.

Back to the Taper and one of my final fellowship tasks: assisting José Quintero, the legendary director and co-founder of New York's Circle in the Square Theatre, in his staging of Tennessee Williams's *Cat on a Hot Tin Roof.*

Watching José in action, I realized I had encountered a special kind of theatrical and personal greatness *and* genius.

On the first day of rehearsal, José gathered the company and spoke for quite a while about his relationship with Williams and what life was like in the theatre world in NYC in their younger days. He talked about finding their honest artistic selves in a community of people dedicated to the work.

José was serpentine: he was all eyes. They protruded from his face with a mask-like intensity, which was quite a juxtaposition with his long and lean body, all elbows and knees.

"His back ain't got no bones," as many bluesmen have sung.

After he talked about his love for Williams, José invited the actress who played "Maggie the Cat" to join him in front of the rest of us. He sat down on a chaise lounge and motioned for her to sit on his lap.

The actress was, by the way, a young Kirstie Alley.

She was reluctant at first. Maybe it was too intimate. Perhaps she was afraid that it would be overtly sexual.

In some ways, it was both.

José knew that for Kirstie to find Maggie, she would need to feel her deeply in her body. Maggie is greatly about unrequited sexual desire.

Kirstie alighted on José's gangly knees and gently reclined into his chest. Her legs rested on his. Then, the most remarkable thing happened—something I can only describe as channeling. José breathed in deeply, and Kirstie relaxed. Suddenly, they seemingly became one person.

José already knew where Maggie was in his body, and as we watched, mesmerized, you could literally see him transfer the Cat's desperate, sensual essence into Kirstie.

It was the damndest thing I'd ever seen.

Later, I realized that José knew himself better than anyone I'd ever met. He was unique in many ways, and he embraced and explored his essential passions through his work.

That was his greatness: knowing and believing in his unique self.

No apology. No lack of confidence. No bullshit. Unadulterated José.

A lesson for us all.

I left the creative cocoon of the Mark Taper Forum in 1983 with a great opportunity to direct at the South Coast Repertory in Orange County.

They brought me on to mount a new play by a guy from Yale, David Epstein, for the 1984–1985 season. It was a world premiere of *Shades*, about an aging hippie who sells sunglasses on a Southern California boardwalk.

It was a wonderful experience. A member of the theatre's staff, the playwright (David) and I held auditions for the ensemble. One of the female characters had a brief topless moment in the play. This turned out to be excellent early preparation for my decades-later work on *Shameless*.

We were down to two choices for the role and decided to take a break. As I left the audition space and entered the lobby, I saw one of the women we were strongly considering for the role talking loudly on a payphone. (Remember them?)

As I passed her, I overheard her say, "And I get to take my shirt off!"

That was and is *the* lesson.

There are two kinds of actors. Really, two kinds of people.

One that *gets* to.

One that *has* to.

One embraces the challenges of their work and relationships—their very lives.

One that rues those challenges by complaining and rejecting—failing to see them as opportunities.

The first group is filled with brave actors and people who will push you to join with them in fighting for greatness.

The second group would love you to accompany them in settling for less than what is possible.

I have been graced, for the most part, to be surrounded by the former. That common trait is as responsible as anything for our collective creativity and success.

As for the *Shades* actress? Obviously, she got the part. And she got to take her shirt off.

While the South Coast Rep gig was a great start, my next move was an even better ending.

An absolute failure. Thank goodness.

Life as a freelance director for hire was possible, but it meant being away from home and family. Having Oli newly in remission was a reminder of what was truly important.

Still, the siren song of the stage was strong, and I followed it to direct a production in 1985 of *The Dining Room* by A. R. Gurney at the Coronet Theatre in West Hollywood.

The playbook described it as "an in-depth portrait of a vanishing species: the upper-middle-class WASP."

The *LA Times* roasted it.

The night after the review ran, I went to the theatre to see how the actors were reacting and to buck them up if necessary.

That proved to be an impossible task. I was pretty low.

After the show, a well-known casting director, Barbara Claman, invited me out for a drink. Although I didn't really know her, I happily accepted. I needed a drink.

Barbara could easily tell that I was miserable. She said, "John, if you are going to take it this hard, maybe you should do something else."

She unexpectedly offered me a job at her casting office. In shock, I gratefully accepted on the spot and began shortly after that.

And so, the curtain dropped dramatically on my directing career, and I was miraculously cast in a brand-new role.

TWO

The Debut

EARLY CASTING CAREER

[CASTING ASSOCIATE JOHN LEVEY]

(38 to 40 years old)

No longer a skinny boy, John is finally (!) embracing adulthood and leaving the theatre behind. He sometimes describes himself as an artist and a hooker...who's been a success at both. In making the transition from his artistic, theatrical roots, John feels a bit like he's whoring himself out because he doesn't yet respect television.

Still, he's grateful for scoring a serendipitous casting associate position working for a movie-of-the-week casting director. The job expands into a career just as his family responsibilities also grow with the birth of his second child, Joanna Claire. Still, the joy of her arrival can't bridge the widening gap between Blaine and himself. Driving to work in the wee hours and home late at night in his bright yellow Honda Civic, you might hear John singing along to Jackson Brown's "The Pretender," especially the lyrics about the conflict between love and money.

Casting is tribal. When you join the profession, it's all about who brings you in because the lineage is critical. While nowadays the Casting Society offers an assistant training and education program, there was no such thing when I was starting out.

This brings me to another analogy I like to use about the casting profession: racehorses. You come in with natural ability, style and taste, but if you're lucky, you find mentors who groom you for longevity and success. As in horse racing, it matters who you come "out of" and are sired by.

And so, yet another lucky accident put me on the right course, with a trifecta of fantastic female role models and trainers. They were all actor-forward casting directors, with a New York bent.

Felt like home to me.

When I joined Barbara, she was working primarily on feature films like *Iron Eagle* with Louis Gossett Jr. and Jason Gedrick. However, I did help her cast a police drama pilot featuring Jack Scalia called *Hollywood Beat.* My favorite project was a sexy little movie called *The Men's Club*, about seven pals who go to a San Francisco brothel for a long weekend. It had a fantastic cast—Jennifer Jason Leigh, Harvey Keitel, Frank Langella, Roy Scheider, Stockard Channing, and Treat Williams, among others—but I especially remember one of the supporting actors, a former lingerie model named Claudia Cron.

In the film, one of the prostitute's specialties was whispering explicit sweet nothings in a man's ear. During the casting process, I read with Claudia. She was very Method; she whispered some rather provocative things in my ear.

I turned bright crimson.

The director, a Hungarian guy called Peter Medak, promptly dubbed me "the thermometer."

For the record, that's about as close to the proverbial casting couch as I've ever gotten. In my experience, it's really not a thing—for casting directors, anyway.

In fact, at the time, I was busy trying to focus on

rebuilding my marriage. Bolstered by my daughter Joanna's (Jo's) arrival in October 1985 and Oli's continued good health (which he and I celebrated by attaching his pillboxes to fireworks and blowing them safely and satisfyingly up at a little park in Santa Monica), things were looking up.

And it all got even better when shortly after that, I got a call from Ilene Amy Berg, my old college friend who stagemanaged many of the plays I'd directed in my early 20s in Rochester. At the time, she was an ABC executive in their movie and miniseries department, producing a lot of great network programming.

"Hey Johnny," Ilene said, "There's a job available at Marsha Kleinman's place. I think you would love her, and she would love you."

Marsha was a disciple of Marion Dougherty, the mother of casting who was famous for bringing the "real" New York actor to Hollywood. (Later, when I was at Warner Bros. in the 1990s, Marion was vice president of casting there. On more than one occasion, I invited her in for a bourbon and loved hearing about how she discovered icons like Dustin Hoffman and Jon Voight. She was quite generous with her stories.)

Ilene couldn't have been more spot on. Like me, Marsha got her start at the Mark Taper Forum. As I recall, the interview went great, and we immediately hit it off. Marsha was a fantastic combination of passion, bluntness and idiosyncrasy. That's a nice way of saying she could be difficult—but in my eyes, in the best way.

Working with and caring for women with big personalities, who some might call "difficult" (like my mother) is my specialty.

At my interview, in addition to talking shop, I couldn't help but gush about Jo. Later, Ilene told me that Marsha called her, saying, "I like him, but he seems more interested in his kid than his job. That makes me nervous."

What a shift from the traditional family structure of my

parents' generation! And almost not getting a great job because of my parental responsibilities, like so many other injustices I've encountered in the business, made me more sensitive to what women routinely experience.

At any rate, Ilene reassured Marsha that I would be a workhorse, and she relented. It wasn't a stretch—I easily buried myself into our work. The truth was that the détente in my marriage was short-lived, and having a special purpose was what I needed.

Marsha's office was a cool little suite on top of the original Tommy Tang's restaurant on Melrose. To the wafting scent of delicious Thai food, we immediately got to work on TV movies like *A Stranger Waits*, which starred Suzanne Pleshette, Tom Atkins, Paul Benjamin, and *The Room Upstairs* with Sarah Jessica Parker, Stockard Channing, Sam Waterston and Linda Hunt, among others. We also cast one of Whoopi Goldberg's early features, *Burglar*.

Casting *Burglar* is the first time my contacts from the theatre world came in handy. Marsha asked me if I knew anyone, and I brought in a woman called Elizabeth Ruscio. Marsha was thrilled with her, and eventually, she actually got the role. Three decades later, I would work again with a Ruscio—this time Elizabeth's sister Nina, who was the production designer on both *Animal Kingdom* and *Shameless*.

While I worked with Marsha for a relatively short time—around two years—she taught me more about casting than anyone else.

Marsha was the one who taught me to really give a damn. Marsha was famous for fighting with networks and studios, regardless of what the consequences might be. (This was something I might have learned too well. However, I appreciated her passion—and learned it was good to bring mine.)

Passionate and intelligent, she was an avid contemporary art collector who, in her spare time, did gymnastics to stay in shape. I remember walking around West Hollywood with her, laughing and talking shop.

We both agreed how lucky we were to find a career where being opinionated was a requirement, not a detriment.

I will always be grateful for Marsha, who regrettably only lived a handful of years beyond our time together. She died of lung cancer at just 54 in 1995.

The third powerful and fabulous woman who solidified my career path was Phyllis Huffman. She too was one of Marion's protégés. Best known for her work with Clint Eastwood, Phyllis became vice president of the television casting department there.

Marsha, a close associate of Phyllis's, was used to getting calls from her when she needed a new staff casting director—my predecessor with Marsha, Kathleen Letterie, went to work for Phyllis.

In 1987, it was my turn. Phyllis called Marsha and asked for a referral. Marsha encouraged my moving over to work for Warner Bros. And as it turned out, a connection preceded my working relationship with Phyllis, which was very defining.

Phyllis's late husband, David Huffman, was a theatre actor who I had known briefly. The pair had two young sons, and so we were around the same phase of life. In 1985, David was in a production of *Of Mice and Men* in San Diego at the Old Globe theatre. During a lunch break in Balboa Park, a teenager grabbed an older woman's purse, and David chased him down. While they were grappling over the bag, the kid stabbed David in the chest with a screwdriver, killing him instantly.

So, Phyllis knew pain. And she wore it. While we never really talked at great length about her husband's death, we forged a personal, human-to-human connection, which we brought into the work.

Going to work for Phyllis and Warner Bros. was a game-changer for me. I got a three-year contract, which paid

$45,000 in the first year and went up by $10,000 per year from there. That allowed us to leave the house we were renting on the Venice–Santa Monica border and buy a modest three-bedroom, two-bathroom home in Van Nuys.

It was an optimistic decision.

It was also the first time I had my own office. Shortly after I arrived at Warner Bros., we moved to that beautiful old building, "the drugstore." You'd come into a large, open waiting room right inside the front door (no security in those days) and check in with the receptionist. Off to the right were my office and Phyllis's.

Of course, Phyllis's office had a deluxe layout, with an inner and outer sanctum. Her assistant sat in the front room, and Phyllis had a luxe private suite with a living room area, desk area and private bathroom. Her desk was for more formal meetings, and the living room was where we met with writers, producers and directors who would come over to talk about pilots or the new season of a show.

My office, on the other hand, was probably half the size of Phyllis's. And it was my job to audition the actors, so it had a simple but comfortable set-up with a couch and a chair. I also had a desk area with a phone—no computer or anything (can you imagine?).

Back in those days, all casting was "live" without the benefit of machines. I'd go through stacks and stacks of manila envelopes with a mind-boggling array of headshots to determine who we'd bring in to audition.

I also remember a whole bunch of offices on the second floor filled primarily with writers who had overall network deals. Diane English, the creator of *Murphy Brown,* was upstairs. It was an exciting time.

The first project I worked on was *Head of the Class*, which starred Howard Hesseman as the teacher for a class of gifted children at a New York City high school. The show had premiered in 1986, so I joined during the second season.

Later, as the original cast started to become too old to reasonably portray high schoolers, I added cast actors Rain Pryor (Richard Pryor's daughter—as Theola June "T.J." Jones) and De'voreaux White (as Aristotle McKenzie—we cast him fresh off his role as the limo driver Argyle in *Die Hard*). Additions like these and a few others made for a more diverse and realistic cast.

I mention this because this is right around the time when networks finally adopted an agenda of diversity. And, of course, this is important—but to me, it can easily fall into a tokenistic trap that I am fundamentally opposed to, which I think of as a kind of "busing for television."

I know this is a loaded statement, but my opinion is always to cast the people who are best for the role. Their talent and ability in the context of the story we're telling are of utmost importance. What is the essence of the character? Sometimes race factors in, but often it doesn't. To me, it's never a "token" decision. That's superficial. Serving the story *and* the community in the best possible way for the most believable and honest portrayal possible: *that* is the ticket.

That said, I've also focused on equity and inclusion— human rights, really—for all people since I was a boy. As I've mentioned, both of my parents were leftists before becoming progressive Democrats. I grew up in that environment. So when something feels like a quota system, it turns me off. Real, systemic change comes when the commitment is to level the playing field and then bring in the best.

This leads us almost to my first career-making opportunity: *China Beach*. But before we get there, a quick story about one that got away—also a defining moment in my career.

That time I fired Annette Bening...

In 1988, I cast a one-camera, half-hour romantic comedy pilot called *Just in Time* about a fictional magazine, the *West Coast Review*. Written by Fred Barron, the show was produced by and starred Tim Matheson as editor-in-chief Harry

Stadlin, a man "determined to turn his magazine around." Annette was cast as Joanna Farrell, a columnist "destined to turn around his life."

Now, Tim is lots of things, including a television leading man. Later, he was excellent in *The West Wing* as Vice President John Hoynes. But there was no chemistry between Annette and him.

So, right after the table read, I was told to fire her. Four decades later, it remains the most absurd act I've ever had to confess to.

What wasn't absurd was the transformative effect Warner Bros. had on me. I was finally dropping a mask I'd worn for a very long time: struggling artist, cloaked in the uniform of poverty and sacrifice. Guided by three strong, creative, smart women, I began to regard television as both a relevant and creative medium.

And I also began to warm to the feeling of success. It was perfect timing, then, to wash up on the shores of *China Beach*.

THREE

The Breakthrough

CHINA BEACH, 1988–1991, 60 EPISODES

[CASTING BY JOHN LEVEY]

(41 to 44 years old)

John, never one to methodically navigate a course, is starting to enjoy the wind in the sails of his casting career. A four-year run on the award-winning China Beach *gives him his first taste of critical success and is the beginning of what will be a long, fruitful working relationship with John Wells's crew.*

While he's on stable shores professionally, his marriage continues to drift out to sea. Pulling up on the Warner Bros.' lot in his sunshiney Honda Civic, you might hear John humming the Supremes' song, "Reflections"— China Beach's *haunting, bittersweet theme.*

Credits of *China Beach*

Shortly after the *Just in Time* debacle and while I was working on *Head of the Class*, Phyllis walked into my office one day, a strange smile on her face.

Plopping down a 120-or-so-page manuscript on my desk, she simply said, "Read this, and talk to me when you're done."

It was the pilot episode of *China Beach*. The show was about the people—nurses, doctors, officers, soldiers, "Donut Dollies" (Red Cross workers tasked with cheering up the troops), prostitutes and other civilians who inhabited the 510th Evacuation Hospital during the Vietnam War. And if you're not familiar with the genesis of the name of the show, it refers to the location of the hospital. "China Beach" was what American and Aussie soldiers called My Khe beach in the city of Đà Nẵng, Vietnam.

It was an exceptional piece of dramatic work.

It had raw, honest reality in it.

It had absurdism in it.

It had the '60s in it.

And, of course, it had women at the center of it, which was the extraordinary part.

The characters were so vivid and three-dimensional. I

remember hearing the show described as a women's locker room set in a man's world. That was precisely it.

Keep in mind that in the mid-1980s, women were still very much marginalized and sexualized on gritty "real world" television dramas. This was a different story in comedy, where women like Mary Tyler Moore, Carol Burnett, Linda Lavin, Candace Bergen, Penny Marshall and Cindy Williams were at the center of shows.

For that reason especially, *China Beach* was surprising and fantastic.

The very next day, I went into Phyllis's office and said, "I love it."

And I honestly did. While there are parts that seem to be written in heaven for a particular actor, this project was made in heaven for me.

With Phyllis and I equally enthusiastic about the project, we met with the show's co-creators, William "Bill" Broyles Jr. and John Sacret Young, the director, Rod Holcomb, and the executive who shepherded the show for Warner Bros., Scott Kaufer.

Even though it was a drama and Scott was vice president of comedy development (under the wonderful Harvey Shephard, who was the president), it was Scott's baby, as he had a previous association with Bill.

Bill is a lanky Texan who was a decorated war hero in the Marines during the Vietnam War. He wrote about his experiences in the autobiographical book *Brothers in Arms: A Journey from War to Peace*. Bill also served as *Newsweek*'s editor-in-chief in the early '80s and has gone on to a successful screenwriting career that includes several acclaimed feature films, including *Apollo 13, Cast Away, Planet of the Apes, The Polar Express* and *Jarhead*, among others. Bill wrote or co-wrote many of the early *China Beach* episodes, and he stayed on as producer and creative consultant throughout the series' four seasons.

John Sacret Young, who we unfortunately lost in June

2021, was the show's co-creator and executive producer. (We'll call him "JSY" to keep things from becoming confusing once John Wells enters the picture.) JSY was a northeastern Brahmin, Princeton educated, extremely bright, delightful—and intimidating as hell. And I think that was very much part of his MO, as a way of meeting new people. He would let them know that more than likely he was the smartest person in the room. And, usually, he was. (Although Bill certainly gave him a run for his money on *China Beach*.)

Scott was an LA boy who always had *the* table at Spago and fantastic seats at Dodger Stadium. Memorably, he and I drove to Bakersfield some years later to watch Hall of Famer Don Sutton pitch on a rehab assignment at the minor league ballpark. So, he may have had silver-spoon taste, but Scott was down to earth, charming and funny.

And then there was the pilot's director, Rod Holcomb, who studied film at San Francisco State and was the son of a police officer. If you're building a driftwood mobile and looking to balance Bill and JSY, Rod was a perfect choice. Cut from a wholly different swath of social fabric, Rod captures the essence of working people and their sometimes brilliant, often troubling and always captivating reality.

Finally, there was my boss, Phyllis Huffman, all five feet, one inch of tough, tenacious, lovely Irish Catholic discipline. Add my community-oriented, storytelling self into the mix, and while the six of us were a strange brew, we were able to conjure a world that hit an honest note for the men and women who came of age while fighting for their lives—and ours.

Once we met, Phyllis and I got to work casting the pilot. While I don't have the original breakdowns, here are the characters we got to cast:

FIRST LIEUTENANT (LATER CAPTAIN) COLLEEN MCMURPHY: A Catholic girl from Lawrence, Kansas,

McMurphy is an army nurse with the 510th Evac Hospital in
Vietnam in the late 1960s. If you were a wounded 19-year-old
boy, 10,000 miles away from home, her arms would be the
ones you'd want to die in. And if you weren't injured, you'd
still long to be in her arms—proof positive you're still alive
and vital.

A side note: McMurphy is loosely based on a veteran
army nurse called Lynda Van Devanter, whose autobiography
Home Before Morning bravely and candidly discussed female
Vietnam vets' struggles with posttraumatic stress disorder and
the unique wounds (physical, emotional, spiritual) that shaped
their lives from their time in service. If the character's name,
McMurphy, sounds familiar, it should—it's a nod to Randall
McMurphy, the protagonist played by Jack Nicholson in *One
Flew Over the Cuckoo's Nest*.

KAREN CHARLENE "KC" KOLOSKI: Part-time prostitute and full-time provider of all things that anyone might
need to alleviate pain and elevate pleasure. KC services the
officers' club, taking care of everyone's corrupt requirements
and personal needs.

MAJOR LILA GARREAU: With natural authority, career
army officer and World War II veteran Garreau represents
old-fashioned American values. And yet, her rules, regulations
and rigid way of doing things are designed to save the women
under her command. (And they often do.)

LAURETTE BARBER: Plucky and unconventional in a
million ways, Barber is a USO singer from Paoli, Pennsylva-
nia, determined to make it big.

CHERRY WHITE: She's the quintessential American innocent (it's all in her name), and a Red Cross volunteer (a

"Donut Dolly") from Iowa, who comes to Vietnam to look for her brother Rick whom she fears is in real trouble.

SP4 SAMUEL BECKETT: Named with a nod to the great Irish playwright who made "Beckett" synonymous with bleakness, Beckett is a preacher's son from North Carolina and a draftee who works in the morgue at China Beach. He and McMurphy have an astonishing connection as the dying men go from her care to his.

CAPTAIN DICK RICHARD: Once again, the name says it all—womanizing head surgeon Richard has the arrogance of someone who plays God, believing he can cut open someone's body and solve all their issues.

CORPORAL BOONWELL "BOONIE" LANIER: This fun-loving all-American boy/marine is having the time of his life as the China Beach lifeguard, throwing parties for GIs on R and R, with all the girls and the hootch anyone needs to get their mind off the war.

CAPTAIN BARTHOLOMEW "NATCH" AUSTEN: The cocky, fun-loving demeanor of this USAF jet pilot undercuts the pressure of his flying missions. It's not hard to see why McMurphy is attracted to him.

STAFF SERGEANT EVAN "DODGER" WINSLOW: This death-dodging ("Dodger") Marine Force Reconnaissance operative is known for his "thousand-yard stare." It's the haunted look that characterizes Vietnam vets who've had their minds traumatically supplanted by the battlefield.

Casting a pilot back in 1988 was a much different beast than it is now because it was all pre-internet. There were no computers on our desks, just gigantic piles of envelopes filled with headshots and resumes, organized by role. And countless telephone calls with agents pitching their actors.

China Beach is when I developed my system of sorting through the pictures and resumes. At the bottom were small boutique agencies and management firms that might have co-star actors (the "D" grouping). The middle section had those that might have co-stars, guest stars or recurring actors (the "C" and "B" groupings). And at the top were managers and agencies most likely to have the series regulars and leads (the "A" grouping).

My process would entail putting a piece of colored paper between the A, B, C and D groupings. I would then go through each group and put another piece of colored paper on top of it to demonstrate that I had been through those pictures and resumes. Next, I'd take the selected actors and put them in separate folders, prioritizing each group by how passionate I was about a particular actor. Finally, I'd give the sorted stack to my assistant to set up appointments.

Sophisticated, right?

My own sorting process wasn't the end of it—of course not! That's what agents and managers are for. I would get calls from them and hear all sorts of pitches about why their person was perfect for a given role. This would send me back into my piles of photos and resumes to give a few actors a second look, this time with the passion of the pitch in my head. And I'd place some of them into the folder to audition, and others would be returned between the two pieces of colored paper.

That process kept going on and on, and then finally, we would start having sessions.

Keep in mind that the process I just described applied to all sorts of roles, but not necessarily the leads. The "A" and even "B+" agents often didn't want their actors playing lesser roles, so they wouldn't even submit them for supporting parts.

So, for the parts with just a few lines, I'd often work with smaller and mid-tier boutique agencies that had tastes I could trust and easy, clear communication. Casting *China Beach* all those years ago taught me how to quickly figure out where I could get the talent I needed. Some agencies represented a lot of BIPOC actors (important for *China Beach*, as so many of the troops and service people were people of color). Others represented a lot of beautiful people, and still others had a full roster of character actors.

While I have always made it a point to have collegial, warm working relationships with agents, managers and actors, I have found it works best as a casting director not to pursue personal relationships with them. I even routinely avoided invitations to lunch, telling them, "Why ruin a perfectly good relationship by getting to know each other personally?"

Now, on to some anecdotes about casting *China Beach*'s series regulars.

FIRST LIEUTENANT (LATER CAPTAIN) COLLEEN MCMURPHY: DANA DELANY

Casting the heart of the show is always a challenge—for the casting director and the would-be stars alike.

As I see it, your work as an actor, and probably elsewhere as well, should be like a good haircut.

You never look like you need one, nor like you just got one. You should just look natural.

In casting, we are looking at several things at once:

Are you talented?

Are you right for the role? Which is to say, do you convey the qualities that the character requires? Under this heading are questions like:

Do you feel vulnerable, or do you feel like you can handle things with grace and ease?

Do you radiate intelligence, or do you feel more instinctive?

Do you lead with your sexuality in a weaponized way or an inviting way?

Do I want to spend the day with your personality and your process?

When casting the *China Beach* pilot, one of the women up for McMurphy illustrated the haircut principle beautifully.

Let me set the stage:

Casting rooms are fraught with tension. Important decisions are constantly being made, so quite naturally, releasing that tension is imperative. Frequently, that is through a kind of dark humor.

There was an actress I was very high on, and I touted her with considerable enthusiasm to Rod, who was directing the pilot episode.

Rod greeted her warmly as he usually did.

Some small talk was next: *Where are you from? Do you have any questions, or should we get going?*

The room settled.

The actress said, "Give me a moment, please."

She turned her back, raised her arms in the air with her palms facing each other, and began rubbing her hands back and forth energetically.

Then she turned back to me, and we began to read the scene. I thought it went well.

When she left the room, I turned to Rod and asked how he liked her.

He rose from his chair, all six feet, five inches or so of him, turned his back to the rest of us, and rubbed his palms together with vigor. It was absurd and hilarious, and Rod made his point without a single word.

Her public process had warned Rod of what a day on the set might look like. Her talent, positive qualities and rightness for the role all took a back seat.

On set, we spend more time with our collaborators in a pressure-filled, intimate setting than we do with our families.

We needed to feel confident that we can look forward to that time with enthusiasm and not dread.

I doubt we would've gotten through one day with the energy conjurer.

And, of course, that was just one possible McMurphy. In general, we might read 25, 30, 35, 40 people for a particular series regular role. The production team would read them all once, and then we'd get together and collectively discuss it. Somewhere between six and 10 would be deemed viable.

From there, we'd read them all again. We'd gather in Harvey's office: the actor, Scott (representing both the production and the studio), studio executives and our production team.

For the record, my assistant was supposed to do the honors of reading opposite each actor, but Harvey called me—the only time he ever did so—to tell me her voice drove him crazy. So my dulcet tones it was.

In the case of *China Beach*, Dana Delany was a top choice early on. At the time, she had a number of credits, mainly soaps and TV movies, but she also had an impressive guest-star turn on *Cheers*. In my opinion, Dana had everything for that part.

She was the girl next door.

She was a bit tomboyish, so she fit in a world predominantly filled with men.

She had great innocence and empathy. I've said it before, but if you were to die in the arms of a woman you didn't know 10,000 miles away from your mom or your high school girlfriend, her embrace would be ideal.

Later, I heard Dana tell the story that she almost didn't get the role because an ABC executive said she wasn't pretty enough. (She confronted him; he apologized.)

I couldn't disagree more.

I knew Dana from back when I worked for Marsha Kleinman. We were casting a made-for-television movie called

Promise about mental illness. James Garner played Bob Beuhler, a small-town big shot who has a schizophrenic brother, DJ, who goes off his meds, played by James Woods. Dana auditioned for the part of a young woman who's dating Bob.

In her audition, Dana read opposite me. In the scene, "Bob" (me) made a joke. Dana was sitting across from me on a couch, and she laughed so hard she fell on the floor. Then she crawled across the floor, pulled herself up on my lap and kissed me.

While she was great, she didn't ultimately get that role. (As I recall, geography, not her skill, was the culprit.) When Dana told the story years later, she liked to say to people that all she had to do to get a series regular job was find a heterosexual casting director, kiss him in an audition, wait five years, and you're a shoo-in.

I love that twist, but it's not how she won the role of McMurphy on *China Beach*.

Helen Hunt also emerged early as a candidate, and she was a bigger name at that point. And of course, she's a fantastic actor. I knew her father, Gordon Hunt, quite well, as he had been the casting director at the Mark Taper Forum. (Later, he was the recording director for Hanna-Barbera cartoons, including *The Smurfs*. He invited me to watch a recording session, and I was amazed to discover that the woman who played Smurfette was an adorable woman in her 70s.)

We narrowed the list down to these two women. In this case, we needed a network test to make the final decision. We convinced the powers that be to finance a screen test. I read opposite each of them on a soundstage on the Warner Bros. lot. They even brought in a palm tree to give the scene a tropical feeling.

I think it was clear to all of us on the production side that it was Dana. I don't say this in a negative way about Helen—she's certainly gone on to do a lot of fabulous work. Innately, though, she is a bit more reserved and was a little less accessible.

With Dana, all is revealed. Her vulnerability and empathy are naked, apparent.

The screen test also convinced the studio and the network, and Dana was chosen. Now on to the women who would balance her on the casting driftwood mobile.

KAREN CHARLENE "KC" KOLOSKI: MARG HELGENBERGER

KC was up next. All you have to know about casting this purveyor of passion is her first appearance in the series: she's leaning in a doorway, smoking a cigarette. A slow pan caresses KC's body, moving from the floor up her bare legs to her skirt and finally alighting on her beautifully made-up face as she takes a drag.

Role-winning actors are very much a combination of what they look like on the surface and their inner qualities. The beautiful, leggy, redheaded Marg conveys a quality that says *I can take care of myself in any circumstances. I don't care who you are and what you've got in your pocket—be it money, a gun, or something else that makes it clear you're happy to see me—I can handle it.*

Marg Helgenberger's performance in that doorway said more than any dialogue could ever have said. Done. Deal.

One of the funniest things that we later learned was that in real life, on a personal level, Marg was more like Dana's character, and Dana was more like Marg's character. But, of course, they were both right for the roles they played.

MAJOR LILA GARREAU: CONCETTA TOMEI

And then we had Major Lila Garreau to cast. Concetta Tomei came in with a booming voice that was at once proud, commanding and forceful. Like she was an opera singer. She had more authority than any man—intimidating in the best way possible.

Concetta was spectacular. And so right for the role.

Rounding out the women were two polar opposites, although there was a core of innocence (about to be lost) with both of them: the characters of Laurette Barber and Cherry White.

LAURETTE BARBER:
CHLOE WEBB

For the role of Laurette, there was a bit of drama out of the gate. We had narrowed it down to a couple of actors, one of which was Jana Marie Hupp. We were told that the studio approved Jana. Phyllis was close friends with her agent, Ro Diamond at SDB Partners, so she called right away with the good news. (Funny how I can't remember what I had for breakfast, but I can remember that.)

And then, Jana was unapproved. These things happen sometimes.

Then, Chandra Wilson, now known for her long-running role as Dr. Miranda Bailey on *Grey's Anatomy*, was hired and fired on day two.

These things also happen.

So we had to scramble to find our Laurette. Chloe was hot from her star turn playing Nancy Spungen in the movie *Sid & Nancy*. And of course, years later, she became well known for playing Monica, Frank's passionate but mentally unstable wife on *Shameless*.

We met Chloe at ABC in Century City, and it was at this meeting that Chloe famously said to the suits sitting around the table:

"I don't do the 'S' word."

I'm sure everyone took that to mean "sex," but that wasn't it at all—it was something more taboo to Chloe: *a series*.

This became clear as soon as we offered her the part, but she agreed to only six episodes, not a long-term deal. Chloe is an iconoclast of the first order and was one of the most fun people to have a margarita (or two or six) with back in the day. And so, we gave her a "special guest appearance by" credit.

CHERRY WHITE: ## NAN WOODS

Nan Woods, who was cast as the Donut Dolly Cherry White, came to us by way of Chicago through Jane Alderman's office. (We later did all of our Chicago-based casting with Jane for *ER*.) What I remember most about Nan was not her audition for the role but her decision to retire from acting at the ripe age of 22 at the end of the second season of *China Beach*.

SP4 SAMUEL BECKETT: ## MICHAEL BOATMAN

This leads us to the casting of the male series regulars. Like Nan, Michael Boatman, a candidate for *China Beach*'s mortician Samuel Beckett, came to us from Jane in Chicago. He was a recent graduate of Western Illinois University and looked even younger than that, thanks to a very short haircut and his incredible protruding ears.

Boatman's youthful look was crucial because one of the notable differences between World War II and the war in Vietnam was the average age of a GI.

In WWII, it was 26 years old.

In Vietnam, it was just 19.

The difference between a 19-year-old boy and a 26-year-old man in any environment is enormous. And in a wartime environment, it must have been profound.

While I was certainly of age to serve in Vietnam, by a twist of fate, I was deemed unable to be drafted by the US military.

That was because I was a felon—albeit an unconvicted one.

Let me explain. In the fall of 1969, the Rochester house I was living in was robbed. When the cops caught the culprit, they found marijuana, which he told them he stole from my home.

This led to a very dramatic arrest of those who were in the house at the time—my roommate, my girlfriend and me. Cops busted through the back door, conducted a full search and unearthed marijuana in pretty much every room of the house. The three of us ended up spending a few terrifying hours in jail. This was before ATMs, so my mom's brother Jack appealed to the bartenders and prostitutes he knew in Rochester to get enough cash to bail us out.

Eventually, the trial judge dismissed the charges because the police didn't do even a cursory check to see if the thief had any reason to be vindictive toward us. And as a result, the warrant was thrown out, along with the evidence. Case closed.

But when my draft notice arrived in 1973, I hadn't had my day in court, so the felony charges were on my record. So, I didn't dodge service, but the accidental timing once again changed my trajectory and kept me stateside during the war. I'm grateful for that and equally thankful that I got to experience the war through *China Beach*.

Back to Michael, who was working the night shift as a security guard when he auditioned for the role on *China Beach*. He handily delivered a stirring performance of dialogue between him and a dead soldier he was embalming.

When we went to the studio and the network, we were confident, as he was so clearly the embodiment of American youth and optimism. But he also conveyed a unique combination of being 19 and wise, in a way that death or proximity to death might be responsible for.

CAPTAIN DICK RICHARD:
ROBERT PICARDO

After Michael was cast, we turned to Captain Dick Richard. His name certainly wasn't subtle, so when Robert "Bobby" Picardo tested in New York, we knew we had our Dr. Dick. He radiated that enormously selfish, roguish charm and could deliver lines with just the right degree of empathy-devoid sarcasm. Of course, the doctor wasn't all bad; you just had to know the character to love him, as he was an embodiment of male entitlement. And Dr. Dick misbehaved all the time. Bobby went on to more famously play another "Doctor," the Emergency Medical Hologram (EMH) in the mid-1990s *Star Trek* television series and films, too.

CORPORAL BOONWELL "BOONIE" LANIER:
BRIAN WIMMER

Casting Brian Wimmer as Boonie, much as it was with Michael, had to do with his ability to convey the quality of innocence even in the most twisted circumstances. Boonie ran the bar, so he knew about prostitution and addiction—GI vices—but nothing was corrupt about him. Brian brought buoyancy to the character, who was another symbolic, emblematic depiction of American boyhood. In fact, at some point in the series, he jumped on a trampoline, and you could see him as a seven-year-old.

CAPTAIN BARTHOLOMEW "NATCH" AUSTEN: TIM RYAN

Natch, the jet fighter and McMurphy's love interest, was a flyboy in all senses of the word. And again, we needed someone who could play the role with a bit of an old soul to reflect the character's battle-worn POV and also youthful exuberance (and sexiness, too). Tim Ryan was an early choice, although his hair was too long. As soon as we cast him, JSY made him cut his hair incredibly short. That was a tactic of his—JSYs idea of youth and innocence for men involved taking away their machismo by cutting off their hair and making their ears stick out.

A very effective tactic, in my opinion. Guys with no protection around their ears look like little boys.

STAFF SERGEANT EVAN "DODGER" WINSLOW: JEFF KOBER

As opposed to the vibrant and fun-loving Boonie or the cocky Natch, Dodger represents the other end of the spectrum: the shell-shocked serviceman. Jeff Kober had that thousand-yard stare down cold, conveying terror, horror and pathos without uttering a word. There was a moment in the series where Dodger and Private Sweetness Elroy, played by former UCLA football player Bobby Hosea, come walking out of the water onto China Beach, fully dressed with weapons strapped across their chest and that vacant, detached look in their eyes.

Jeff and Bobby were breathtaking. It was an image that became emblematic of the series, a poetic shot that conveyed a palpable sense of being lost and arriving from nowhere. Their only lifeline is believing the rah-rah macho rhetoric that football teams and army brigades are famous for—now known as "locker room talk."

And so, our driftwood mobile, made from the all-American men and women who washed up on the shores of *China Beach*, was complete for the pilot and six episodes that made up the first season. That was the genius of the writing. It was so strong that under the guidance of JSY, Bill and Scott, Phyllis and I could put together not just a cast of talented actors but also people who were perfect for the roles.

Once the series got the green light, it was my baby, and Phyllis went back to running the casting department. She had a close relationship with JSY, which was good and bad. Often we went wildly over-budget, but JSY was of the mind that we were making a television show, not a budget.

I think Phyllis often enlisted Harvey, along with Beverly Nix, who was the head of business affairs, to tell John that he couldn't do various things. The studio spent a lot of time and energy trying to reign JSY in, frankly, to almost no avail.

The show's success, which saw JSY directing a number of episodes and becoming more deeply involved in all aspects of the show, gave the studio an opportunity. They brought in John Wells to run the *China Beach* writers' room starting in Season Two. He had an overall development deal as a writer/producer at Warner Bros. Television as a producer. John would go on to write 16 episodes of the series, rising to supervising producer (Season Three) and ultimately co-executive producer (Season Four).

John was also brought in to contain JSY's instincts.

Along with John came some new colleagues who became lifelong friends: writers Lydia Woodward and Carol Flint, and director and supervising producer Mimi Leder. Appropriately for the story, they were all powerful, talented women. We would go on to collaborate on several other John Wells productions, including *ER*, *The West Wing* and *Shameless*, among others.

What Bill, John and JSY accomplished was to elevate the dramatic formula that *Hill Street Blues* created—the multi-layered, multi-dimensional, A, B and C plots anchored by the ensemble's interior landscapes and interpersonal relationships —to the next level.

Like great jazz musicians, they took the basic rhythm from *Hill Street*'s standard and played it with their own personality and instrumentation. They evolved dramatic storytelling on television, and I'm grateful as hell to have been a part of it all.

Adding new inhabitants to the world you've created while continuing to evolve the richness of a series is always an exciting challenge. *China Beach* proved to be nearly impossible, but not because we didn't have quality candidates.

It's because Season Two had to be cast during the infamous writers' strike of 1988, which ran 153 days, from March 7 until August 7. Shortly thereafter, in late August, the show began to garner critical acclaim with several Primetime Emmy Award nominations and one win (for Outstanding Achievement in Costuming for a Series). So, we were off and running.

A new regular was to be added for the upcoming season, but there was a perplexing problem: no script.

How do you meet and assess actors for a role that doesn't exist?

I came up with the idea that we should get folks to tell two personal stories: one centered around a triumph and another around a humiliation.

I was sent to New York City to meet actors.

It was there that I met with Nancy Giles. She was taller than me by several inches—I'm not quite five feet nine. Nancy is over six feet tall.

She radiates a curiosity and an intelligence that would eventually lead her to a role as a comically inclined political observer and commentator.

I don't remember her triumph, but her humiliation has stayed with me all these years.

Nancy described the tiny space she lived in. It was a basement room, where the only light came from a sidewalk-level grate.

Late one night, a man stood on that sidewalk and urinated in that space. It wasn't the facts that grabbed me but rather the way she expressed them—after all, the simple act of urinating on the sidewalk in NYC was not that unusual.

She held on to her dignity and the hopes she had for her future and saw the absurd humor in her circumstance.

I brought her to the attention of the writer-producers, and they also responded positively to her.

Later, when the strike ended, a role was crafted for a female GI in the China Beach motor pool, Private Frankie Bunson. We brought Nancy to ABC in Century City, which was then housed in a giant corporate building.

The test went well, and she was approved. I was told I could give her the good news.

Nancy had a few minutes' head start on me, but I caught up to her at the elevator bank. She was already in the elevator, and I managed to join her as the doors closed behind me.

I excitedly told her that she got the gig.

Nancy began to cry and slid her long-legged body to the floor at my feet.

Several corporate executives were waiting for the elevator when the doors opened.

What the hell? they must have thought. None of them crossed the threshold.

It was her triumph and my embarrassment.

Later that season, we also added the Air Force officer Wayloo Marie Holmes, a reporter for the Armed Services Network who longs to strike it big as a journalist. She also wants to be friends with McMurphy, whose approval would go a long way to build Holmes's confidence, along with access to great stories.

In a sense, we brought in this character to replace Nan, who was leaving *China Beach* and her acting career after

Season Two. Megan Gallagher was another version of an American innocent: ambitious, smart, attractive and guileless. Again, just right for the role of Wayloo Marie.

We made an interesting and unusual casting decision in Season Two. Jeff Hyers had played a character called Dewey in Season One, Episode One, "Home." In it, McMurphy has put her anger aside in helping deliver a baby for a pregnant Viet Cong woman who threw a grenade in a bar, killing Dewey on the night he was slated to leave Vietnam.

Ned Vaughn, an Archie-esque redhead, beautifully portrayed youthful innocence as Dewey, and we brought Ned back as Corporal Jeff Hyers, a good-natured combat medic who hails from Georgia. We ended up killing him off again during a routine patrol in Season Three.

This couldn't happen today because the networks are adamant about not having people appear in the show more than once—worse because Ned played two different characters, both of whom died tragically.

Troy Evans was another later addition to the *China Beach* cast in Season Three as Master Sergeant Bartholomew "Bub" Pepper, but unlike the rest, Troy was acting from lived experience. He served for two years in the jungles of Vietnam in the 25th Infantry Division.

When Troy returned home to Montana, he had a severe case of alcoholism and PTSD, which led to bar fights, jail and eventually, a one-man show about his life called *Troy Evans' Montana Tales and Other Bad Ass Business.*[1]

John Wells caught the show and introduced us to Troy. He was the perfect person to play the World War II vet, Sgt. Pepper (again, a not-too-subtle referential name) who embodied a true American: latent danger under an affable facade. These same qualities would come in handy later when we cast Troy as Officer Frank Martin in *ER*, who later became a desk clerk in the ER.

Rounding out the Season Three additions was Ricki Lake,

whom we cast as sassy Donut Dolly Holly Pelegrino, who explores her sexual freedom for the first time in Vietnam. This was Ricki's first big TV role after doing some big films with John Waters (*Hairspray* and *Cry-Baby*).

There was a moving and compelling episode called "Holly's Choice," written by Carol Flint, which was told backward about Holly being impregnated by a GI and her decision to have an abortion. Imagine the timing: it was 1990, and back then, the topic was extremely controversial. It showed both sides with Catholic pro-lifer McMurphy and Dr. Richard, too. KC supports her decision, and in the process shows how the only difference between Holly and her is that she took money for her services.

KC slept with officers for money, and Holly slept with men out of the goodness of her heart.

We all have our motives, after all.

Beyond casting series regulars, our department was always busy staffing the 510th Evac Hospital and related locales. Sometimes there was a big guest star, but often they were small parts. (I know, there are no small parts, only small actors. Semantics.)

So, in any given scene, we might be filling the officer's club with patrons and a one-or-two-line actor to order a beer from Boonie. Or we'd have to fill the hospital with injured soldiers who came into McMurphy's care.

One memorable casting decision involved me. There was a part in the pilot for a guy called "the burnt soldier." I portrayed that character (and all others) when the women who read for the role of Laurette Barber were auditioning. When it came time to shoot the pilot with Chloe in place, Harvey asked me to be our burnt soldier. I respectfully declined. Not only did I not want to spend all day in makeup because the character was burned by napalm from head to toe, but I also firmly believe that actors, not casting directors, should get acting jobs.

Throughout the series, we cast several well-known or soon-to-be-well-known actors in the series. Topping the list was Nancy Sinatra, who made a guest appearance as herself on a celebrity USO tour in the Season One episode, "Chao Ong." She later had a development deal at Warner Bros. television.

A notable side story: years later, in 1996, I cast James Farentino as George Clooney's father, Ray Ross, on *ER*. James had been charged with stalking his former girlfriend, Tina Sinatra, Nancy's sister. All I knew was that a restraining order was involved.

Cut to a date I was on shortly after my divorce at a local bar/restaurant with a nice young woman. I felt a tap on the shoulder, and I turned to see Nancy. Before I could utter a word, she slapped me across the face harder than I've ever been whacked by anybody in my life.

She turned on her heel, walked back over to the bar to join a friend, and minutes later, a $250 bottle of Krug champagne arrived at our table.

I think you could say I'd been Sinatra'd.

Later on, in Season Three, we cast a famous episode called "Independence Day," one that taught me an important lesson. Dana was involved in casting a guest star who was to become a love interest for her: an enlisted man named Sgt. Vinnie Ventresca, aka the Dog Man.

At Dana's urging, we ended up casting the enormously talented and equally troubled Tom Sizemore. Even at our first meeting, Tom demonstrated both his prodigious talent and his propensity to tell the world to go screw itself.

The lesson I learned was that involving your lead too much in the casting of somebody she's going to play opposite sets up a condition that can be problematic. Because if you go with her choice, and it's the wrong choice, the show suffers.

Similarly, if you go with someone else, then she's unhappy on day one of shooting. That doesn't work either.

That question of how much involvement a series lead

should have has reared its head on subsequent series I've cast, including various lead actors on *ER* and Emmy Rossum on *Shameless* making suggestions for guest stars that may not have necessarily been the best choices.

And when that happens, I revert to what I learned on *China Beach*. I'm a firm believer that the lead actor should read with the possible guest actors who might join the cast. Then we should thank them graciously and excuse them while we decide what's best for the show.

At the end of Season Three, we cast another significant actor in what turned out to be an acclaimed and also somewhat controversial episode, "Warriors." Don Cheadle played a character named Angel, who is part of a grizzled bunch of marines that report to Frankie Bunson when she is mistakenly promoted to sergeant. (The correct commander was a man named Francis Bunson.)

A fun side note: the episode was directed by the original Hutch of *Starsky and Hutch* fame, David Soul.

One of the things I take the most pride in about *China Beach* was how true-to-life we were in casting the show. According to the *New York Times*, in 1967, when the pilot episode took place, Black Americans represented approximately 11 percent of the civilian population, yet comprised 16.3 percent of all draftees and 23 percent of all combat troops in Vietnam.[2]

Our cast reflected that fact, and very honestly so.

Now, I knew Don a little bit personally because when my ex and I lived in Venice just before *China Beach*, we decided to turn the garage in our tiny house into a guest bedroom and a playroom for Joanna. Some of Don's CalArts friends, including actors Glenn Plummer (who had a role in an early *China Beach* episode and later played Timmy Rawlins on *ER*) and Dave Duensing (who played a "giggling grunt" in the *China Beach* pilot), built it.

The night they finished the remodel—stunning with blue

carpet and walls to match—Don came over with Glenn and Dave. Someone put on some rock 'n roll, and our two-year-old daughter danced with Don for what seemed like hours. When he turned to leave, he said to me, "John, in 25 years when she marries a Black man, it's because of tonight."

Needless to say, I'd be thrilled if she married a man like Don.

China Beach was also where some other notable actors got their start. When I received the Hoyt Bowers Award for Lifetime Achievement in 2009, my Second Chair, Melanie Burgess, and her husband, a film editor named James, generously offered to make a highlight reel of all the shows I have cast.

Watching some cuts, Melanie suddenly exclaimed, "Stop! Go back!" She had spied Vince Vaughn, who played a motor pool grunt in the first episode of Season Three, "The Unquiet Earth."

Sadly, I don't have any memory of him having an audition. He wasn't "Vince Vaughn" then. I'm pretty sure he was just Grunt Number Three.

We also had some high-profile guest directors (besides David Soul). The most memorable to me was Diane Keaton, who directed an episode in Season Four called "Fever." One of the things that was most notable about *China Beach* is that it followed the characters home to convey that for them, the war didn't end just because they left Vietnam.

The episode was about McMurphy returning to her hometown of Lawrence, Kansas in 1970, trying to re-acclimate to a civilian nursing job and life with her neurotic mother. We also see a flashback to China Beach three years earlier, when she reluctantly responds to a surprise birthday party thrown for her by Dr. Richard, Dodger, Boonie and others.

I was trying to concentrate on my job, starting with reading with actors. But it was Diane *effing* Keaton.

One of the parts was for a Vietnamese "bar girl"—a prostitute. The actress was young, shy and clearly a bit freaked out by Diane.

The scene was a seduction of sorts, with not a lot of dialogue.

After the first time through, Diane approached the young actress and whispered in her ear. She then returned to her seat and said that we should run the scene again.

This time the young actress stood out of her chair and approached me, her hands reaching for my belt.

I was paralyzed for a second and then reached out and grabbed her hands. I stopped the scene.

Keep in mind that this was long before we had intimacy coordinators on set. It was a much more "method" time.

Diane wasn't happy—she chided me. "Too real for you, Levey?"

Damn right it was.

Years later, I brought a date to a party at Mimi Leder's house.

Diane came walking over to us, greeted me warmly and playfully asked, "Who's the blonde, Levey?"

Still trying to direct me in some way, but I'll take it.

Other big names who showed their face on *China Beach*, albeit fleetingly, included Adam Arkin, Annabelle Gurwich, Vivica A. Fox, Megan Mullaley, John Slattery and Raymond Cruz.

Thanks to my prepubescent son, who joined me in catching some rising comedians at the Comedy Store, a young actor named Michael Rappaport came to my attention. (Shockingly, Michael was *not* doing blue material.) After his set, Oli turned to me and said, "He was good, dad. Not so funny, but you should put him on *China Beach*."

He was right. A chip off the old block. And so, I cast Michael in Season Four in a guest star role, "Kravits," in an episode called "One Small Step."

Stephen Baldwin appeared as a delusional GI convinced he was Chuck Berry in Season Two ("All About E.E.V.")—a relatively lighthearted commentary on race. And on the other end of the spectrum, Mykelti Williamson (later known for his role as Bubba in *Forrest Gump*) played a character named Jean Jacques Rousseau in Season Two, in the episode "Promised Land."

Again, the name says it all. The 18th-century philosopher and political theorist Jean-Jacques Rousseau famously wrote *Discourse on Inequality*. He also said: "Man is born free and everywhere he is in chains."

In "Promised Land," there is an honest and horrifying depiction of a racially charged, violent incident that breaks out in the camp after the news of Martin Luther King, Jr.'s assassination hits *China Beach*.

The truth is we discovered how controversial it was as we were doing it. This was an excellent illustration of JSY's anachronistic and rebellious instincts.

His goal and all of ours, really, was to convey the human cost of war, the emotional damage and the lengths people go to in deferring, deflecting and burying the damage to somehow continue on.

Part of what I think made the show so real, so believable, and ultimately, so respected was an accident of creativity that brought a group of people together who were right for that project. They knew, embraced and fulfilled their roles with a fully collaborative, cooperative, teamwork approach.

The feeling I got from *China Beach* and throughout my career when working on a project that's destined to be unique and timeless is akin to falling in love. You don't do it on purpose. But you can tell when it's happening to you.

But I digress. Because I was innocent enough at the time to follow my leaders, listen to the script and instinctively vibe with my colleagues.

The series went on to great acclaim, garnering multiple

award nominations and wins, including Primetime Emmys (Dana for Outstanding Lead Actress in a Drama Series, 1989 and 1992; Outstanding Sound Mixing for a Drama Series, 1990; Marg for Outstanding Supporting Actress in a Drama Series, 1990; Outstanding Achievement in Costuming for a Series, 1988), Golden Globes (Best Television Series - Drama, 1992), a Humanitas Prize (1989), and a Peabody Award (1990). Phyllis and I were nominated for a Casting Society of America Artios Award for the pilot, Best Casting for TV, Dramatic Episodic 1989. I received two subsequent Artios nominations in 1989 and 1990 in the same category.

It was great to help shine that kind of light on the project. But it wasn't about me. Casting is something I lead—I like to say I produce the casting on the shows in which I'm involved.

This is important: casting is a very collaborative act. I get to say *no* and *maybe*, but ultimately several of us get together before we say *yes* to an actor.

And I'm very much aware of that. Again, that goes back to my days as a young man in the '60s in college, where being a member of a community meant everybody doing their job. The spotlight belonged on the production—that way the collaborative effort was always the beneficiary.

And certainly, JSY got much of the credit (not to mention most of the blame) for *China Beach* because he was the leader. But that was just his role in the community.

The real rewards for me, though, were the friendships and collaborations that were formed and cemented in *China Beach*. The driftwood mobile analogy I like to use for casting? It works beautifully for the art the Wells crew created on our first series together.

Unbeknownst to all of us at the time, that mobile would hold strong for multiple series for more than three decades.

This feels like forever—like your freshman year in college, where you end up meeting some of your best friends, and you don't realize it at the time.

China Beach had that kind of magic. And soon, we'd go from a fictional gritty medical hospital in Vietnam to a gritty inner-city hospital in Chicago.

But first, a brief interlude where I experienced *Growing Pains* and ended up in *Brisco County's* Wild West—and said happy trails to my marriage.

FOUR

The Interlude

GROWING PAINS, THE ADVENTURES OF BRISCO
COUNTY, JR. 1991–1994

[SERIES CASTING BY JOHN LEVEY]

(44 to 47 years old)

While the home fires are burning out, John is burning the midnight oil. One of just a few to survive the Lorimar–Warner Bros. merger, he settles in with a new boss, a new office and the prospect of a new life as a divorcé.

Watching John pull out of the Warner Bros. lot in his now-beat-up, faded yellow Honda Civic, you might hear the strains of Nina Simone's "I Get Along without You Very Well (Except Sometimes)."

This chapter of my life was about making changes. Some small and some not so small.

It was both the lull before the storm (professionally) and the perfect storm necessary to finally level things (personally).

In terms of my marriage, it was a series of minuscule mistakes. And some that were not so insignificant.

For example, when Blaine's mother died, I stayed in Los Angeles. I think we talked about it and reached that decision together. But really, what was I thinking, prioritizing my work life over her emotional needs?

Our split was a self-fulfilling prophecy as a child of divorce. It seemed inevitable. I truly did not expect that I was entitled to be happy at home and at work.

And I think I contributed to the inevitability of our split. As it turns out, I'm sort of constitutionally opposed to change. And yet, every time I've had a major transition in my life, it's turned out to be of great benefit.

So, while I suffered greatly during our divorce, it turned out great from many points of view.

I was a better and more complete father when my relationship with my children was directly between them and me.

I found another source of partnership and love that's lasted more than 20 years. Spoiler alert: In those two decades, Blaine and I have maintained regular and friendly contact. We are both close with our now-grown children, and that is a lifelong tie that binds us.

I consider all of that to be something of a miracle—a happy accident.

Back to the early '90s and the biggest benefit of personal turmoil for my career: I was free to bury myself in my work.

Once *China Beach* came to an end, my colleague Patricia Noland and I worked under Warner Bros. VP of Casting, Marcia Ross, out of the old drugstore building on the lot. We were put on the popular sitcom *Growing Pains*, which was having its own growing pains as its heartthrob, Kirk Cameron, started to age out of being a draw for teenage girls.

The penultimate chapter of the show was focused on adding a new cast member in the seventh season, Luke Brower—a homeless boy who lives with the Seavers. If you know anything about Leonardo DiCaprio's mythology, this was his "big break" early in his career.

Now, it would be nice to say that I cast him in that role, but really, Patricia was primarily responsible.

I was busy hashing out the penultimate chapter of my marriage on a family trip, which included my mother, to the Florida Keys.

It was shit-or-get-off-the-pot time.

Blaine and I were either going to tell my mother that our marriage was ending, or we would try to figure out some way to make it work. I honestly wasn't sure which direction it would go.

As luck would have it, toward the end of our trip, I ended up in traffic on the longest bridge in Florida, the Seven Mile Bridge, alone with my mother. Ironically, as we were stuck, things back in LA were moving at a rapid clip. Patricia had spent the day at the network and finally managed to get Leo approved to become a series regular.

Of course, there was drama playing out on the Seven Mile Bridge, too. I was still trying to pretend that there was some hope for Blaine and me.

But Mom was none too flattering about Blaine (there had always been a bit of tension between the two), and I could see what she was doing. She was trying to be the bad guy who didn't accept "because she's my wife!" as a response to why I thought we should (or had to) stay together.

By the time we reached our destination, I, too, had arrived at the sad but final conclusion that Blaine and I had reached the end of our marriage. Nothing was anyone's "fault." We had become two people sharing a house and children, but nothing else.

We simply grew apart.

When we arrived back in LA from Florida, Blaine made it official by contacting an attorney. I did the same and moved into an apartment.

Even though it was a straightforward case of "irreconcilable differences," it took a couple of years to finalize.

Finally, I remember sitting in my lawyer's conference room one day. The man didn't have a fax machine or an answering machine because he didn't want to be reliably reachable. And suddenly, the truth hit me.

I realized that it was in no one's best interests but mine to get things resolved. Our lawyers would happily drag things out as long as was necessary—or, more accurately, as long as we bought the story that we couldn't hash things out on our own.

As two people who knew a few things about communal living and its aftermath, I realized we could work it out.

I drove to our family home, now just about officially Blaine's house, and waited for her to return. Not that I thought she was scared of me, but I recall getting out of the car very cautiously and asking if we could speak.

She agreed.

So, I climbed into the passenger seat of her mom-car, and we negotiated the final remaining points in our divorce agreement.

And then it was done.

Word to the wise: especially when there's not much left to talk about—when you reach the point where the amount the lawyers will make exceeds what you'll be left with—work it out.

A postscript on other endings, too. At the end of *Growing Pains'* seventh season, Leo got offered a leading role in the film *This Boy's Life.* So while Patricia had negotiated his entrée on the show, I went to the studio to facilitate his exit.

I told the studio head, Harvey Shephard, "I know we could stop him, but we shouldn't. It's the right thing to do to let him do this movie, and it can only help us if the show gets picked up for another season. Leo becoming a movie star will be something our viewers love."

Harvey agreed, and he let Leo out of his contract.

And, of course, ABC didn't pick up *Growing Pains* for an eighth season anyway, so it turned out to be the right call. Leo went on right away to do *What's Eating Gilbert Grape?*, garnering best supporting actor Oscar nominations and becoming the superstar he was destined to be.

The last project I did over at the old drugstore building with Patricia was casting the pilot for an inventive show called *The Adventures of Brisco County, Jr.* created by Jeffrey Boam and Carlton Cuse, the duo who had written the script for *Indiana Jones and the Last Crusade.* (Carlton went on to create the monster hit television show, *Lost.*)

I always called it a "two-reefer Western" because it was trippy as hell. It had a mystical science fiction element in the trappings of a traditional western.

So it wasn't a shocker that the man we ended up casting in the titular role, Bruce Campbell, performed a hilarious and surreal audition for Patricia and me in our tiny office. At the time, Bruce was best known for his work on the *Evil Dead* movies (created by his childhood buddy, Sam Raimi), and, of course, today, he's gone on to become an iconic, cult-classic actor.

I don't remember the script, but I do remember Bruce doing a front flip in Patricia's and my face. It was shocking, terrifying and hilarious all at once. We figured he was either going to kick us in the kissers, break his neck or possibly both.

From the make-your-audition-memorable files, Bruce kicked ass.

Literally.

More changes were afoot as the Warner Bros. and Lorimar merger, which was official as of 1989, finally shook things up in my world. In the early fall of 1993, two dozen people were let go, and only a handful of us from Warner Bros. TV was retained by the new studio, which I quietly and affectionately dubbed "Warnermar."

Besides me, Gregg Mayday stayed on as senior VP of movies and miniseries, David Sacks remained a current programming exec, and Henry Johnson continued as VP of production.[1] Leslie (Les) Moonves was in charge of the whole operation, now officially known as Warner Bros. TV Production. And Harvey was out—he stepped into being an independent producer for Warner Bros.

While I don't know this for sure, I believe that John Wells had put in a good word for me with Les. He, in turn, suggested to his senior VP of casting, Barbara Miller, that she absorb me into her department over at Building 140 on the Warner Bros. lot.

Barbara was a seasoned casting director who'd been the head of casting at Lorimar since the mid-1970s. She was impeccable, dressed to the nines every day at work, commandeering all casting activities from her large, well-appointed suite.

If you were on her good side, she was kind, funny, and generous.

If not, watch out.

The bottom line was that Barbara had a lot of rules, mostly designed to maintain her power position and authority.

The casting directors had almost no institutional contact with executives from other departments, not even business affairs.

Barbara controlled all of the series regular deals. Not current programming. Not development. Not production. Not publicity.

So, when I first arrived at "Warnermar" from the smaller and more interactive original Warner Bros. TV, Barbara sat me down and succinctly delivered her message:

"There will be a lot of changes, and you are making all of them."

Clear as a bell.

I wanted to fit in. I wanted to play ball. Truly.

However, what she ordered me to do is outside of my nature. Given my '60s background, I'm suspicious of authority. Independent, naturally. And a bit of a rebel.

The project that I had brought over was, as mentioned, *The Adventures of Brisco County, Jr.*

One day upon arriving at work, I checked my voicemail. There was one message that stood out: a female voice with a sweet Southern accent explaining how she thought I had blocked her access to a role on the show.

Unlike her accent, the message she left on my machine wasn't sweet at all. She was damn mad and quite explicit about her wish to do me harm.

I saved the voicemail. And I called security.

They came and retrieved the message to begin an investigation.

I then went down to Barbara's office to tell her the story. I tried to downplay my worry.

After I finished, she looked at me kind of sideways and said, "You have voicemail?"

It seems her staff wasn't permitted that luxury. The assistants had to cover the phones on a rotating basis, even during lunch. Barbara always wanted someone there to answer the phones in person.

Her wrath over my using voicemail was honestly more unnerving than that disgruntled actress.

Life at Building 140 was a night-and-day difference from the old drugstore building. There was a long hallway with a few executive offices at one end that housed about a dozen of the casting directors who reported to Barbara.

I was down the hall next to my dear old friend, Deedee Bradley, who I worked with at Barbara Claman's office when I began my casting career. And across from me was my close friend (and later collaborator on *The West Wing*), Tony Sepulveda. Also surrounding me were good friends and colleagues Leslie Litt, Megan Branman, Ellie Kanner, Geraldine Leder, Mark Saks and Ted Hann.

To get to the reception area, actors would come through the back door of Building 140—not the front door. After a while, we'd call down to have two or three actors at a time wait in the long hallway filled with about 35 chairs for all the different shows we were casting.

I only wish I had the wherewithal to have the receptionist in the front waiting room take a photograph every hour or so of the people sitting in the waiting room. It would've been a brilliant piece of photojournalism because, at any given moment, you might find a six-year-old missing both front teeth sitting next to a drag queen or a Hell's Angels biker.

I always liked to go and get the actors myself from the long hallway rather than just call them in. That way, I could have a brief interaction with them if I felt that they were flipping out or flipping in. I was always happy to answer questions.

As I see it, one of my responsibilities is always to put the actor at ease by being a human being myself. So they can be a human being *themselves*. I always have tried to make the environment regular and not fraught with tension and pressure as much as possible.

After collecting the actor, we'd head into my office. I would usually sit in a chair, and they would sit or stand opposite me, depending on what we were casting. And we might talk a bit about the project, especially if it was a pilot since they wouldn't know much about it.

If it was a producer's session, generally speaking, the writer and producer would sit on the couch so that the director could sit in a single chair. That way, everyone would have a fairly good eye line to observe the actor.

And I would be in the center of the room to read the parts with the actors—something I did all the time.

Here's a note about giving actors notes: I have always said that there are two reasons I would give an adjustment and two reasons why I wouldn't.

The two reasons to give an adjustment are:

1. The actor is of considerable interest, but the performance doesn't feel right. I then will goof around with them to see what their muscle and range are.
2. They are very right for the role, but they have made some wrong assumptions. That way, I can guide them to make stronger choices that may help improve their performance.

The two reasons *not* to give an adjustment are:

1. The actor is not fascinating or right at all.
2. The actor is just simply wonderful, and I don't want to mess with it.

So, I've often told actors don't strategize and wonder why there was or wasn't an adjustment: it could be good news, *or* it could be bad news.

Also, because of my background as a teacher and a director, my adjustments tend to be process oriented, not results oriented.

So, for example, "Would you pick up the pace, please?" is results oriented.

I might say something like, "Would you love them a little bit more?" Or, "Can you be a bit more concerned about what he thinks of you?" And, "What if you were really angry at him, and you wanted to humiliate him quietly?"

This kind of adjustment gives them something to play that will help their process.

One last story from *Brisco* that has nothing to do with the acting process but is a final note about my own process as a product of the '60s.

We had a role for a kind of shaman ("Dr. Milo") who traveled the area in a horse-drawn carriage of sorts, peddling herbs and spices for the episode "Stagecoach."

We thought it would be kitschy if the famed LSD guru and former Harvard math professor Timothy Leary would play the part.

We met Timothy in Carlton's office. He arrived on time and was reasonably well put together. Also present was a young rising star producer, John McNamara.

We chatted about the show, the role and some details of production.

Every so often, Timothy would kind of stop mid-sentence and stare at me. It was odd but not alarming in any way.

Eventually, he spoke directly to me: "You get me," he said, nodding his head knowingly. "They don't get me, but you get me."

I wondered exactly what he meant. I was older than the others in the room and certainly closer to his age or that of his disciples.

But I think it was more than that.

I think he could tell that I had taken his advice to turn on, tune in and drop out at one point in my life.

Of course, he was right.

But not anymore. I was respectable, responsible and ready for the next chapter. A new kind of doctor was guiding my way—all the way to Michael Crichton's County General Hospital's *ER*.

FIVE

The Game Changer

[CASTING BY JOHN LEVEY, CSA]

(47 to 48 years old)

This 47-year-old man who had been in monogamous relationships his entire life is newly single, which is both terrifying and exhilarating—the dominant emotions evoked by the new series he's casting, ER. *His parenting life, like the show, picks up plot lines mid-stream, as John has two days with each kid per week.*

If there's a theme song to John's life, it would have to be the iconic, the heart-pumping, electronic jazz of the ER *theme song by James Newton Howard—come for the initial adrenalin rush, stay for the hopeful pickup and sexy sax that signals better things are coming.*

Closing credits of *ER* Season One, 1994-1995 (which ran
through Season 12, 2006)

Unlike other hit projects organized in boardrooms and
carefully orchestrated for greatness, *ER* has a legendary beginning that started back in 1974 when Michael Crichton first
decided to chronicle his time in an emergency room as a
young medical student. His TV series pilot script, entitled "24
Hours," was quasi-documentary style—fast-paced, a jumble
of stories stacking on top of each other, with no slow begin-
nings or logical conclusions.

A series of middles, set against the backdrop of life and
death.

Michael, already a prolific and wildly successful non-
fiction writer and novelist, was coming off of directing his first
film, *Westworld*. What's fascinating to me is that an amusement
park filled with nefarious robots apparently felt less scary to
him than making his next project something that people had
never seen before.

And so, Michael shelved the script for 15 years until he
brought it up with Steven Spielberg as a possible next project
in 1989.

In the same conversation, he told Steven about another
project he was working on—a little something about

dinosaurs. The two decided dinos before doctors, and once again, "24 Hours" was shelved.

Or, perhaps more accurately, tucked away in a closet. Because that was the story I heard. Five years later, Anthony "Tony" Thomopoulos, who headed Amblin's Television Division, unearthed the script from a storage closet.

He read it—presumably intrigued as it was written by Michael Crichton, creator of the 1993 hit film *Jurassic Park*— and thought it would make a great television show. Somehow he got it to Warner Bros. and Les Moonves. And then John Wells was tapped to develop and run the show.

This is where I came in. I can vividly remember reading the script and knowing it would be something unlike anything we'd ever seen before. It was urban, high-charged—and very, very urgent.

An emergency. This wasn't some old-fashioned doctor show with a kind-hearted patriarch who's making house calls to families in distress. It reflected that poor Americans and, in particular, people of color, use the ER for their primary care. It signaled an emergence of a new genre.

The feel of the script and its pacing were unique. The storytelling structure and technique told me that the show would need a visual style that reflected the urgency. It was jarring.

Because after all, we, the viewers, weren't there to see the car accident, heart attack or fall from the ladder. And usually, we didn't know the story's end, either.

Later, sometimes for the A storyline, we did find out how challenges were resolved.

But most of the stories had no beginning and no end, just a riveting middle.

Here's the breakdown I received to cast the heart of the ensemble back in 1994—thankfully preserved by my dear friend and esteemed colleague, Kevin Scott. You'll notice from the time we did the casting until the actual pilot was shot, that the characters, including all of their names, evolved.

BREAKDOWN
To: Agents
From: Barbara Miller/John Levey
Date: 2/9/94.
RE: "ER" - 2hr pilot for 1hr drama series for NBC
Prod. Co: WARNER BROS TV IN ASSOCIATION WITH AMBLIN ENT.
Location: LA
Dir: ROD HOLCOMB
St. Date: Approximately 3/15/94
Writer: Michael Crichton
Exec. Prods: Michael Crichton/John Wells
Co-Prod: Tony Thomopoulos
SR VP Casting: Barbara Miller
Casting Dirs: Barbara Miller/John Levey
Casting Assts: Roberta Heiman/Kevin Scott

WRITTEN SUBMISSIONS TO: John Levey
300 Television Plaza
Bldg. 140, RM. 135
Burbank, CA 91505
***NOTE: Please send duplicate submissions with pictures to Barbara Miller at the same address in RM. 133.**

SEEKING:

Dr. RICHARD GREENE: 28 to 35. Medical resident, married with a kid. His wife and family are pushing him to become a dermatologist. Make a lot of money, set your own hours. But he's drawn to emergency medicine. Danger, poor pay, lousy hours—but he makes a difference in people's lives—isn't that why he got into medicine in the first place?

DR. PAUL BENTON: Surgical resident, 33. Black, confident. A risk-taker, a high wire act. Looking down the throat of real success. Three hundred grand a year. A Black man floating through a white world—alone.

DR. COLLEEN LEWIS: Mid-30s. Ambitious. Talented. A real sports nut. Her dad's daughter. Her long-term relationship has just ended. Badly. They were engaged, and he left because she couldn't do it all.

TOM ROSS: Too handsome for his own good. Late 20s to early 30s. Pediatrician, drinker, womanizer. When will he stop screwing up his life? His list of old girlfriends is long. Way too long.

DR. JOHN CABOT: Intern. Mid to late 20s. From a very wealthy family, his father, a well-known cardiologist. Cabot is vaguely hapless, and a lot of our fun will be in watching him grow. Mature. Take on more. But we'll also have fun watching Ross, and especially Benton, torment the hapless kid. And surprisingly—we'll see him begin to succeed.

Now, here are my recollections of casting *ER*'s initial core ensemble:

DR. DOUG ROSS:
GEORGE CLOONEY

George had a development deal at Warner Bros. Television, and a top prospect for him was an NBC pilot for a buddy cop show. Now, keep in mind that this was in the time of buddy cop movies, buddy cop shows, buddy cops all around. Now, that show wasn't bad, but it wasn't innovative or great.

As I've mentioned, Les Moonves was the president of Warner Bros. Television at the time, and he put an enormous emphasis on what he called "the count." This referred to how many pilots we made. He really wanted to make more than Universal, MGM and any other production company.

It was vital to Les to be the volume leader.

In fact, when I first came over to Warner Bros. TV when the merger happened, an executive named Larry Little told Les that I had said, "Oh, shit, I'm going from quality to quantity."

That wasn't exactly true. Not that I didn't say it (I did), but while Les was interested in quantity, he was also interested in quality. And he believed both could co-exist. He confronted me with that alleged quote at some point early on in my days after the merger, but I somehow managed to live through that.

Back to Clooney's potential buddy show. There was a lot of pressure from the top because of Les's interest in "the count." With George attached, the show would have certainly gotten picked up.

Now to a legendary story from George's own mouth—one I'd love to believe is true, but I don't quite recall it this way. George once told somebody that I had snuck him a copy of the *ER* pilot script to his dressing room on *Sisters* in a brown paper bag like it was a dirty magazine.

As the story goes, it was clearly the sexy choice and all he needed to make his decision.

But the bottom line is that somehow George did, in fact, get a copy of the script. And he wisely recognized that to play Dr. Ross would end his streak of seven or eight failed pilots.

George was everything that every show was looking for back then: a funny, smart, sexy, somewhat dangerous, somewhat vulnerable, 30-something leading man.

And so it wasn't surprising that NBC wanted him for the

buddy cop show or that Les thought he could get two birds with one stone—with George being the big, hunky stone.

But George always has had a fantastic commercial instinct: as an actor, a director and a producer.

He really knows what he wants to do.

But he also knows what he *ought* to do.

And so George came into a meeting with the pilot's director, Rod Holcomb, John Wells, Barbara Miller, and me in Barbara's office. Rod talked about how he thought he was going to shoot the pilot. And George was very production savvy, so he understood Rod's image. John talked about the script and the things about it that he loved. Barbara and I just listened.

As I recall, George told us a fantastic story of the night of the Northridge earthquake on January 17, 1994, a few weeks earlier, where he ended up outside his house at 4:31 am in the backyard, under a tree with his roommate, naked, with their pet pig.

As he told us, "Just another Saturday night, naked with a pig."

George was Doug Ross.

Needless to say, he passed on the buddy cop show. He actually took a small cut from his overall deal to do *ER*. That's how much he knew it was his ticket.

Side note about the pig comment: I don't think he meant to insult either his pet pot-bellied pig, Max, or any of the women he had been with, but he was making fun of himself. This is one of George's extraordinary qualities: humility, mixed with his enormous confidence. And that's so appealing to everybody, men and women.

George is the definition of charisma.

And he's also the definition of generosity and humanity. George was famous for knowing the names of everybody's assistants in the hallways of Building 140. If he was going to have a meeting with Les about a script and with producers, he'd walk down that hallway full of casting directors…and he wouldn't necessarily bother saying hi to any of us. But he always warmly greeted our assistants by name.

DR. MARK GREENE:
ANTHONY EDWARDS

One day early on in the casting process, it just so happened that John Wells had a meeting in Building 140 on the second floor where all of the Warner Bros. TV executives' offices were located.

On the way back, he popped into my office on the first floor, where all of us casting directors sat. I was standing in my then-assistant and forever dear friend Kevin Scott's office (my space was just behind his). On a shelf was a giant pile of folders labeled "Dr. Greene."

Oddly enough, at that particular moment in time, Tony's picture was on the top of the pile. He was a submission from Innovative, a well-respected boutique-y agency, up there with Gersh and Paradigm.

If you think back on what Tony looked like in *Top Gun*, and you juxtapose that with what he looked like in *ER*'s pilot, his appearance was quite different. Some of the leading man qualities he possessed as "Goose" in *Top Gun* went down the shower drain with some of his hair. And he became more of an empathetic, lovely, relatable adult.

John took one look at his picture, and he said, "Wow, that's a great idea."

And it sure as hell was.

Ultimately Tony tested opposite an actor called Chris Fields, who today is the artistic director of one of LA's most important small theatres, The Echo Theatre Company.

With Tony in the role, *ER* had its everyman hero to root for. Early in the series, I remember sitting on the couch watching dailies (not my favorite activity) with Barbara.

After about the tenth time seeing Tony comfort a patient, Barbara hollered out to her assistant: "Get my doctor on the line and cancel my appointment for next week. I'm only going to see Dr. Mark Greene from now on."

And that really encapsulated what I think America felt: he was the heart and soul of the show. Tony played Dr. Greene in such an understated and selfless kind of way—the way we like our heroes to be—not braggadocio saviors but just do-your-job heroes.

Which, of course, in our post-pandemic world, we now know is precisely the kind of heroes our medical workers truly are.

MEDICAL STUDENT/DR. JOHN CARTER: NOAH WYLE

Of all the roles I've ever cast, Noah's audition might be the most memorable for several reasons. It had to do with who was in the room and what transpired naturally (and hilariously).

As was usual in those days, I was on the phone. It was the kitchen phone, which was mounted on the wall with a 25-foot cord so I could wander, in this case, into Kevin's space in the front office.

John, Rod Holcomb (the pilot director) and a third man breezed past me and settled on the couch and matching chair in my larger space.

A chair was set up for the auditioning actor in the middle of the room.

I entered briskly, wanting to appear cool and efficient.

I was introduced to the third man—the author of "24 Hours"—now officially *ER*'s pilot episode.

Michael Crichton.

(Later, a few months after the pilot had been shot and we had been ordered to series, I met Michael a second time. This time, Steven Spielberg was there, too. When John introduced us, the two men rose in tandem—quite a sight as Michael was 6'10" and Steven is 5'8." Michael seemed to rise forever as Steven stopped abruptly on the way. I had to laugh out loud. Sorry, I digress, back to Noah's audition...)

The first actor up was a young man I didn't know.

It was Noah Wyle.

I had had several phone calls from his agent, Ilene Feldman, a woman whose taste and independent spirit I admired, who had a small agency bearing her initials (IFA).

She could have had a much less risky job at one of the established agencies but wanted to do it her way.

Noah had done some work in films that had not yet been released, so I couldn't make up my mind about his talents or his rightness for Dr. John Carter.

I agreed happily to audition him without producers present out of respect for the agent.

She insisted that he had to be seen by the decision-makers immediately.

After three or four similar calls, I relented, and now here we were.

Noah approached me and said he wanted to do a scene that wasn't part of the audition plan: his first blood draw.

I agreed.

There wasn't much dialogue in the scene, so he asked if I'd please sit in the chair and offer up my right arm for his use.

Again, I agreed.

He tied something around my bicep and produced a pencil—the kind where you hit a button, and the point emerges.

He shook it and began to look for a vein.

He was unable to find one.

He started over.

He failed again.

And again. And again. And again.

Michael laughed quietly at first, then more and more robustly.

It was a happy coincidence that I had relented on the one day the series creator attended auditions in my office.

And, of course, Noah was so right for the role. Looking back, I refer to this epic day in casting history as his "25-million-dollar audition." (Not that I know the exact figure he made from the series, but Google seems to feel this amount is about right.)

A side note about character development: A few seasons into *ER*, it was revealed that Dr. Carter's older brother, Bobby, had died in childhood from leukemia. (As you can imagine, this hit particularly close to home for me, considering my own son's early diagnosis.)

When Noah learned of that painful fact of his character's background, he remarked that knowing about his deceased brother might have impacted his performance.

But actually, my gut says it was the other way around. John's ability to pick up nuances in the dailies likely led him to notice an extra dash of compassion and sweetness in Noah's/Carter's interactions with kids. The character's back-story was thus likely shaped by Noah's instincts, not the other way around.

The detail of the older brother's death also explains Carter's mother, Eleanor's, emotional distance and coldness to her surviving son. (The wonderful Mary McDonnell ulti-mately played her.)

DR. SUSAN LEWIS:
SHERRY STRINGFIELD

Just as we were about to begin casting *ER*, John and I flew to New York to do some work with casting director Francine Maisler, who today is known for countless award-winning films and TV shows. At the time, however, *Reality Bites* was perhaps her most notable credit.

It happened that we were sitting on the plane in first class, and near us was Sherry Stringfield, who had just come off a spectacular turn on the first season of *NYPD Blue* (1993–1994) playing Manhattan Assistant District Attorney Laura Kelly. Publicly Sherry had expressed some unhappiness with the show, so she was released early from her contract.

John and I both thought she was the cat's meow.

So, we told her, "Get a hold of the *ER* script. Take a look at it. There's a role, Dr. Lewis, and we think you'd be great."

Somehow, Sherry did. And her audition went beautifully. Her quality is all about the understated hero, which was what *ER* was all about.

The hero that didn't need attention.

The hero that came from a real family with an effed-up sister who we meet later on in the first season (Chloe Lewis, played deliciously by Kathleen Wilhoite).

Dr. Lewis is that understated everywoman, empathetic person that Sherry genuinely is.

That's why she got the job and what she brought to the show.

I remember in the pilot episode, Sherry had a very memorable scene with Miguel José Ferrer, who was George's cousin in real life. He played a 40-year-old husband and father of three named Mr. Parker, and she delivered the diagnosis of lung cancer to him. (Ironically, Miguel died years later of esophageal cancer at the relatively young age of 61.)

In the show, he asked her how long he had to live. Her answer was six months to a year.

When he presses her if that's for sure, she answers, "Mr. Parker, if there's one thing you learn in my job, it's that nothing is certain. Nothing that seems very bad, and nothing that seems very good. Nothing is certain. Nothing."

And her delivery of that line was so deep—it's what she didn't say that said it all.

DR. PETER BENTON:
ERIQ LA SALLE

Casting Eriq La Salle as Dr. Peter Benton on *ER* was no small feat. Doing it put me in direct conflict with one of Barbara Miller's hard and fast rules: we casting directors were not permitted to compete with each other for actors.

Everybody had to produce an interest list regularly, and if an actor was high on someone else's list, we were to stay away.

I was interested in Eriq La Salle for the *ER* pilot right from the start, but another casting director already had dibs on him.

Later, Eriq was hired for the other show—*Under Suspicion* —but the role was reduced from a series regular to a guest player for budget reasons, as sometimes happens.

In the meantime, we had moved along in the process of casting *ER*. We had George. We got Tony, Sherry and Noah all in that one incredible session at Lori Openden's NBC casting office.

The last role was Dr. Benton.

We tested the terrific actor Michael Beach.

Legendary NBC executive Don Ohlmeyer said, "You've got four-fifths of a great ensemble. You can have Michael if you feel strongly."

Not exactly high praise, but we were still leaning toward Michael—for about five minutes longer.

After leaving the meeting in Lori's office, John Wells and I were walking down the hall toward the elevator when Les Moonves hurried to catch up to us.

"Whatever you do, don't pick up Michael's option yet," he urged.

Already damned by Don's faint praise, we agreed to pass

on Michael for the role of Dr. Benton. (Ironically, he ended up in a supporting role on *Under Suspicion*.)

And so, I had no choice but to defy Barbara's rule.

We saw Eriq several days later after he returned from shooting his guest role in Portland.

I remember him in medical scrubs, lying in the hallway outside my office, stretching like a ballplayer before a big game.

He came in and read.

It was clear that we had the final one-fifth of this historical ensemble.

That all happened several days into the shoot.

Later, after *Under Suspicion* only lasted a season, Michael joined the *ER* cast in a crucial guest star role in Season Two, Al Boulet—physical therapist Jeanie Boulet's husband. Notably, Al is diagnosed as HIV-positive and infects Jeanie in one of the show's more honest, real and heartbreaking turns.

Tackling the significant issues of the time was always one of the most compelling aspects of *ER*.

A win-win from breaking Barbara's rules.

Back to Eriq: I always admired the hell out of him because he took the responsibility of playing a surgeon on a popular television show, and being a role model, very seriously.

If you want visceral proof, just watch the scene from Season Six, Episode 22, "May Day," where the doctors do an intervention with Carter, who is abusing painkillers. Carter storms out, and Benton follows.

It's those unspoken moments that say it all.

Noah breaks down, Eriq pulls him into a brotherly hug, and you can feel it.

That's not just acting. That's something beyond.

A side note about chemistry and connection in story-telling: My opinion is that it takes a brilliant creative mind to make magic out of what is invisible.

As I've mentioned, John always believed that as a

showrunner, if you watch the dailies carefully, you'll see things that you didn't even intend.

For example, two people will cross paths in the hallway, and the palpable chemistry between them could lead you to make a romantic connection. Or it could lead you to make a mentor-mentee connection.

So that's how John discovered the relationship between Noah and Eric early on. Noah was a medical student, so remember, he wasn't on a surgical rotation; he was on an ER rotation. Somehow, though, whenever those two were on screen together, John saw potential, and he let that relationship evolve naturally.

It did, and it paid off big time.

Ultimately, showrunners are like sports coaches: the best ones adapt their philosophies and systems to their players. And the worst ones hold tightly—well, rigidly—to their idea of what's the best.

John is fantastically flexible in that regard, and totally willing to discover, which is great. In this way, he encouraged all of us to be open to how things unfold.

NURSE CAROL HATHAWAY: JULIANNA MARGULIES

In the grand tradition of *Hill Street Blues*, a guest star in the *ER* pilot became a series regular: Julianna Margulies.

(For *Hill Street* fans, officers Bobby Hill [Michael Warren] and Andy Renko [Charles Haid] were both shot in the pilot. Renko was supposed to die, and Hill was to be a recurring character, not a lead—but thanks to high scores with test audiences, both survived and became central to the show's success.)

Nurse Carol Hathaway's suicide attempt was supposed to be a success, although her death was implied but not proclaimed in the pilot. But then Julianna's performance, along with her character's relationship with Dr. Ross, tested so incredibly well that there was really no choice but to give her a miraculous recovery.

I agreed with the audience's take on her performance. I had actually tried very hard to get Julianna on *The Adventures of Brisco County, Jr.* early on, but somehow those producers just didn't see a beautiful Jewish girl in the Old West.

So, when *ER* came along, I thought she would be fantastic as Nurse Carol Hathaway. And oh, you know, once in a while, you're right.

I was right. She was a *wow*.

This brings me to casting what I dubbed "the trampoline." It's those recurring characters and guest stars that pop in and out as the working people who populated County General, informing its personality and pace.

In fact, discerning our trampoline was one of John's first tasks. Michael's script was filled with non-descript characters: "doctor," "nurse," "orderly," and "EMT." So, when we first started to talk about the script, I innocently asked John, "How do we know if the nurse on page 42 of the script is the same nurse from page 12?"

So, that was the first thing that John did to the script: identify those doctors and nurses and create character arcs for them, too.

Then the fun began.

I moved all of the furniture to the side and sat in the middle of my office floor, surrounded by pictures and resumes of actors we liked very much but weren't right for any of the leads.

Kevin stood in the doorway and would say something like, "female of color, nurse, 45." And I would pick five or six women from the 30 or 40 pictures surrounding me on the floor and hand them to him.

Kevin would then paperclip them together and attach an index card with the character's name—in this example case,

"Nurse Haleh." (We ultimately cast Yvette Freeman in that role, which she played in 184 episodes, beginning with the pilot and ending with the series finale in 2009.)

Or Kevin would say, "28-year-old EMT, ladies' man, open to any ethnicity," and I would hand him five or six photographs and resumes, and he would clip them together and label them.

We would then set up sessions that way. And every time I gave him five or six pictures, he would give me a half-dozen more from the big pile of our favorites to replace on the floor.

This wasn't just a job for the pilot episode. Keeping the trampoline fresh was an ongoing process for 15 seasons, all 331 episodes. As I once told *Backstage,* "Everybody who speaks, grunts, groans, moans, cries out in pain—that's our responsibility."

Because we didn't have a clear sense of who everybody was beyond John's spare sketches, we didn't put out breakdowns for most of the guest parts on *ER.* My floor was kind of like my mainframe—our own handmade computer system.

How I did my work then is how I've always done it and still do it to this day. I consider a number of angles, from the actor's representation to their background, experience and face.

Then I rely heavily on my nerve and instinct to assess their life force. In this case, it was always about the tension and bounce they'd provide to the trampoline.

Because the show was set in a county hospital, a few unique elements came into play. Because we were dealing with sick people, I was always acutely aware that empathy had to be on display in every room and in every situation.

That's a particular affect an actor would either have —or not.

I can take care of myself, so I can take care of you, was the predominant ethos I was looking for in the medical staff.

Also, racial balance was a central focus for casting *ER.* We were telling honest, raw stories from a county hospital's emergency room's POV. We were acutely aware that rich people only go to the ER for actual emergencies. Otherwise, they see their own doctors.

But basic care for the poor, the urban and the disenfranchised often takes place in the ER.

So everyone, from our trampoline to our recurring guest stars, was chosen with a responsibility to an honest portrayal of an inner-city *ER* and the people who inhabit its hallways.

Keep in mind that we did all of this casting before studios and networks had policies and procedures concerning racial balancing. We assembled an incredibly diverse supporting cast, and we did it without being told to.

That was a function partly of the script and the arena, and partly because of our personal cares and concerns. Our own casting office was balanced in terms of gender and race, and it just made sense to us.

THE TRAMPOLINE: MEDICAL AND RELATED WORKERS

These are in alphabetical order, for all 15 seasons—please note this list is as inclusive as possible, from my recollections and research. They are indicated in the following order: Actor, Character Name, Character Position or Description and Years of Appearance. Also, I've indicated those performances that garnered Emmy nominations and wins.

Actor	Character Name	Character Position	Years Appearance
Alan Alda	Dr. Gabriel Lawrence	ER attending physician (Emmy -nominated)	1999
Mädchen Amick	Wendall Meade	Social worker	2004–2005
Sam Anderson	Dr. Jack Kayson	Chief of Cardiology and board member	1994–1999, 2001–2005, 2007
Perry Anzilotti	Perry	Anesthesiologist	1994–2004, 2006, 2008
Shiri Appleby	Dr. Daria Wade	Intern	2008–2009
Amy Aquino	Dr. Janet Coburn	OB/GYN chief	1994–2009
Ed Asner	Dr. James McNulty	Runs a street clinic	2003
John Aylward	Dr. Donald Anspaugh	Chief of Staff, general surgeon and board member	1996-2009
Abraham Benrubi	Jerry Markovic	Desk clerk	1994–1999, 2002–2006, 2008–2009

Paul Blackthorne	Dr. Jeremy Lawson	Invasive radiologist	2004
Alexis Bledel	Dr. Julia Wise	Intern	2009
Michelle Bonilla	Christine Harms	Paramedic	1999—2009
Conni Marie Brazelton	Conni Oligario	ER nurse	1994–2003
David Brisbin	Dr. Alexander Babcock	Anesthesiologist	1998–2002
Clancy Brown	Dr. Ellis West	SPG doctor	1997–1998
L. Scott Caldwell	Dr. Megan Rabb	Director of Neonatology	2004, 2006
Jordan Calloway	K.J. Thibeaux	Volunteer	2005–2006
Scott Michael Campbell	Reilly Brown	EMT	1996
Laura Cerón	Chuny Marquez	ER nurse	1995–2009
Don Cheadle	Paul Nathan	Medical student (Emmy-nominated)	2002

Morris Chestnut	Frank "Rambo" Bacon	ICU nurse, father of Deb's (Jing-Mei's) daughter	2000
Megan Cole	Dr. Alice Upton	Pathologist	1996, 1998, 2000–2001, 2003
Brendan Patrick Connor	Reidy	Paramedic	2006–2008
Ellen Crawford	Lydia Wright	ER Nurse	1994–2003, 2009
Julie Delpy	Nicole	Runner for Central Supplies and Luka Kovač's girlfriend	2001
John Doman	Dr. Carl Deraad	Chief of Psychiatry	1999–2001, 2003
Malaya Rivera Drew	Katy Alvaro	Medical student	2006–2007
George Eads	Greg Powell	Paramedic	1997–1998

Ron Eldard	Ray "Shep" Shepard	Paramedic	1995–1996
Christine Elise	Harper Tracy	Medical student	1995–1996
Julie Ann Emery	Nikki	Paramedic	2001–2003
Omar Epps	Dr. Dennis Gant	Surgical intern	1996–1997
Charles Esten	Dr. Barry Grossman	Orthopedic surgeon	2007–2008
Troy Evans	Frank Martin	Desk clerk	1994–2009
Jorja Fox	Dr. Maggie Doyle	ER intern, resident	1996–1999
Yvette Freeman	Haleh Adams	ER nurse	1994–2009
Mike Genovese	Al Grabarsky	Police officer	1995–1996, 1998–2000
Jami Gertz	Dr. Nina Pomerantz	Psychiatrist	1997
Sara Gilbert	Dr. Jane Figler	ER intern, later resident	2004—2008
Erica Gimpel	Adele Newman	Social services liaison	1997–2003

Matthew Glave	Dr. Dale Edson	Surgeon	1996–1999, 2001–2002
Robert Gossett	Dr Everett Daniels	Hospital board member	2008
Mariska Hargitay	Cynthia Hooper	Desk clerk, also Mark Greene's lover	1997–1998
Glenne Headly	Dr. Abby Keaton	Pediatric surgeon	1996–1997
Mary Heiss	Mary	ER nurse	2000–2008
Lynn A. Henderson	Pamela Olbes	Paramedic	1995–2009
Justin Henry	James Sasser	Medical student	1997
Djimon Hounsou	Mobalage Ekabo	Custodian	1999
Glenn Howerton	Dr. Nick "Coop" Cooper	ER resident	2003
Michael Ironside	Dr. William "Wild Willy" Swift	Chief of Surgery and ER chief	1995, 1998, 2002

Kristen Johnston	Eve Peyton	Chief ER nurse	2005
Penny Johnson Jerald	Lynette Evans	Nurse practitioner	1998–1999
Julia Jones	Dr. Kaya Montoya	Intern, medical student	2008–2009
Tara Karsian	Liz Dade	Social worker	2005–2006, 2007, 2008–2009
Daniel Dae Kim	Ken Sung	Social worker	2003–2004
Ed Lauter	Dannaker	Fire captain	1998–2002
James LeGros	Dr. Max Rocher	Pediatrician	1998
John Leguizamo	Dr. Victor Clemente	ER attending physician	2005–2006
Dinah Lenney	Shirley	Surgical charge nurse	1995–2004, 2006—2009
Harry Lennix	Dr. Greg Fischer	Infectious disease specialist	1997
Brian Lester	Brian Dumar	Paramedic	1996—2009

Louie Liberti	Tony Bardelli	Paramedic	2003—2009
Julia Ling	Mae Lee Park	Surgical intern	2006–2007
Bellina Logan	Kit	ICU, pediatrics and surgical nurse	1996–2003; 2005; 2008
Donal Logue	Chuck Martin	Flight nurse and Susan Lewis' significant other (ultimately ex)	2003–2005
Chad Lowe	Dr. George Henry	Medical student	1997, 2005
William H. Macy	Dr. David Morgenstern	Chief of Surgery, head of the ER (Emmy-nominated)	1994–1998; 2009
Joe Manganiello	Officer Litchman	Police officer	2007
Deborah May	Mary Cain	County nursing director	1996–1997, 2002
Mary McCormack	Debbie	Doctor in Africa	2003–2006

Kristin Minter	Miranda "Randi" Fronczak	Desk clerk	1995-2003
Lily Mariye	Lily Jarvik	ER nurse	1994–2009
Vanessa Marquez	Wendy Goldman	ER nurse	1994–1997
Kari Matchett	Dr. Skye Wexler	Acting Chief of Emergency Medicine	2007–2008
Chad McKnight	Officer Wilson	Police Officer	1995, 1996, 1999–2000, 2001–2004, 2006
Elizabeth Mitchell	Dr. Kim Legaspi	Psychiatrist	2000–2001
Rolando Molina	Rolando	Desk clerk	1995–1996
Sumalee Montano	Duvata Mahal	ER nurse	2002-2005
Angel Laketa Moore	Dawn Archer	ER nurse	2006–2009
Julian Morris	Dr. Andrew Wade	Surgical intern	2008–2009

Demetrius Navarro	Morales	Paramedic	1998—2009
Bobby Nish	Danny Yau	Police officer	2005–2006
Charles Noland	E-Ray Bozman	Desk clerk/trainee Nurse	1995–1997
Leland Orser	Dr. Lucien Dubenko	Attending trauma surgeon, chief of surgery	2004–2009
Kip Pardue	Ben Parker	ER nurse	2006–2007
Busy Philipps	Hope Bobeck	Medical student	2006–2007
Glenn Plummer	Timmy Rawlins	Desk clerk	1994–1995, 2006–2007
CCH Pounder	Dr. Angela Hicks	Surgical attending	1994–1997
Victor Rasuk	Dr. Ryan Sanchez	Intern	2008–2009
Gina Ravera	Dr. Bettina DeJesus	Radiologist	2006–2008
Kyle Richards	Dori	Nurse	2000—2006

Ron Rifkin	Dr. Carl Vucelich	Senior vascular surgeon	1995–1996
Lucy Rodriguez	Bjerke	Nurse	1996; 2000–2003
Emily Rose	Dr. Tracy Martin	Intern	2008–2009
Rick Rossovich	Dr. John "Tag" Taglieri	Orthopedic surgeon	1994–1995
Vyto Ruginis	Wright	Paramedic	2006—2007
Monté Russell	Dwight Zadro	Paramedic	1995—2009
Dahlia Salem	Dr. Jessica Albright	Surgical chief resident	2005–2006
Nadia Shazana	Jacy	Nurse	2001–2008
Michael B. Silver	Dr. Paul Myers	Psychiatrist	1995, 1997–2000, 2003, 2005, 2008
Pamela Sinha	Amira	Desk clerk	1999–2001, 2003–2005
Maury Sterling	Dr. Nelson	Psychiatrist	2004, 2006

Rossif Sutherland	Lester Kertzenstein	Medical student	2003–2004
John Terry	Dr. David "Div" Cvetic	Psychiatrist	1994
Meg Thalken	Dee McManus, Rottman	Chopper EMT, flight nurse	1996, 1999–2001, 2005, 2008
Dearon "Deezer D" Thompson	Malik McGrath	ER nurse	1994–2009
Stanley Tucci	Dr. Kevin Moretti	Chief of emergency medicine (Emmy-nominated)	2007–2008
Lisa Vidal	CFD Lt. Sandy Lopez	Firefighter	2001–2004
Emily Wagner	Doris Pickman	Paramedic	1994—2009
Gedde Watanabe	Yoshi Takata	ER nurse	1997–2003
Bresha Webb	Laverne St. John	Medical student	2008–2009

Mare Winningham	Dr. Amanda Lee	Chief of emergency services	1998–1999
Lisa Zane	Diane Leeds	Risk management and one of Doug Ross's girlfriends	1995

THE TRAMPOLINE: STAFF SIGNIFICANT OTHERS AND FAMILY MEMBERS

These are in alphabetical order, for all 15 seasons—please note this list is as inclusive as possible, from my recollections and research. Again, I've indicated those performances that garnered Emmy nominations and wins.

Actor	Character Name	Character Position	Years Appearance
Khandi Alexander	Jackie Robbins	Peter Benton's sister	1995–2001
Bonnie Bartlett	Ruth Greene	Mark Greene's mother	1997–1998
Michael Beach	Al Boulet	Husband of Jeanie Boulet	1995–1997
Julie Bowen	Roxanne Please	John Carter's girlfriend	1998–1999
Lisa Nicole Carson	Carla Reece	Peter Benton's girlfriend	1996–2001

Kieu Chinh	Lin Chen	Jing-Mei "Deb" Chen's mother	2003
George Kee Cheung	Mr. Chen	Jing-Mei "Deb" Chen's father	2003–2004
John Cullum	David Greene	Mark Greene's father	1997–2000
Steven Culp	Dave Spencer	Elizabeth Corday's boyfriend	2004
Vondie Curtis-Hall	Roger McGrath, also played Henry Colton/Rena (a patient, Emmy-nominated)	Carla Reece's husband	1994 (Roger McGrath), 2001 Henry Colton/Rena)
Oliver Davis	Alex Taggar	Samantha Taggart's son	2003–2005
Rebecca De Mornay John	Elaine Nichols	Carter's cousin's ex-wife	1999
Garret Dillahunt	Steve Curtis	Samantha Taggart's ex-husband	2005–2006
Paul Dooley	Henry Lewis	Susan Lewis's father	1995–1996; 2004

James Farentino	Ray Ross	Doug Ross's father	1996
Sally Field	Maggie Wyczenski	Abby Lockhart's mother (won an Emmy for this role)	2000–2006
Frances Fisher	Helen Kingsley	Kerry Weaver's biological mother	2005
Paul Freeman	Dr. Charles Corday	Elizabeth Corday's father	1998, 2001–2002
Danny Glover	Charlie Pratt	Greg Pratt's father	2005
Rose Gregorio	Helen Hathaway	Carol Hathaway's mother	1996–1999
Chloe Greenfield	Sarah Riley	Tony Gates's adopted daughter	2006–2009
Michael Gross	John "Jack" Carter Jr.	John Carter's father	2001–2004
Christine Harnos	Jennifer "Jenn" Greene (later Jennifer Simon)	Mark Greene's wife	1994–1998, 2001–2002

Estelle Harris	Mrs. Markovic	Jerry Markovic's mother	2006
Cole Hauser	Steve Curtis	Samantha Taggart's ex-husband	2004
Marg Helgenberger	Karen Hines	One of Doug Ross's girlfriends and his father's boss	1996
Hallee Hirsh	Rachel Greene	Mark Greene's daughter	2001–2002, 2004, 2009
Ernie Hudson	Colonel James Gallant	Michael Gallant's father	2006
Michelle Hurd	Courtney Brown	Kerry Weaver's girlfriend	2006–2007
Stacy Keach	Mike Gates	Tony Gates's father	2007
Anupam Kher	Ajay Rasgotra	Neela Rasgotra's father	2004
Kiron Kher	Mrs. Rasgotra	Neela Rasgotra's mother	2004

Nancy Kwan	Lin Chen	Jing-Mei "Deb" Chen's mother	2000
Piper Laurie	Sarah Ross	Doug Ross's mother	1995–1996
Amy Madigan	Mary Taggart	Samantha Taggart's mother	2009
Mary McDonnell	Eleanor Carter	John Carter's mother (Emmy -nominated)	2001
Trevor Morgan	Scott Anspaugh	Donald Anspaugh's son	1998
Thandie Newton	Makemba "Kem" Likasu-Carter	John Carter's girlfriend/wife	2003–2005, 2009
Henry O	Mr. Chen	Jing-Mei "Deb" Chen's father	2004
Judy Parfitt	Isabelle Corday	Elizabeth Corday's mother	2000-2002
Andrea Parker	Linda Farrell	One of Dr. Ross's girlfriends	1994–1995

Valerie Perrine	Cookie Lewis	Susan Lewis's mother	1995
Sheryl Lee Ralph	Gloria Gallant	Michael Gallant's mother	2006
Ving Rhames	Walter Robbins	Peter Benton's brother-in-law	1994–1996
Beah Richards	Mae Benton	Peter Benton's mother	1994–1995
Jonathan Scarfe	Chase Carter	John Carter's cousin	1997–1998, 2001
Tom Everett Scott	Eric Wyczenski	Abby Lockhart's brother	2002–2003
Lois Smith	Gracie	Samantha Taggart's grandmother	2007
Frances Sternhagen	Millicent "Gamma" Carter	John Carter's grandmother	1997–2003
Georgiana Tarjan	Helen Hathaway	Carol Hathaway's mother	1994–1995

Marcello Thedford	Leon Pratt	Greg Pratt's brother	2002–2003
Mark Valley	Richard Lockhart	Abby Lockhart's ex-husband	2000–2003
Fred Ward	Eddie Wyczenski	Abby Lockhart's father	2006–2007
Matthew Watkins	Reese Benton	Peter Benton's son	1999–2001, 2009
Kathleen Wilhoite	Chloe Lewis	Susan Lewis' sister	1994–1996, 2002
Cress Williams	Reggie Moore	Police officer and Jeanie Boulet's boyfriend/ husband	1998–2000, 2008
Victor Williams	Roger McGrath	Carla Reece's husband	1998–2001
Shannon Woodward	Kelly Taggart	Samantha Taggart's sister	2009
Yvonne Zima	Rachel Greene	Mark Greene's daughter	1994–2000

The pilot season when we shot *ER* was exciting from the start.

I'd visited the old hospital in East LA (the Linda Vista Hospital in Boyle Heights) that was to be the set. (Exteriors were shot in Chicago, and eventually, the set was built on the Warner Bros. lot in Burbank.)

It was perfect—filled with the echoes of the real people whose stories played out there over many years.

From discolored water stains at the bottom of a corner of the wall to linoleum that had been buffed and cleaned to the best of the janitorial staff's ability but was scuffed beyond repair, it was the way a real inner-city metropolitan hospital would be.

Of course, I had sat through countless auditions, studio tests and network tests to come up with the ensemble cast and trampoline we've already discussed.

The pilot was in the can.

The Warner Bros. testing was so through the roof that the executives at NBC thought something was wrong with it.

This was a good thing, because, across town, CBS had their own doctors lined up on a hospital show called *Chicago Hope.*

Our stories were pulled from the pages of the *Daily News.*

Theirs were from the glossy pages of *People* magazine.

The duel was set to start with their premiere on September 18th, 1994, and ours on September 19th, 1994. (A Sunday and a Monday night, respectively, until they went head-to-head on Thursday nights starting on September 22nd, 1994.)

They had older, more established stars attached.

They had a splashy storyline for their pilot about conjoined twins needing to be surgically separated at birth.

We had stars-to-be.

We were younger.

Our pilot started and ended with an exhausted Dr. Greene. In between, in no particular order, everything from a hangnail to an ectopic pregnancy, a gunshot wound, an abused child, stomach ulcer, cancer, an overdose and an aneurysm were discussed and shown in various stages.

One of the pilot's storylines was especially telling: a terrific series of scenes that traced an elderly couple through the realization that the woman was dying through to the moment of her death.

The wife, "Mrs. Franks," was played by Herta Ware, Will Geer's wife.

The husband, "Mr. Franks," was in the remarkable hands of John Randolph, a wonderful veteran actor, theatre man and activist whom I'd met along the way in the early '80s.

John was from an earlier world—one where ideals and ideas mattered more than fame or wealth.

He had a craggy, handsome face that contained and revealed what he had experienced, thought and felt. He was an open book and a truth-teller, not a pretender.

In the final scene, when Herta's eyes closed and her death had clearly and simply happened, John kissed her eyelids gently and began to softly sing, "That Old Black Magic."

He didn't try to "perform" the song. He sang it because it clearly had emotional meaning for the two of them and the life and love they had shared.

It was then that I knew for sure that we had something special within our grasp if we could stay true and simple and real. And, for the most part, over 331 episodes, we did.

Back to the dueling pilot episodes.

It was no contest.

We clobbered them on our way to an audience that reached 40 million people.

It felt otherworldly.

It felt great.

It was the embodiment of collaborative teamwork.

A community of people with roles to play that functioned with a love of the work with no expectations and surprising results.

It was a lesson learned in "24 Hours." One down, 330 episodes to go.

SIX

The Star-Maker

ER, 1994–2009 (330 EPISODES + THE PILOT)

[CASTING BY JOHN FRANK LEVEY, CSA]

(48 to 62 years old)

John at midlife settles into what for some would be the role of a lifetime: casting director for a 15-year series that wins hundreds of awards, launches countless careers and changes the face of television. Flush with cash, John does what any other red-blooded American man would do: buys a house for his mother across the street from his home.

The addition of "Frank" to his credit is so she can see her (maiden) name on the small screen. Of course, she's not the only woman in John's life— an initially secret love affair with a Warner Bros. executive leads him back to monogamy. As John drives his Honda Civic to the Warner Bros. lot, you might hear him humming along to Third Eye Blind's "Semi-Charmed Life." (Not his choice—it's what's playing on the radio station his kids left on—but it does make a lot of sense...)

Closing credits Seasons 13–15 of *ER*, 2006–2009

As I thought about writing the *ER* section of this book and what the series meant to me, I must confess I realized it had much to do with coming to grips with success. While many people fear failure, I would say I had a fear of success.

I was terrified that it would mean somehow I wasn't myself anymore.

Quickly, though, I discovered my fear was unfounded. And I attribute that to my '60s values of fighting for equity and diversity and seeing myself both as an individual and as a part of the whole.

The idea that 40 million people would tune in on Thursday nights at 10 o'clock—more than the number of people who voted in some non-presidential elections at that time—could easily go to one's head.

But that wasn't where my mind went. Instead, I'd think about how instrumental the series was at sharing real-life, honest perspectives and information about mental health issues, drug addiction, alcoholism and even STDs—more than any government agency.

I also like to believe that a whole generation of people went to medical school to be doctors and other medical professionals because of *ER*. That's because we cast real people who grappled honestly with the very things they portrayed.

A few examples:

We cast an actor named Richard Frank (my mother's maiden name, but we were not related) in 1994 to play an HIV-positive person in part because he *was* HIV positive. And it was an extraordinary experience in many ways—topping the list is that it brought the AIDS epidemic home. He was among the first with the deadly disease whom I'd been aware had it. (According to AMFAR, 1995 was the year AIDS deaths reached an all-time high in the US.[1]) Richard was so right for the role.

We also cast several other actors to play HIV-positive and AIDS patients. At one point, a guy asked me in the middle of a casting session, "When will this shoot?"

I think I said something like "Next week, Wednesday," and he said, "My T cell count is zero. I won't be alive by next Wednesday."

Wow.

Casting gives you a chance to experience things that aren't part of your life.

Another example was when we cast an episode where the script called for a group of Black teenage gang bangers who come into the hospital seeking revenge against a rival crew.

The talent pool seemed inauthentic to me.

I wanted to go for something that felt more real—*was* more real.

I got the contact info of a guy named Paul Ehrmann, who was a substitute teacher in an inner-city school. Paul had done some acting, was a published poet and later became a novelist. A true man of letters and ideas.

I explained my situation to him, and with his customary enthusiasm, he agreed to help.

Paul brought a van full of 15- to 17-year-old boys to my office at Warner Bros. Many of them had never even been out of their neighborhood, and none of them had ever been on a film and television studio lot.

Somehow in the ensuing chaos, we picked the teens whose looks were the most interesting.

There was one speaking part of a line or two. Out of the boys, I noticed one young man with a unique face, dotted with freckles. He also had haunting hazel eyes and almost a red tint to his hair and his complexion.

We chose him for the dialogue and the likely close-up.

The shoot went without any issues.

The young men all got some money.

The speaking role got the most.

The scene was worth the effort for many reasons, among them the fact that Paul and I became lifelong friends.

Sadly, the story of the teen doesn't have a happy ending.

Some years later, I got a phone call from that young man's mother. It turns out he had been killed in a gang-related incident, and she wanted information on how to access his residuals, which were stuck in a SAG account. I, of course, helped her as much as possible, and to this day, I am haunted by the other path that the naturally talented young man might have taken.

And a third story, from the perspective of a viewer and then some:

On the Friday morning after Episode Four ("Hit and Run") had aired the previous night, the phone rang in my office.

My ever-upbeat and level-headed assistant, Kevin, stood in the doorway between our offices in Building 140.

He had a quizzical look on his face.

"It's a woman from NBC," he said.

When the network calls, it's rarely good news.

In fact, the network *never* called me in those days.

I picked up gingerly.

"Hi John, I'm Linda Mancuso from NBC. I'm the current

executive on *ER,* and you made me cry last night. Thank you."

She went on, complimenting the casting of a mother and son. The mother thought her son might have hearing loss or deafness. It turned out that she had schizophrenia and was suffering from hallucinations. So she heard things when the son, of course, did not.

Linda had found both the mother and child to be so real that she was moved to tears.

I had never gotten such a call before, and I've never gotten another like it since.

Linda became a dear and trusted friend up until her sad and way-too-early cancer death less than a decade later.

Then it was my turn to cry.

At any rate, we had a lot of come-to-Jesus, real-life experiences through the work on *ER* where we had to confront what was going on in the world.

That's a gift we would never have had if we were casting *Friends* or almost any other show on television.

And beyond what we put out to the world, the behind-the-scenes reality was equally grounding and humbling.

We were truly a family.

Sure the actors got a lot of the accolades, as well they should. It was their faces—and asses—on the line.

But in the background, there were hundreds of people, from the art department to music, costumes and makeup, editing, production design, sound, production management, my casting colleagues—you name it—they made the show tick for 331 episodes over 15 years.

I think George still uses the guy who did his hair on *ER.*

People got married, had kids, got divorced, and some (a few of them close to me) passed away. We had triumphs and tragedies in our lives, and we were there for each other, congratulating each other and commiserating with one another in a profoundly personal way.

Of course, there were the fans, too. (Still are!) I got a chuckle when I read a *New York Times* interview with Amy Poehler, and she confessed her pandemic TV viewing:

"I'm rewatching all the seasons of *ER* for the third time. I'm so obsessed with *ER*. I did Seth Meyers's show, and I was telling him about a friend who knows Julianna Margulies, and I texted that friend because I want to get dirt. Because Dr. Ross might be charming, but he's a terrible doctor. Fight me on that."[2]

I wouldn't fight her on that or anything else. And here's the real scoop (dirt, as it were):

Those were remarkable days. That level of camaraderie, collaboration, and building and maintaining community was transformative.

It certainly changed my life.

Now, it would be remiss of me not to talk about winning an Emmy—my first, shared with Barbara—for the pilot and Season One of *ER*. It seems like the right time, so here's the truth:

It was great and kinda weird at the same time.

It was known as a "Jury Award," which means it was among a few announced before the event.

It was also the first year that casting was included. God knows what the delay was.

Barbara and I shared the award with Junie Lowry-Johnson, the casting director of *NYPD Blue* and a peer for whom I have great respect.

Her relationship with the Steven Bochco group was very similar to mine with the John Wells camp.

Interestingly, both men graduated from Carnegie Mellon University—Steven preceded John. They both are contributors to a massive shift in television programming, turning toward a much more realistic view of life. (Past-tense in Steven's case, as he sadly passed away from complications of cancer at just 74 in 2018.)

Their cops and doctors were different from Joe Friday and Marcus Welby.

I'm not sure if the other nominees knew that Junie and I would be announced that night, but it sure took the edge off of the time before our turn came.

As I recall, Junie and her longtime colleague spoke first as Barbara and I waited in the wings.

In what felt like a dream, the actress Shirley Knight announced that Barbara and I had won an Emmy in our category. Very generously, Barbara allowed me to speak first. Exhilarated beyond belief, I spoke loudly and with great excitement:

"Hi. Barbara and I would like to thank everybody who touched this work and made it better. And if we haven't thanked you in person, we will the next time we see you. Having a job that you care about, that is demanding, rewarding and fun, with people that you love and respect, is a miracle. And Barbara and I both have such jobs.

Good luck is the place where opportunity meets hard work. And Barbara and I feel fabulous about standing in that place this evening. I want to take a special moment to thank my son, Oliver, who is here with me tonight, and my daughter, Joanna, who I recklessly promised could come next year. Barbara?"

Jo with me at a later Emmy Awards ceremony—
promise fulfilled!

Barbara was decidedly briefer. She simply said, "Thank you, everybody. Thank you."

Later, Lydia Woodward, a dear friend who was a writer on *China Beach*, then *ER* and more, teased me by saying she didn't know I had a background in radio as an announcer.

Over the years, I did get more relaxed at such events, and eventually I could be myself. But that first time was still fraught with getting used to being part of such a successful series.

Back to *ER* and the ongoing challenge of casting series regular roles on a hit television show. As I told *Backstage* in 2004:

> You have to have fabulous talent. You have to have a great, winning likeability. They have to fit into the balance of making an ensemble and re-making an ensemble. It's kind of like making a mobile. If you hang a beautiful piece of turquoise here, but you don't have anything to balance it on the other side—that's contrasting in color, that has the right weight and size—then the whole thing tips over. We just kept plugging away and trying to keep the ensemble fresh, exciting, smart, winning, likable, charismatic, sexy.[3]

That summary of the work of our casting team held true all through the run of the series. Even in the final season, we added characters played by some of the most talented actors of our time. Here are my recollections of shifting the ensemble and keeping "the mobile" fresh.

SEASON TWO: September 21, 1995–May 16, 1996

JEANIE BOULET: GLORIA REUBEN

This resilient physician assistant contracts HIV from her husband, and living with the disease informs her life personally and professionally. (Jeanie was a recurring character in Season One: a physical therapist hired by Dr. Peter Benton to care for his aging mother.)

John and I both knew Gloria because she was one of the backup singers with Chloe Webb in the pilot of *China Beach*. She came up and ultimately was cast because she embodied what most of the other actors (and characters they played) had in common: that heroic quality. Gloria and her fictional counterpart, Jeanie, consistently exhibit an absence of selfishness and no need for attention.

That quality was amplified when we went to the storyline of her contracting HIV from her unfaithful husband, Al (played by Michael Beach, who as mentioned, almost became Dr. Peter Benton).

SEASON THREE: September 26, 1996–May 15, 1997

DR. KERRY WEAVER:
LAURA INNES

Dr. Weaver arrives at County General in Season Two and becomes the chief resident in Season Three. Weaver is the queen of making unpopular decisions (in part because of her administrative position, and also it's her character). She is also a walking contradiction: empathetic to patients (perhaps in part because of having survived congenital hip dysplasia and needing a cane to get around), often condescending to co-workers. Over time, she naturally climbs the professional ladder at County General, going from attending physician to chief of emergency medicine and ultimately, hospital chief of staff.

Laura was in *The Louie Show*, a comedy by Diane English, starring Louie Anderson. Diane famously created *Murphy Brown*. I knew Diane because, during the early years of *China Beach*, my office was next door to the office of Murphy Brown's casting director, Andrea Cohen.

At any rate, there was a guest shot that we thought Laura would be perfect for on *ER*. So I reached out to Diane and asked for her kind indulgence for us to consider Laura for this role, even though she was under contract for *The Louie Show*. Diane gave me her permission, and Laura came in as a guest.

It went so well that I then had to ask permission to expand Laura's role to a guest arc of multiple episodes. This was when the kind indulgence turned less, well, kind.

Diane, who was, like most showrunners, fiercely protective

of their series, sent me a little note that said in no uncertain terms: *Back off—no.*

And then, fortunately for us and less fortunately for them, *The Louie Show* was canceled after just six episodes. This allowed us to expand Laura's role to a series regular. There was, however, a controversial element in that Laura was playing, among other things, a disabled person. We worried that this might be a point of contention—it certainly would be today—but luckily, all went off without a hitch.

This situation was a milestone in many ways, as it spoke to the growing importance of authenticity. While absolutely I understand that from the perspective of inclusivity, I have some questions about how that plays out for actors. For example, you don't have to be a killer to play a killer on a cop show. So I'm not sure why you have to be a disabled person or a lesbian to play a character that embodies those qualities. That said, I would do my damndest to cast someone who brings authenticity to the role.

As an actor, a lot of what you use is yourself. But also what you use is your imagination.

At this point, in the mid-'90s, I thought access was my responsibility and the best person for the part should get the job. It's always a difficult balancing act.

At any rate, the story of how Laura joined the cast—from guest star to recurring and lead—repeatedly happened with several key actors on *ER*. Once again, I give all the credit to John. He sees something on film: in the dailies, in the final cuts, and then he moves on instinct.

Like George, John has an enormously successful commercial sense, and he knows what a good addition could be. By Season Three, we had fat budgets. The show was nominated for and won several prestigious awards, including Emmys, Artios Awards, People's Choice and NAACP Image Awards, among others. Barbara and I were nominated again for an Emmy (Outstanding Casting for a Series) in 1996 and were nominated and won again in 1997. And we received Artios awards for Best Casting for TV, Dramatic Episodic in 1995, 1996 and 1997.

Life was already changing for all of us in very abundant ways.

Shortly after Laura joined the cast, I vividly remember an especially hectic day at my casting office.

Keep in mind this was still 1996. Technology had not yet emerged in our daily lives.

Imagine:

No email.

No electronic submissions.

Just piles of envelopes filled with agents' ideas of actors who might be right for the available roles.

On *ER*, there were always lots of roles available. And they almost always had real emotional content.

It was, after all, the emergency room.

Phones were ringing.

Envelopes were being opened.

Pictures and resumes were being sorted.

My assistant called out to me that John Wells's office was on the line. I picked up the phone and was greeted by John's assistant Susan's husky, New York-y voice.

She said there was to be a meeting in 15 minutes in the conference room adjacent to John's office.

I asked what it would be about.

Susan said that she couldn't tell me.

I tried to say that I was swamped. She said it wasn't optional.

Shit.

I walked the two or three football fields over to the conference room. Lots of my colleagues were already gathered.

We were told that Michael Crichton, Steven Spielberg and John Wells were sharing some profits with us. The room was buzzing.

The appreciation being expressed by our three leaders was unprecedented.

I took my envelope and began to walk back to my office. One of the prop guys was 20 yards ahead of me, carrying an infant (not a real one, of course) by one foot.

It was so odd and yet so unique to the world of *ER*.

I stopped and decided to open the envelope. My expectations were low.

$5,000? $10,000? Maybe a little more?

A fella can dream, I thought.

I glanced down and had to look twice. Okay, more like a half-dozen times to be sure my eyes weren't playing tricks.

It was over $100,000.

I fell to my knees—not in prayer but in astonishment.

I used that money to buy the small house across the street from my modest home in Burbank and moved my aging mom from New York City to become my neighbor for the final years of her life.

Later, I bore witness to the incredible (and deserved) bonuses the original cast received.

Tony, George, Eriq, Noah, Sherry and Julianna were summoned to the president's office.

I believe they each received a million bucks.

Wow.

They came downstairs, and I happened to be in my office doorway in Building 140. The hallways were lined with posters of present shows on the Warner Bros. TV roster, and on a short hallway around the corner were more posters of long-ago hits.

The cast gathered together in front of their own poster.

It was a glorious picture that I could only capture with my mind's eye. (Remember, we didn't have instant cameras in our hip pocket then like we do today with our cell phones.)

It is still the definition of success for me.

But what besides money comes with success?

A responsibility to keep doing what got you there in the first place.

The discipline to pay attention to the details.

To do your preparation with consistent effort and care.

To create and maintain a safe and collaborative environment.

To represent the show with grace.

To speak out on matters of import.

To grow and change with your ascendency.

Success is an opportunity and a responsibility. And, for some, a burden they are unable to meet. For example, Sherry left the show in Season Three—despite being contracted for five seasons. This was at least partly because she didn't love being a public person (although she did come back after the birth of her daughter in Season Eight, stayed through Season 11, and came back for the series finale).

Change was in the air for all of us.

Exhilarating and terrifying.

SEASON FOUR: September 25, 1997–May 14, 1998

By Season Four, *ER* was the show to beat, so inevitably, perhaps, we took a bit of a hit. Even though every episode was rated number one in the time slot, there was a perception the show had perhaps "jumped the shark."

Time to get creative.

And luckily, we had the budget to go from five series regulars to 10 (and later more—12, then 14 at a height). We had the enormous gift of being able to experiment, and if it didn't work, no worries. That's what happened, for example, with Maria Bello, who played Anna Del Amico for Season Four only, and Kellie Martin, who joined in Season Five and only lasted until Season Six. (Although she did get a splashy, albeit horrific, ending at the hands of a person with schizophrenia in a delusional state.)

DR. ANNA DEL AMICO:
MARIA BELLO

An ambitious medical intern, Dr. Del Amico joins County General wishing to double-board in both pediatrics and emergency medicine. She butts heads with Dr. Ross and ends up as a doctor consultant in Carol Hathaway's clinic.

I honestly don't remember Maria's audition, but clearly, we thought she was right for the role. She was playing a pediatrician, and in real life, she is extremely dedicated to philanthropic work to help children and women especially.

Maria is a television star through and through—meaning she exhibits a combination of beauty, intelligence, relatability, mystery, humor and even danger—she just needs the right vehicle. Of course, she went on from *ER* to star in several notable series including *Prime Suspect*, *Goliath* and *NCIS*, among others. And John later cast her in a film he did, *The Company Men*. As I recall, there was something about a sex scene she did with Tommy Lee Jones, but that's a story for someone else's memoir.

DR. ELIZABETH CORDAY:
ALEX KINGSTON

This British doctor moves to Chicago to become experienced in trauma surgery, only to find that things are a bit different in the US. After her sponsorship ends, she becomes an intern, learns the ropes (through hardship and hard work) and finds true love with Dr. Greene.

In Season Four, we saw the addition of Alex Kingston as Dr. Elizabeth Corday. John had seen her in the critically acclaimed Masterpiece Theater presentation, *The Fortunes and Misfortunes of Moll Flanders*—a period piece that aired on PBS that I would've called a "crinoline drama"—and loved her, so he recommended we meet her.

And of course, we did, and Alex was great for years. I

have many fond memories of table reads where Julianna would play Alex's part in her "British" accent, and Alex would play Julianna's in her "American" accent, just for fun.

SEASON FIVE: September 24, 1998 – May 20, 1999

LUCY KNIGHT:
KELLIE MARTIN

A "by-the-book" medical student, Lucy gets along well with everyone, save her resident, Dr. Carter. Theirs is an uneasy relationship from their first meeting until the day Lucy and Carter endure a violent attack.

In Season Five, we brought in Kellie Martin to play medical student Lucy Knight. Like others, John took note of her in a role that resonated with him: Becca Thatcher on *Life Goes On* (a show that I once filled in to cast the last season or so for my dear friend Deedee Bradley). John was very enthusiastic about her, so he wrote the part of Lucy specifically for Kellie.

As a side note, although I love Kellie, I found that she didn't quite have the pace, tempo and urgency that an ER demands. She admitted that even the medical jargon was difficult for her. (Although I would certainly trip over words like "renal vein thrombosis," too.) If she were a musician, she'd play pretty songs, like ballads, beautifully. But in my opinion, she wasn't necessarily the instrument for frantic *ER* music.

SEASON SIX: September 30, 1999–May 18, 2000

With George's departure in Season Five, it was time to get strategic. Clearly, he left us with enormous shoes (pants?) to fill. We made several moves, though, to try.

First off, John had the brilliant idea of introducing Alan Alda as Dr. Gabriel Lawrence in the first few episodes of Season Six as an off-kilter doctor in the early throes of

Alzheimer's disease and a foil for Dr. Greene. That gave us a terrific bit of cloud cover (which led to an Emmy nomination for Alan), so we could do some experimenting with new intriguing and sexy male leads and one female lead to fill the empathetic role of the pediatric doctor.

It worked in some ways and not as much in others.

DR. ROBERT "ROCKET" ROMANO:
PAUL MCCRANE

Sarcastic and mean-spirited, surgical attending physician Rocket Romano is an excellent antagonist who later gets his comeuppance when he memorably loses an arm in a helicopter accident (Season Nine).

First, we elevated Paul McCrane, who played Dr. Robert "Rocket" Romano, from a recurring character (beginning in Season Four) to a series regular (Season Six). Paul is a short man—perhaps a bit shorter than me, and I'm around 5'9"—but he's so much taller in stature driven by vibrating intensity.

Paul was perfect, then, to play a sort of asshole character with great affection. He didn't apologize for that quality at all, which is why he played "soulless" so well.

DR. LUKA KOVAČ:
GORAN VISNJIC

Emergency room attending physician Dr. Kovač is haunted by survivor's guilt of an unfathomable tragedy that took the life of his wife and two children during the Croatian War of Independence. He comes to America and County General hoping to find a new lease on life.

Next, we brought in Croatian actor Goran Visnjic as Dr. Luka Kovač, who was sent our way by Kristin Harms, the then-president of John Wells Productions. She had seen Goran in something that caught her eye (understandably) and thought of him immediately for the role.

I think the one thing that worried some people was that he

was reminiscent of George's physical appearance. And we didn't want to accentuate the notion that he was replacing George. (Although truthfully, he most certainly was.)

What Luka shared with George was that he was a guy who you could do love stories around. And we certainly gave him his fair share of sexual scenarios.

Plus, there was an excellent backstory for his inner life and external actions because of the Serbia-Croatia political strife.

DR. CLEO FINCH:
MICHAEL MICHELE

This skillful new pediatric fellow is hardworking, no-nonsense and dedicated. Her professional demeanor, unfortunately, doesn't make her personal life easier. Finch struggles with strain on her relationship with Dr. Benton, thanks to his distrustful mother and some of Benton's own biases surrounding her biracial background.

Speaking of love stories (and filling George's massive shoes/pants when he decided to leave after his original contract was up at the end of Season Five), we brought in Michael Michele as Dr. Cleo Finch in Season Six. Eriq strongly felt that it was time for Dr. Benton to have a relationship with a Black woman after a long string of relationships with white women.

John agreed, but ultimately it was one of the few colossal failures of the series.

While Michael is among the most beautiful women that ever lived and has many talents, she lacks the vibrancy, intensity and depth of a pediatric doctor à la Doug Ross. Her tenure at County General lasted just a couple of seasons.

DAVE MALUCCHI:
ERIC PALLADINO

What this eccentric second-year resident lacks in maturity, competence, diplomacy and warmth, he often makes up for with street smarts, humor, and occasionally, inspired insight. Still, his deficits are his undoing, and he makes tragic (and sometimes plain stupid) mistakes that can't be undone.

Eric Palladino joined the cast as a second-year resident, Dave Malucchi. While Eric did a great job, he also happened to make his debut when there were too many cast members. While he provided both some comic relief and intensity as a bumbling and sometimes dangerous would-be physician, he ultimately left in Season Eight after being fired from County General for having sex with a paramedic in an ambulance.

DR. JING-MEI "DEB" CHEN:
MING-NA

Once a medical student at County General, Jing-Mei Chen returns years later as a resident in a position paid for by her wealthy parents through a generous donation to the hospital.

In mid-Season Six, we saw the return of Ming-Na as Dr. Jing-Mei "Deb" Chen, reprising a recurring character she portrayed in Season One. When we first cast her, she was "Ming-Na Wen," but she dropped her surname shortly after.

I think that there may have been some wish on the part of the network to diversify County General, and John had always appreciated Ming-Na's work. So she was reinstated in the rotation as a third-year resident.

NURSE (LATER DR.) ABIGAIL "ABBY" LOCKHART:
MAURA TIERNEY

Initially a labor and delivery nurse, Abby decides to study medicine and joins County General as a third-year medical student. And then, due to an angry ex and financial difficulties, it's back again. Abby is often caught in the middle of yo-yo situations, which might just feel like home judging from her bipolar mother.

Finally, Maura Tierney came in first as a guest star at the beginning of Season Six, and then as a series regular in the second half of the season playing nurse Abigail "Abby" Lockhart.

I adore Maura Tierney and her talent. She was so funny in the NBC comedy *NewsRadio*, and wonderful in many other roles, so we brought her in. I must confess I have a particular soft spot for Maura, as both of the significant adult women in my life are Irish Catholic.

It's about the complexity, I believe. It's why the Irish are so great at being poets and singers of sad songs and passionate revolutionaries. And she was just the right choice for a complicated character, as her role evolved to portray Abby's ambition to be a doctor, her complex relationship with both doctors Kovač and Carter, a battle with alcoholism and an incredibly complicated relationship with her bipolar mother, Maggie Wyczenski, played brilliantly by Sally Field.

Maura ultimately brought so much emotional depth to the show that I think, in some ways, she was not so much a replacement for Sherry's character, Dr. Lewis, but Anthony's Dr. Greene, who died in Season Eight.

There's one more Season Six casting story worth sharing, but unlike the rest, this is the one that got away.

For me, anyway.

The legendary Jeanne Moreau.

As a boy in the '50s and early '60s, four women dominated the horizon of female sexuality for me.

Of course, the first was Marilyn Monroe. After all, she had been married to Yankee great Joe DiMaggio.

The second was Brigitte Bardot.

The third was Sophia Loren.

And the fourth was Jeanne Moreau, a French film star.

Monroe and Bardot were all sex.

Loren was so formidable as to be intimidating.

Moreau had sex, class, style and intelligence.

The more I grew up, the more her combination of qualities resonated.

We were casting Dr. Corday's mother, Isabelle Corday, and she had to complement Alex Kingston—a tall order.

I suggested Moreau. My colleagues were skeptical about the chances of her saying yes, but still, I thought it was a great idea.

After some research, I found her agent for America was someone I didn't know at William Morris in their London office.

We connected on the telephone eventually. (Remember, we were still in the time of no email!) As I recall, the time difference was quite an obstacle.

The script was sent.

Ms. Moreau expressed interest.

We began to iron out the details of her deal, including travel, hotel and other matters.

All of Warner Bros. television executives were on a retreat somewhere, myself included.

Amid all of the team-building exercises in the conference room, I kept stepping out to continue discussions with the agent and the producers.

We finalized the deal.

I reentered the conference room and interrupted the company to announce my joy.

Everyone shared my excitement.

Sometime later, Ms. Moreau finally arrived in Los Angeles.

I met her briefly on the set on her first day.

She was already unhappy because she had been picked up by transportation in a van.

A few minutes later, a production assistant who had no idea who she was approached her. Ms. Moreau was smoking a cigarette on stage.

The PA told her that she couldn't do that.

Ms. Moreau left for the airport almost immediately.

No one had treated her as the star she was.

I was crushed.

We pivoted and cast the tremendous Judy Parfitt as Isabelle Corday, and she did an excellent job. With all due respect, though, my boyhood self couldn't help but pine for Ms. Moreau.

SEASON EIGHT: September 27, 2001–May 16, 2002

By Season Eight, we were back on the hunt to add substantial actors to County General's ER.

MEDICAL STUDENT MICHAEL GALLANT: SHARIF ATKINS

Coming off active military duty, this third-year resident exhibits grace under pressure and heroism in the ER and out of it. Still, there is collateral damage from his tours of duty, and his dedication to the military often interferes with his personal life.

I had known Sharif because he did a TNT pilot that I cast for Carol Flint (whom I worked with on both *China Beach* and *ER*) called *The Big Time*. Sharif played a three-piece jazz bandleader, and he sang and played for his audition. As a great jazz lover, that was one of the most enjoyable auditions I've ever been a part of.

So, when shortly after that we were told to cast the second Black male doctor for the series, Sharif immediately came to mind. And of course, he did an outstanding job through the audition process and got the job, which started as a recurring guest star role and was quickly elevated to series regular.

DR. GREGORY "GREG" PRATT:
MEKHI PHIFER

Sharp, brash and arrogant, this ambitious intern sets himself up for conflict, especially with his superiors, including Dr. Carter and Dr. Romano.

Also joining the cast in Season Eight was Mekhi Phifer as Dr. Gregory "Greg" Pratt, whom I had enjoyed in the Eminem film *8 Mile.*

Mekhi has a terrific intensity, incredible realness, and is authentically himself. In real life, he came through relatively humble means and advanced himself through sheer effort— that goes for both the character and the actor.

This, as I've mentioned, is critical to an actor's success. If you bring your truth to a role, you will create an honest, believable, multi-layered character. And then you adapt your authentic self to the backstory circumstances that are in the script.

This is not to say actors can't create a believable character without having dealt with similar real-world circumstances. If you don't have authentic experiences that match up with the character's, then that's what imagination is for.

That's the other half of the actor's toolbox.

SEASON 10: September 25, 2003–May 13, 2004

Season 10 brought a couple of strong actresses to County General, starting with an actress who received an unprecedented action by John.

MEDICAL STUDENT (LATER DR.) NEELA
RASGOTRA:
PARMINDER NAGRA

This talented, intelligent, diligent and reserved British medical student is a quiet heartthrob and endures significant heartache at County General.

Parminder had played a lead role in *Bend It Like Beckham* (as soccer player Jess Bhamra). John saw the movie, loved it, loved her and brought her in. We had a general meeting in John's office, which included Andrew Stearn, then the ranking television department executive at John Wells Productions, and Jinny Howe, a dear friend and also an executive in John Wells Production television department.

In that meeting, John did something I had never seen him do before and have never seen him do since: he offered Parminder the job on the spot. And his instincts were, as always, absolutely correct. Parminder brought a whole new set of sensibilities and spice to *ER* and was a great addition.

NURSE SAMANTHA "SAM" TAGGART: LINDA CARDELLINI

A hardworking and hardscrabble nurse and single mother, Sam is haunted by a past that includes a long line of alcoholic family members and a violent ex—which seeps into her present.

Also joining County General was Linda Cardellini as Samantha "Sam" Taggart. Like so many of the other successful ER cast members (and indeed, actors), Linda is another natural person—she's a blue-collar, Italian American gal from Northern California.

Linda at the time was known for her "brainy" roles, like Lindsay Weir on *Freaks and Geeks* and Velma in the 2002 movie *Scooby-Doo*. ER gave her a chance to play a grown-up version of a smart woman who grapples with serious personal issues. What started as a short, year-and-a-half contract ended up being a six-year run on the series.

SEASON 11: September 23, 2004–May 19, 2005

DR. RAY BARNETT:
SHANE WEST

A rockstar doctor and a real rockstar, Dr. Barnett has to manage conflicting priorities.

Shane West was Andrew Stearn's idea to enhance the commerciality of the show. And Shane is a lovely, extremely good-looking guy. He brought a certain sort of rockabilly swagger to the part.

Personally, I never believed him as a doctor.

SEASON 12: September 22, 2005–May 18, 2006

DR. ARCHIE MORRIS:
SCOTT GRIMES

Always the joker, Dr. Morris starts as a relatively inept resident, but has the last laugh as he evolves into a capable physician.

Scott Grimes joined County General as Dr. Archie Morris in Season 12 as a series regular, promoted from a recurring guest star. Because he's a redhead, he gave us a wonderful, unique look that we hadn't had yet.

Plus, Scott is hilarious in real life, so his character was allowed to have a sort of sarcastic sense of humor. I appreciated it, as *ER* was filled with dark humor.

PARAMEDIC/MEDICAL STUDENT TONY GATES:
JOHN STAMOS

A Gulf War vet and serious flirt, the strong-willed, sometimes rebellious Tony Gates deals equally in confrontations and romantic liaisons.

The reason Tony Gates began as a recurring character had to do with Stamos's (and I'm calling him that because we have so many "Johns" in the mix already—myself and Wells) prior commitments, so he was first introduced as a paramedic. (Once he was freed up, he became a series regular in Season 13.)

Stamos and I had met years earlier when he auditioned as George was leaving the show. Even with all of his accomplishments and success, Stamos told me that being brought in to audition for *ER* was a big deal for him.

"I crapped my pants," was the direct quote.

Unfortunately, that first go-round didn't go well.

We both knew it.

Later, my dear friend and colleague Geraldine Leder (Mimi's sister) and I worked on a comedy pilot developed for Stamos.

It was a romantic comedy.

It was funny and not so funny because Stamos had "history" with lots of the women who were reading for the part opposite him.

He felt he couldn't share some of that with Geraldine, but he could with me.

Locker room talk and all that jazz.

Cut to a few years later, and the time for Stamos and *ER* was right. What was striking and admirable was that he embraced storylines about his vulnerability, which never happened when he was the lead in, say, *Full House* or *Jake in Progress*.

Because of this, Stamos became a wonderfully three-dimensional character, with his flaws juxtaposed against that incredibly handsome Southern California Greek face.

A sweet memory I have is of a beautiful note Stamos sent me that arrived along with an expensive bottle of red wine (my favorite). It said something like, "Thank you for allowing me to prove that I'm better than I thought I was."

And another memory I have related to Stamos has to do with a legendary comic. It was not quite so sweet.

Stamos has lots of friends in show business. Some, of course, are peers he has worked with.

Others are people who you might not expect.

Stamos has a deep respect for the history of show business and the greats that came before him.

One of those was Mr. Don Rickles.

Stamos lobbied the writers to create a role for him, and eventually, they did.

I was given the parameters of the deal.

I called the agent and made the offer.

Mr. Rickles was displeased and declined the role.

Later, Stamos told me that Don was more than unhappy —he was livid.

He threatened me (never directly, as we had no personal contact) with mayhem and violence.

Stamos thought it was funny.

I wasn't so sure.

SEASONS 14 AND 15: September 27, 2007–May 15, 2008; September 25, 2008–April 2, 2009

Among the last, but certainly not least, final additions to the main *ER* cast made in Seasons 14 and 15 included David Lyons as Dr. Simon Brenner and Angela Bassett as Dr. Catherine "Cate" Banfield. Both were notable in different ways.

DR. SIMON BRENNER:
DAVID LYONS

Charming, cocky and connected (he's the son of a surgeon and leading hospital board member Donald Anspaugh, played by the late John Aylward) this ER attending physician is a survivor in every sense of the word.

We brought David in because we had seen him in an

Australian hit drama called *Sea Patrol.* He's a great-looking guy and a strong actor, and we knew he'd be an excellent addition.

But his time on *ER* stood out for another reason: it was the first time in 14 seasons that the production ever shut down, costing the show a small fortune and the show's producers a load of stress.

David had a visa problem, so we ended up sending him to an embassy in Canada to wait for the paperwork rather than back to London, where he was living. The most memorable thing about this incident was the line producer being furious that we had allowed an immigration snafu to make him shut down for three or four days.

Even though they could well afford it.

DR. CATHERINE "CATE" BANFIELD: ANGELA BASSETT

This tough-as-nails, humorless attending physician has a mysterious personal history with the County General.

Angela was brought in by John, and she was, as we say in the business, a "great get," with so many incredible performances under her belt at that time, including her iconic portrayals of Tina Turner in *What's Love Got to Do With It* and Dr. Betty Shabazz in *Malcolm X*. She is the consummate star— spectacularly talented and a beautiful, intelligent, powerful, unapologetic person of great authority.

Perfect for the permanent chief of the Emergency Department.

Now, that's a wrap on the series regular additions. A quick anecdote related to the trampoline (detailed in the last chapter):

During the run of *ER*, I developed an issue with one of my eyes.

It was called a "macular pucker."

That always made me laugh because of its aural proximity to "motherfucker."

It is like a thin layer of plastic wrap that should be smooth and flat, which develops wrinkles and needs to be peeled away.

Surgery was scheduled.

During the prep, several medical staff gave me extraordinary reassuring attention.

I heard the sound of three languages: English, Spanish and Tagalog.

As I was fading under the power of the anesthetic, I was later told by one of the nurses that I had said: "Shit, I fucked up *ER*—everyone is Filipino!"

If we ever cast a reboot, I'll keep that note in mind.

All I can say is hooray for the trampoline on television and in real life—especially in our post-pandemic world.

As I did in the last chapter, I want to be sure to include the names of the people who made *ER* such a groundbreaking television series.

So, I believe it's worth noting all the luminaries who came through County General's doors as patients. Here's a list in alphabetical order, for all 15 seasons. Again, please note this list is as inclusive as possible, from my recollections and research. I've indicated those performances that garnered Emmy nominations.

Actor	Character Name	Character Position	Years Appearance
James Belushi	Dan Harris	A father who has a car accident with his son	2001
Chadwick Boseman	Derek Taylor	A boxer with a facial injury	2008
Ernest Borgnine	Paul Manning	A man coming to terms with the death of his wife of 72 years	2009 (Emmy -nominated)
Red Buttons	Jules "Ruby" Rubadoux	Carter's patient with heart issues who blames the doctor for his wife's death 10 years earlier	1995, 2005 (Emmy -nominated)

Veronica Cartwright	Norma Houston	A mother who fights her adult son with terminal cystic fibrosis being taken off life support	1997 (Emmy -nominated)
Jessica Chastain	Dahlia Taslitz	A faulty caretaker of a brain-damaged father	2004
Rosemary Clooney	Mary Cavanaugh a.k.a. "Madam X"	An Alzheimer's disease patient	1994 (Emmy -nominated)
James Cromwell	Bishop Stewart	Coaxes a confession from Dr. Luka Kovač before dying from lupus	2001 (Emmy -nominated)
Kat Dennings	Zoe Butler	A victim of parental battering	2006
Kirsten Dunst	Charlie Chemingo	A child prostitute	1996

Zac Efron	Bobby Neville	A gunshot victim	2003
Dakota Fanning	Delia Chadsey	A 6-year-old car accident victim with leukemia	2000
Colleen Flynn	Jodi O'Brien	A pregnant woman with complications gets treated in the ER by Dr. Greene with tragic results	1995 (Emmy -nominated)
Penny Fuller	Mrs. Constantine	A bipolar patient with cellulitis	1996 (Emmy -nominated)
Josh Gad	Sgt. Bruce Larabee	A combat medic stationed in Iraq with Michael Gallant	2005
Joanna Gleason	Iris	An allergy patient, infomercial director, briefly Mark Greene's romantic interest	1996

Judy Greer	Tildie Mulligan	Drove her car into the lake because the GPS told her to go straight	2009
Kathy Griffin	Dolores Minky	A Ranger Scout troop leader with a diarrhea -infected troop	1995
Christina Hendricks	Joyce Westlake	A domestic abuse victim	2001
Marilu Henner	Linda	An obnoxious mother-in-law who had a fight with her son's bride at the wedding	2009
Keegan-Michael Key	Witkowski		2001
Jeff Kober	Toby & Matt's dad	A father of a family who was hit by a drunk driver while making a snowman	2002

David Krumholtz	Paul Sobricki	A patient with schizophrenia who stabs John Carter and Lucy Knight	2000, 2002
Swoosie Kurtz	Tina-Marie Chambliss	A televangelist using her health issues to raise money	1998 (Emmy -nominated)
Shia LaBeouf	Darnel Smith	A young patient who has muscular dystrophy and uses a wheelchair	2000
Ray Liotta	Charlie Metcalf	A regret-ridden, dying alcoholic	2005 (won an Emmy for this role)
Lucy Liu	Mei-Sun Leow	The mother of a child dying of AIDS	1995
Lin Shaye	Margaret	A woman who's worried and scared about her mom, who is battling dementia	2009

Ewan McGregor	Duncan Stewart	A convenience store gunman	1997 (Emmy -nominated)
Sanford Meisner	Joseph Klein	A man saved by "extraordinary measures" in the ER who had signed a DNR	1995
Eva Mendes	Donna	A babysitter concerned with the well being of the girl she's caring for	1998
Jeffrey Dean Morgan	Firefighter Larken	A firefighter undergoing a leg amputation	2001
Bob Newhart	Ben Hollander	An architecture model-maker losing his sight	2004 (Emmy -nominated)
Nick Offerman	Rog	A rocker whose bandmate is rushed to the ER	1997

Jared Padalecki	Paul Harris	A son who was brought in after a car accident with his father	2001
Aaron Paul	Doug	A Jesse-Pinkman-like" character	2003
Kal Penn	Narajan	A doctor who sews stitches on a patient's head	2001
Chris Pine	Levine	A drunk teen patient	2003
Danny Pudi	Mahir Kardatay	A brother who confronts his sister's boyfriend while she's being treated for stab wounds	2006
Josh Radnor	Keith	Alderman John Bright's lover with syphilis; treated under the table by Kerry Weaver	2003

Charlotte Rae	Roxanne Gaines	An eccentric "cat lady" who uses the ER as her primary care facility and pharmacy, much to the frustration of hospital staff. (At one point, she makes pot brownies the interns and doctors accidentally eat.)	2008
Alan Rosenberg	Samuel Gasner	A man who's been waiting for a heart transplant and won't last the night without it	1995 (Emmy -nominated)
Katee Sackhoff	Unnamed	Jason's girlfriend	2002
Susan Sarandon	Nora	A grandmother asked to consent to donate her grandchild's organs	2009

Adam Scott	David Kerstetter	A car accident victim	1995
Wallace Shawn	Teddy Lempell	Creates a love potion that may have worked for Jerry	2009
JK Simmons	Gus Loomer	A car accident victim	2004
Octavia Spencer	Maria Jones	A pregnant woman considering a third abortion	1998
Eric Stonestreet	Willie	A man who tried to make his ears look Vulcan	2000
Gabrielle Union	Tamara Davis	An overachieving high school student who has an "accident"	2000
James Woods	Dr. Nate Lennox	An ALS patient and Abby Lockheart's teacher in medical school	2006 (Emmy -nominated)

Bruce Weitz	City of Chicago Alderman John Bright	Kerry Weaver's patient; treated for syphilis	2003
Forest Whitaker	Curtis Ames	A patient who files a lawsuit against Dr. Luka Kovač	2007 (Emmy -nominated)
Bradley Whitford	Sean O'Brien	The husband of a pregnant patient in Mark Greene's care	1995
Anton Yelchin	Robbie Edelstein	A 10-year-old car accident survivor	2000

One of the most amazing things about *ER*—and why we had the budget to stop productions and bring in marquee names—was its incredible staying power. Throughout 15 seasons, the series was nominated for 375 industry awards and won 116 (according to the very helpful resource, Wikipedia).

In our final year (2009), for example, Rod Holcomb won a Primetime Emmy for Outstanding Directing for a Drama Series. The show also won a GLAAD Media Award for Outstanding Individual Episode ("Tandem Repeats") and a Television Critics Association Heritage Award. Angela won an NAACP Image Award for Outstanding Supporting Actress in a Drama Series.

But in the end, while the accolades are lovely, it's the experience that matters. After all, work is the sum total of our days, and if you have meaning, purpose and camaraderie in your chosen vocation, you're a lucky person.

I am so lucky that way.

That's why in accepting an Emmy in 1997 for Outstanding Casting for a Series, an honor I again shared with Barbara, I said in my two-sentence acceptance speech that *ER* was "the greatest show I've ever had a chance to work on with my best friends in the business."

That was, and still is, the truth.

Of course, I might qualify it as the greatest *medical* show because at the same time we were casting *ER*, we were also casting the greatest *political* show I've ever had the chance to work on with my best friends in the business.

So, let's leave *ER* now and take a trip down memory lane to *The West Wing*.

SEVEN

The Media Darling

THE WEST WING, 1999-2001 (SEASONS ONE AND TWO)
44 EPISODES; OVERSAW SEASONS SIX AND SEVEN

[CASTING BY JOHN LEVEY, CSA]

(52 to 53 years old)

What do you do when you're riding high? The answer for this casting director isn't about getting high off your own stardust. Instead, it's about taking on more. Professionally, it's about letting loyalty steer while casting two dramas simultaneously—the ongoing juggernaut of ER *and the new Aaron Sorkin project,* The West Wing *(finally in a three-person team with Kevin Scott and Cheryl Kloner).*

Personally, it's being a full-time dad to a newly minted teen (Joanna, 13) and finally being ready for a second chance at love with a friend(+) and colleague from Warner Bros. No time to listen to music or dwell on what car was being driven—John is full-throttle, full-time.

Credits for Season One of *The West Wing*

When *The West Wing* came across my desk in late 1998, it was a real jolt to the system, as an Aaron Sorkin project tends to be.

Right away, I loved the challenge of it all. Everybody told us that politics doesn't work on television, so it was like, *challenge accepted.*

I read the pilot script...again...and again...and again because I wanted to get to know Aaron in particular.

I already knew his longtime collaborator from *Sports Night,* Thomas ("Tommy") Schlamme. Tommy had directed the first episode of *ER,* Season Four, "Ambush," which was shot live. (It aired September 25, 1997.) From that experience, I knew he was highly organized, gifted and meticulous as hell.

So, as usual, I started talking to agents and managers. We were still in the pre-technology days, so it was the envelopes and stacks of headshots and resumes as I've described. Auditions weren't recorded. It was truly the last of the auteur days, and we were unencumbered by excessive network oversight.

The process was much freer then.

This was a good thing. Aaron's approach is by far the most unique of anybody I've ever worked with in Hollywood.

First off, his writing. For example, there might be a scene between a congressman and Josh Lyman (President Jed Bartlet's White House deputy chief of staff and chief political advisor), and it would be two and a half pages long. Let's say the role we're casting is the congressman.

No page number.

As a casting director, you'd have to know more than the words on the page. You'd need an understanding of where the scene is in the script. Is it in Act One or Act Three? Is it a stand-alone scene or one of a handful?

The answers to these questions are essential because it is crucial to know what pond you're fishing in for talent.

And secondly, Aaron's hands-on approach to casting was (and is to this day) very different from any other show creator I've worked with.

Some casting directors are encyclopedic. They watch everything and know everybody. They can rattle off the third replacement in Aaron's *A Few Good Men* on Broadway and that kind of minutiae. So they are steeped in Sorkin.

I'm not that way.

As I've said before, I'm that '60s guy who's a vibist. I know what you are from what I absorb when I'm sitting in the room with you. I get you, and I get a sense of where to put you.

I think that's my strongest skill.

In some ways, I jump to conclusions.

That is, I know if I'm going to like and trust you almost immediately.

I don't know how I know that, but I do.

I read people. I pay attention to body language, eye movements and behavior. From that, I instantly get your vibe.

What matters is that the things I'm getting from you will be part of your performance. It's those tangibles and intangibles I know the audience will get from your essence.

So. I would never put somebody who I can't trust in a role where believability is crucial.

For example, I'd never put someone who I don't think is sexy in a part where sexuality is important. And that's not about being pretty, handsome or having a great body: it's more about being in touch with your sexual and sensual self.

It's also about having the understanding that you *get to* do what you do. As I mentioned earlier, believing your work is something you *have to* do is a fast track to inauthenticity and, in the acting world, a poor performance.

Anyhow, that's a slice of how I usually dig into figuring out who's right for the role and who isn't.

As soon as casting began for *The West Wing* pilot, I learned I would have to make a 360° turn from my usual process and put my vibist ways on ice.

Aaron insisted on reading with every actor.

That meant that during auditions, I was relegated to playing the role of host.

This was extremely difficult for me for several reasons. I lost my capacity to "feel" an actor. Also, when I'm reading with actors, I help impact the pace. For example, I can send messages with my eyes and with my reading to the actor to try to bump them in a direction.

It's kind of like being the rhythm section in a small group of musicians. If I feel that it's getting too legato, I can make it a little more staccato.

This gives a clearer picture of an actor's pitch, tone and style.

Aaron and I are similar in this approach. His reading with actors is all about pace—he tells them how fast they need to go. (Really, really fast, for the record.)

So, he's really in the flow of the audition performance.

I had a hard time initially understanding how he could watch the scene as carefully and thoughtfully as other creators when he was part of the action.

It took time for me to understand Aaron's process fully.

So, while I was the one who'd send out breakdowns and

take a first look at the pictures and resumes for the pilot and first two seasons, I didn't get too hung up on anyone I'd think should be of interest, who could become a cast member.

I would always show five or so options because I was never sure what Aaron saw in a given actor. It was never what I thought. It was all about who grabbed Aaron's attention.

And ultimately, that was the deciding factor.

With *The West Wing*, you could tell that Aaron was building his repertoire. Prior to the show, he had *A Few Good Men* on Broadway, which he later adapted into the iconic film in 1992.

As I mentioned, he and Tommy created *Sports Night* on ABC, where the relationship between the two main characters was the exact relationship between Josh and Sam on *The West Wing*.

If you're a fan of Aaron's, you might notice that some of the *Sports Night* dialog made it to *The West Wing*, along with lines from *A Few Good Men* and *The American President*.

Now, I'm not suggesting that Aaron plagiarized himself. What I think he did, smartly so, was to use his unique and compelling dialog as a thread through his projects.

The other thread, of course, is Tommy.

While their relationship was incredibly respectful, it was also inter-independent.

Also, it was very competitive. Both Aaron and Tommy are alphas.

In comparison, *Southland,* which was completely Chris Chulack's project, had John at the helm. (We'll discuss *Southland* in more detail later.) Chris controlled the set and created his own environment, and John stayed out of that. Still, he deferred to John in some ways.

It was a similar situation between Rod Holcomb and JSY on *China Beach* and Rod and John on *ER.*

This exhibits a different way of two strong people working together.

And so, *The West Wing* could've theoretically been touchy,

but in my opinion, John laid pretty low. It was his prestige off of *ER*'s success that got the pilot ordered.

Then it was the excellence of the project, thanks to Aaron and Tommy, that got it ordered to series. And it was John who kept the show in good graces with the network and Warner Bros. Television. He also became the one who, unenviably, had to try to rein in Aaron financially. (This was not a new role for John—he did the same for JSY and *China Beach*.)

I learned quickly this was no easy task.

For example, I would call Aaron every once in a while. And I'd say, "I just read the next episode's script. And I've done a preliminary budget, and you're 40 percent over the pattern."

Inevitably, he would say something like, "Why are you telling me that?"

I would think to myself, *"Because you're the executive producer, and you should be concerned with that as well as the storytelling."*

This element of my job—producing the casting—I actually enjoy. That involves being fiscally organized and responsible.

Now, ultimately, the line producer and the executive producers can decide, *Fuck it, we're going over the pattern this week because it's vital to the story*, but they should be informed of that.

John is known for being a responsible producer so, when he decides to spend, it's because there's a story-related reason to expand the budget, not because John doesn't care about the budget.

And I would say he was able to ultimately rein in Aaron, and for matters of budget, not having anything to do with the success of the storytelling.

Still, I pride myself in the role I played in casting the incredible core ensemble and other key parts in the pilot, Season One and Season Two. Here are my recollections of putting together a dynamic driftwood mobile of actors who went on to win 100 awards from 288 nominations, including

98 Emmy nominations and 27 wins over the run of the series. (Two Emmys, in 2000 and 2001, were for casting, an honor I shared with Kevin and Barbara—thanks, Wikipedia, for keeping count!)

The following is the original breakdown of the pilot episode's lead characters, along with some others who would become part of the trampoline. And a few were just guest star roles for this initial episode. I'd like to thank my dear friend and colleague Cheryl Kloner, who preserved the original breakdown (on paper!) and sent it to me for use in this book.

DELIVERED NOV 16 1998

LN Executive Producers: John Wells, Aaron Sorkin
Producer: Kristin Harms, John Wells Productions/WBTV
Director: TBA

"THE WEST WING"
Writer: Aaron Sorkin
Pilot/NBCSr.
V.P. of Casting: Barbara Miller
Draft: 2/6/98
Casting Directors: John Levey/Kevin Scott
Sr. Casting Coordinator: Cheryl Kloner
Casting Coordinator: Maxine Harris
Start Date: Approx. 2/1/99
Location: Pilot TBD: Series L.A

WRITTEN SUBMISSIONS ONLY TO:
JOHN LEVEY/ KEVIN SCOTT
300 TELEVISION PLAZA
BUILDING 140, FIRST FLOOR
BURBANK, CA 91505
SCRIPTS AVAILABLE 11/18

NOTE: DIRECT ALL SUBMISSIONS AND INQUIRIES TO KEVIN SCOTT' S OFFICE.

DUPLICATE SUBMISSIONS (COVER LETTERS ONLY) TO BARBARA MILLER AT THE ABOVE ADDRESS.

[SAM SEABORN] Early 30s, Sam is the deputy communications director at the White House. The subordinate to Toby Ziegler, Sam works closely with Leo, Josh, Toby and C.J., planning the appropriate presidential response to the events of the day. Not the most well-read guy in the world, Sam works in the White House but is strictly a political animal, knowing nothing of the history of the White House, and under the mistaken impression that FDR is the 16th president of the United States. While the rest of the staff wrestles with the main events of the day (the president's broken ankle, the Cuban refugees headed toward Florida and Joshua's major gaffe on yesterday's *Meet the Press*), Sam deals with a little personal problem all his own. The woman he met and went to bed with last night is not just cheerful and attracted to him: she's also a part-time hooker, the kind of faux pas that can ruin an ambitious man's career for good...SERIES REGULAR

[JOSHUA LYMAN] A youthful man in his 30s, Josh is the deputy chief of staff, working directly beneath Leo Jacobi, and is a highly regarded brain. Josh helped elect President Bartlet, and during the campaign, had an affair with gifted political consultant Mandy Hampton. He broke up with Mandy after he was tapped to go to the White House and she was let go, but he's clearly still very much attracted to her. A very liberal Democrat who has nothing but contempt for the Religious Right, Josh is in the doghouse after a disastrous appearance on *Meet the Press*, during which he smugly denounced Mary Marsh, a spokesperson for Christian Family Values. Believed to be on the verge of losing his job, Josh is on tenterhooks throughout the day and even agrees to apologize to Mary Marsh for his thoughtless sarcasm. Delighted to learn that Mandy is back in town (and not so delighted to find she's working for the opposition), Josh gets a surprise when the president shows up unexpectedly to back him during a conference with Mary Marsh and Reverend Al Caldwell....(8) SERIES REGULAR

[TOBY ZIEGLER] In his 40s, a rumpled and sleepless communications director at the White House, Toby is Sam's boss and works closely on a day-to-day basis with Leo, Sam and C.J. A man with a cynical sense of humor, Toby worries about the political implications of every decision and is very peeved with Joshua for his uncalled-for remarks on *Meet the Press*. After raking Josh over the coals for having vastly exceeded the parameters of his instructions, Toby tries to preserve Josh's job by arranging a peace meeting. But when Toby attends the pow-wow with Mary Marsh and Reverend Caldwell, he blows his own stack when he thinks Mary is making anti-Semitic cracks about Josh and himself...(13) SERIES REGULAR

[MADELINE "MANDY" HAMPTON] A fine-looking, instantly likable woman in her mid- to late 30s. Mandy is a top political consultant who had an affair with Josh during Bartlet's presidential campaign. Intelligent and ambitious but sometimes a bit scattered, Mandy did not go to the White House along with everyone else; Josh got tapped for his slot, and Mandy went off to a $650,000 per year consulting job. However, Mandy has just returned to Washington with a new job as political consultant for her lover, Senator Lloyd Russell. Intrigued to be back in the same town with Josh, Mandy intends to stage-manage Russell's bid for the presidency, and hopes to be fighting toe-to-toe against Josh all the way. Quite pleased to have lunch with Josh, she lets him know that their new relationship will be personally friendly but professionally adversarial...(30) SERIES REGULAR

[LEO JACOBI] 55 years old and professorial. Leo is the president's chief of staff. A stickler when it comes to his cross-word puzzles. Leo knows the president quite well and regards him as a klutz and a spaz. Leo is furious with Joshua for having behaved foolishly on *Meet the Press* and chews Josh out royally but appears to have no intention of firing him. None too thrilled with the lack of solid intelligence about the Cuban refugees, Leo clearly keeps a careful watch on the pulse of the nation, despite the fact that no two economists can agree on anything. A man with a dryly sarcastic sense of humor, he hits the ground running when Josh brings him evidence that Senator Lloyd Russell is running for president against Bart-let....(2) SERIES REGULAR PLEASE SUBMIT ACTORS OF ALL RACES AND ETHNICITIES.

[C.J. GREGG] In her 30s, compact and athletic and quite coolly competent, she lives in Georgetown, and is the White House press secretary. Used to working closely with Toby and Joshua, C.J. is in charge of briefing the press, conducting press conferences and deflecting their awkward questions with grace and skill. She spends most of the day evading questions about Joshua's gaffe, and fears that the press are bloodhounds on Joshua's scent. She tries to moderate the tempers during the conference with Caldwell and his supporters...(3) SERIES REGULAR PLEASE SUBMIT ACTORS OF ALL RACES AND ETHNICITIES.

[PRESIDENT JOSIAH (JED) BARTLET] The president of the United States. Bartlet is a Democrat from New Hampshire and is a descendant of one of the original signers of the

Declaration of Independence. Looking every bit the country lawyer. you wouldn't immediately guess that he's brilliant, which he is. "While the left hand is lulling you with folksy charm, you don't even hear the right hook coming." Regarded by his staff (especially Leo) as a klutz, Bartlet has just added to his reputation by riding a bicycle into a tree and spraining his ankle. When he returns to the White House, he reveals why: he was in a rage because an anti-abortion movement called Lambs of Christ has sent his 13-year-old daughter a Raggedy Ann doll with a knife stuck in its throat. Still furious but under control, he wastes no time in kicking Reverend Al Caldwell out of the White House and ordering him to denounce the LOC publicly. He demands that his staff re-focus their attention on the real problem: the Cuban refugees...(60) SERIES REGULAR

[DONNATELLA MOSS] Josh's assistant, known as "Donna," is 25 and sexy without trying too hard. She is devoted to Josh but resolutely refuses to bring him coffee—until today, when she's half-certain Josh is going to be fired. She's been his assistant for two and a half years and believes that Josh was instrumental in winning the election for President Bartlet. She later cancels for the president's daughter, who has received a particularly memorable piece of hate mail...20 lines, four scenes (7) POSSIBLE RECURRING ROLE

[CATHY] A pretty Asian American woman, Cathy is Sam's secretary, a very competent woman who keeps Sam's head screwed on a little straighter. She gives Sam the bad news that he must give a tour of the White House to a group of fourth graders and is mildly appalled by Sam's desperate efforts to evade the responsibility...one speech and 16 lines, five scenes (36) POSSIBLE RECURRING ROLE

[DAISY REESE] Mandy's assistant, Daisy, is a chain-smoking 25-year-old super-brain. Quite furious that her boss has totally screwed up the details of their move to new offices in Washington, Daisy is convinced that she's going to spend countless fruitless hours sorting through cartons, all because Mandy misplaced the guide to the boxes' contents. Sarcastic and needling, Daisy doesn't try for an instant to hide her disdain for Mandy's boo-boo...one speech and 14 lines, one scene (30) POSSIBLE RECURRING ROLE

[BILLY] A well-known Washington reporter, Billy is a hard-working member of the press corps, who tries hard to get Sam to give him a statement about Joshua Lyman's future. Convinced from Sam's stonewalling that Josh is on his way out the door, Billy spreads that rumor far and wide among the members of the working press...11 lines, three scenes (1) POSSIBLE RECURRING ROLE

[MALLORY O'BRIEN] A young teacher of a fourth-grade class, she brings her students to the White House and is given a guided tour by Sam Seaborn. When it's clear that Sam is utterly ignorant about the history of this most famous building, she takes him aside for a dressing-down and is none too impressed with his lame defense. She reveals to him, with some irritation, that she is the daughter of Leo Jacobi, and clearly regards him as a moron...three speeches and 13 lines, two scenes (51) POSSIBLE RECURRING ROLE

[MARGARET] Leo's secretary, Margaret, isn't sure that Leo's dictated letter to the *New York Times* is for real, and later brings President Bartlet a note...one line, two scenes (12) POSSIBLE RECURRING ROLE

[MRS. JACOBI] The wife of Leo Jacobi, and the mother of Mallory O'Brian. She tells Sam when "POTUS" is calling for him. She still holds a grudge against Sam because he made a pass at her once, not knowing she was Leo's wife...two lines, one scene (3) POSSIBLE RECURRING ROLE

[MRS. LANDINGHAM] The president's private secretary, she worriedly asks Leo about the president's health and lets him know she doesn't appreciate flippant chat about the president's physical awkwardness...five lines. one scene (11) POSSIBLE RECURRING ROLE

[CHARLIE] 19 years old, fresh-faced in a Brooks Brothers suit. Charlie is taking a year off from Georgetown to work as the president's personal aide. He carries Bartlet's duffel bag and briefcase when he returns to the White House...no lines, one scene (60) POSSIBLE RECURRING ROLE

[LAURIE] An attractive woman at a hotel bar. She checks Sam out and later goes to bed with him. A devotee of pot, Laurie smokes furiously after sex and is miffed (maybe a little hurt) when Sam excuses himself to go to work at 5:30 in the morning. Unaware that "POTUS" stands for president of the United States, Laurie accidentally swaps pagers with Sam, and coos with glee when he calls her: then is quite let down when she learns he just wants to swap pagers. Under close questioning from Sam, she reveals that she is indeed a hooker, but that she went to bed with him because she liked him. She has no intention of telling the press about their liaison and reassures Sam that his career is safe with her...two speeches and 33 lines, four scenes (3)

[MARY MARSH] A well-groomed middle-aged woman, she is a prominent member of the Religious Right, a spokeswoman for Christian Family Values, who is insulted by

Joshua during a face-to-face on *Meet the Press*. She later attends a peace conference at the White House and takes Josh's apology with ill grace. Remarkably ignorant for a religious spokesperson, Mary can't keep the 10 Commandments clear in her head and is accused by Toby of making an anti-Semitic remark...two speeches and eight lines, two scenes (18)

[REVEREND AL CALDWELL] A prominent member of the Religious Right, Caldwell is a good friend of Mary Marsh. He's also on good terms with the first lady and is her advisor on the topic of teen pregnancy. Offended by Joshua's intemperate remarks to Mary Marsh, he leads a peace meeting at the White House with Toby and Joshua and takes Joshua courteously to task for his "hostility and contempt." After having a hard time controlling the equally intemperate remarks of his associates, Caldwell is treated to a withering display of outraged anger on the part of the president, is politely booted out of the White House, and is ordered to denounce the Lambs of Christ if he wants to ever return again...one speech and nine lines. one scene (56)

STORYLINE: This is the story of a day in the life of the West Wing of the White House during the administration of PRESIDENT BARTLET and the actions and decisions made by his staffers.

Now, let's get into stories about casting the series regulars.

PRESIDENT JOSIAH "JED" BARTLET: MARTIN SHEEN

The first thing you have to know about casting the role of the president on *The West Wing* is that Aaron initially didn't envision showing the fictional leader of the free world at all.

He was going to be more of a presence off-camera than on-camera.

Otherwise, Aaron would have probably called the show *The Oval Office*.

The initial focus of the show was to be on the senior staffers who make all the behind-the-scenes moves when it comes to policy and politics.

And so, we auditioned a number of people for the role of the president when we thought it was going to be a guest star. Jason Robards, Alan Alda (who later signed on to play Senator Arnold Vinick), John Cullum and Sidney Poitier were all in the running.

But then, I think Martin Sheen's people approached the production and expressed some interest in the role. This made perfect sense: after all, he had played the Bobby Kennedy role, A.J. MacInerney (chief of staff) in *The American President*, so Aaron knew him quite well.

And, of course, we all knew Martin's work for decades— for me, going back to the film *Badlands* in 1973 with Sissy Spacek. (Boy, did I love the young James Dean-like Martin in that role—he was fantastic. I also loved Sissy, and I credit her for establishing my "type.")

Plus, Martin comes from the great activist tradition of his friend, pacifist Jesuit priest and poet Daniel Berrigan. He was a significant figure in the nonviolent protest movement during the Vietnam War. Like Berrigan, Martin's social activism was an enormous part of what we all loved about him.

It's part of his ethos.

And so, one of the reasons why he was so right for Jed Bartlet was that both men allowed their core values to influence their decisions. (Policy decisions in Jed's case.)

For example, there's a terrific moment in the famous capital punishment episode, "Take This Sabbath Day," when Jed calls his childhood priest, Father Thomas Cavanaugh, to ask for advice. He has to make a snap decision about whether to commute a federal prisoner's sentence who had killed a pair of drug kingpins.

Side note: Karl Malden, in the final role of his career, played Father Cavanaugh. He brought with him the Bible from *On the Waterfront* (another of my all-time favorite films) that he'd had for around 45 years.

Jed asks Father Cavanaugh to call him "Mr. President" and not "Jed" because he has to function and feel like the president of the United States instead of like the man the father knows so personally.

While that's some brilliant dialogue that many people probably didn't get, the point is that you could feel Martin, the actor, inhabiting the character so completely.

We always used to tease and say that during *The West Wing*, Martin actually thought he was the president.

Perhaps predictably, then, once Martin had a few episodes under his belt, the importance of the role grew in accordance with what he had to offer.

That's how Martin became a series regular, eventually racking up multiple awards and Emmy nominations for Best Lead Actor in a Drama Series for almost every season.

A side note about Martin: He's exemplary as Number One on the call sheet. It's a big responsibility when you're in the first slot on the call sheet—it's not the same as number three or number five.

You're the leader.

There's an old Jewish expression: "When the fish stinks, it stinks from the head."

When a show smells "good," it's because the person at the top of the call sheet is generous, open and interested in other people. They welcome people on their first day and thank them on their last.

Their actions exemplify their commitment to the quality of the project in every way possible.

That's Martin in a nutshell. He is the father and grandfather of many great leaders—the actors who have served under him and who've gone on to be Number One on call sheets.

That quality is something I value in him terrifically.

And I feel that I have tried to do that with the men and women who have worked in my offices over the years in various capacities, as assistants, associates, second chair, junior partners—whatever you want to call them. To this day, I'm thrilled with the successes of people like Kevin Scott and Sara Isaacson and the quality of work from Melanie Burgess (Renfroe), Kim Wong and Tawni Tamietti.

Not to say that I'm in the same league with Martin Sheen, but I can say that working with him on *The West Wing* made an indelible impression and set the leadership bar high.

WHITE HOUSE CHIEF OF STAFF LEO MCGARRY: JOHN SPENCER

John Wells and I had recently worked with Spencer (again, so many "Johns" that I'll call him "Spencer") in New York on a show called *Trinity* that aired just four episodes (in 1998) before being canceled.

As is often the case, New York actors have a particular theatrical bent. And Spencer was no exception—he was a real actor's actor. He inhabited his work in a way that's not typical of television.

Suffice to say, though that series didn't go far, we knew how terrific Spencer was.

Aaron, too, knew Spencer and reportedly has said that he imagined him in the role but guessed he wouldn't be available.

The pilot script is said to have been so moving to Spencer that he decided to walk back on a vow not to do any more TV dramas. (The long hours weren't his favorite, but playing a man in recovery was both relatable and enticing to him.)

And so, Spencer delivered a powerhouse performance,

reading early on for the part of Leo. Everyone in the room—especially Tommy and Aaron—was blown away.

It's no wonder that Spencer went on to high-profile accolades for his performance as Leo, including a Primetime Emmy in 2002.

The only person I can recall who read for the part was comedian and then shock-jock Jay Thomas. He did a hilarious ten-minute riff on Rob Lowe's 1988 sex tape from the Democratic National Convention.

Hilarious and certainly memorable, but Spencer was still clearly right for the role.

DEPUTY WHITE HOUSE CHIEF OF STAFF JOSH LYMAN:
BRADLEY WHITFORD

There's a lot of mythology around the casting of Josh, including the notion that Aaron wrote the part with Brad, a longtime friend, in mind. Brad also loved the part and "desperately wanted" it. It's been reported that both Tommy and I objected to him playing a lead role—supposedly, I thought he lacked sex appeal, and Tommy questioned his depth—but that's not exactly true.

Nor is it the whole story.

The half that's missing is that Rob Lowe read once for the pilot, and then his manager, Bernie Brillstein, said, "He's never going to read again, so make an offer or go away." (I'm paraphrasing, but that was the gist.)

So, while Aaron absolutely had Brad in mind for something, we weren't clear until very close to production which part he would play. Because if Rob was in, he was Sam. But if Rob said no, Aaron wanted Brad in the more prominent role, which was Sam.

But Brad didn't feel it. And I didn't either, nor did Tommy.

And we were all right.

Brad was Josh. He was not Sam. It's not because he lacked depth or sex appeal.

It was simply that he was right for the role.

That's why Brad made an impassioned call to Aaron, telling him that he was calling in a favor because he knew in his bones the role he was right for.

So, to be clear, my reservations weren't ever about Brad playing Josh. Brad has a puppy quality—meaning he's enthusiastic and excitable—and quite a problem solver. He was every bit right for the role, which was later validated with multiple Emmy nominations and a win in 2001 for Outstanding Supporting Actor in a Drama Series.

Fortunately, everybody finally said, "What are we doing? This is stupid. We can have Rob and Brad, and we can have them in the right roles. Let's relent and stop this power play with Bernie Brillstein. Let's just make him feel like he won. And we can have them both."

And so we did.

DEPUTY WHITE HOUSE COMMUNICATIONS DIRECTOR SAM SEABORN: ROB LOWE

That's essentially the story of how Rob was cast as Sam, but it's worth adding that his audition was fantastic.

As far as my driftwood mobile metaphor goes, you can see it all taking shape. You have Brad as the gung-ho problem solver. Rob plays the self-assured, "I'm right, and I've got the goods," kind of guy.

As I told *The West Wing Weekly* podcast, "Rob is a completely well-made bed. His shirt is tucked in, his tie is tied well and it's always in place…he's a real leading man in that way."[1]

Here's a quick story about Rob's humility and heart. After

we got the first Emmy for *The West Wing* in 2000, I was asked to bring the statue down to the set. And Rob was so lovely and complimentary. Then, very politely—worth noting because, you know, he's not a demure cat—he said, "Hey, would it be all right if I hold it? This is as close as I'll ever get to one."

Of course, I let him. And then, the following year, he was nominated for an Emmy for Outstanding Lead Actor in a Drama Series (along with Martin). While he didn't win for *The West Wing*, he's still a busy actor. So there's time.

But back to casting *The West Wing* and casting the third role in the mobile that would create necessary conflict—the ambivalent one.

WHITE HOUSE COMMUNICATIONS DIRECTOR TOBY ZIEGLER: RICHARD SCHIFF

In casting Toby, two wonderful actors came to the fore. While they had some things in common, there were also notable differences.

One, of course, was Richard Schiff.

The other was Eugene Levy of *Schitt's Creek* fame.

Richard embodied the specter of worry that trails the character everywhere, much like Peanuts character Pig-Pen's cloud of dirt. He exuded the equivocation that comes from a mind that sees all sides of an issue at once.

As I mentioned, these qualities meshed perfectly opposite Sam's certainty and Josh's "go get 'em" spirit.

Richard was really right for the role. And that was validated by his win for Primetime Emmy for Best Supporting Actor in a Drama Series for Season One.

On the other hand, Eugene was so damn funny and skilled. He understood the world.

He gave the funniest and best audition that *didn't* get the job I have ever seen.

WHITE HOUSE PRESS SECRETARY C.J. CREGG: ALLISON JANNEY

When it came to casting C.J., the cast's lack of racial diversity started to factor in. At one point, we were very seriously considering CCH Pounder, whom we had, of course, worked with on *ER*.

While CCH is always fantastic, she wasn't our CJ.

It was Kevin, formerly my assistant, now my second-chair partner, who found Allison. He watched reams of videotape of people we didn't necessarily know, and he brought her to my attention. She had played several supporting roles opposite marquee names in significant projects, including movies like *The Ice Storm*, *Primary Colors*, *Drop Dead Gorgeous* and *American Beauty*.

It was clear Allison could hold her own opposite heavyweight talent. Plus, she is so damn funny, smart and fast—all three prerequisites for working with Aaron and Tommy.

I heard Richard say that when he saw Allison waiting to audition it sealed the deal for him. He said if they were serious about her, then he knew they knew what they were doing. (This insight was prescient; Allison went on to win two Primetime Emmys for Best Supporting Actress in a Drama Series and two for Lead Actress in a Drama Series, with a ton of other nominations and awards in between for her performance as C.J.)

Now, back to the network pushing for diversity. Had we been casting *The West Wing* nowadays, where diversity is a non-negotiable, CCH would likely have won the C.J. role.

I say "likely" because, of course, we are talking about Aaron Sorkin. Even in today's world, where you have many powerful lobbies to answer to (along with a call for greater authenticity, which I applaud), Aaron, like me, can be a bit of a brat.

When you're a brat, you don't like to be told what to do.

It's hard to listen to somebody telling you that you have to make a choice that you don't feel serves the storytelling in the best way possible simply because the optics will look bad.

So Aaron got Allison through, but the network still insisted on adding a Black character to the cast.

What did Aaron do? The first person of color he added in episode two ("Post Hoc, Ergo Propter Hoc") was the president's physician, Captain Morris Tolliver, played by Ruben Santiago-Hudson.

The character died before the end of the episode in a helicopter crash.

In my opinion, this was basically Aaron's way of saying *vaffanculo!* to the network.

Of course, he ultimately acquiesced and created the role of Charlie Young.

PERSONAL AIDE TO PRESIDENT BARTLET
CHARLIE YOUNG:
DULÉ HILL

While Charlie Young was a character in preliminary drafts of the pilot, he didn't appear until the third episode as a, well, young (21-year-old) aide to President Bartlet who helped with personal issues (not policy or politics). Some of this had to do with the network's response to pressure from the NAACP to diversify the all-white, primarily male cast.

Again, it was Kevin's idea to bring in Dulé to audition. While he did have several guest star roles under his belt, I only knew him as a tap dancer. (Dulé was in *The Tap Dance Kid* on Broadway, primarily as an understudy for Savion Glover.)

This turned out to be an enormously successful decision. Dulé was fantastic—the perfect fit for the role and *The West Wing* (with a 2002 Primetime Emmy nomination to prove it). And he's now on the popular remake of *The Wonder Years*.

SENIOR ASSISTANT TO WHITE HOUSE DEPUTY CHIEF OF STAFF DONNA MOSS: JANEL MOLONEY

(Recurring Season One, Full Cast Member Season Two)

When you're casting in any Aaron Sorkin project, you have to ask yourself this question first: How fast can they go?

Because you know the dialog is going to be flying around. It's like watching professional ping pong players: You can't even see the damn ball. It just goes flying back and forth across the net.

If you're going to be playing with a partner who is that quick and facile, you've got to be able to hit the linguistic ball back over the net.

The bottom line is that some wonderfully talented actors can't talk fast enough to play a role in something Aaron's created.

And there are some actors whose facility may mask an absence of depth, but they can talk fast enough to play an assistant to a main character. They can walk, talk and do all that famous Sorkin stuff.

Janel is one of those people.

She was on *Sports Night,* but it wasn't because of Tommy or Aaron that I brought her in. In fact, I don't think I made the connection, believe it or not.

She won the part of Donna, rightly so—initially a minor recurring role. But thanks to the onscreen chemistry she had with Brad, a "Josh-Donna" moment had to be a part of each episode. This led to Janel being promoted from a recurring role in Season One to a full-on cast member in Season Two (for which she received a Primetime Emmy nomination in 2002).

ABBEY BARTLET:
STOCKARD CHANNING

(Recurring Seasons One and Two, Regular Seasons Three to Seven)

On the first day that Stockard was on set, Barbara Miller and I went down to say hello. As head of Warner Bros. casting, I think Barbara had met her many times over the years. I had seen Stockard on Broadway, of course, but I had never actually been in the same room with her.

To be frank (and I am John *Frank* Levey, after all), she wasn't terribly friendly.

Now, she was getting ready to shoot her first scene in a big job opposite Martin in a prestigious show. I've since read that her whole first day was a whirlwind, as she had just flown cross-country from Toronto, was thrown into formal attire with hair and makeup, and dropped unceremoniously on set to play a scene in an episode called "The State Dinner."

The job was to act with a person she had never met before and make it like they'd been a happily married pair for 25 years.

A tall order, to be sure.

At any rate, she made it clear to me that she didn't care who I was. And I probably took it more personally than she meant it.

All of that said, Stockard was absolutely right for the role —and the proof was in the Primetime Emmy nominations and win (for Season Three) she garnered. She was the perfect wife for President Bartlet, suffering through all the decisions he had to make. Stockard exuded a certain ethos that said, "Buck up, Jed. Just do your job."

A good reminder for sensitive me, too.

MANDY HAMPTON:
MOIRA KELLY

Moira came from Gersh's enormously ripe pool of television actor talent, and I liked her right out of the gate. However, while she is a wonderful actress, her time on *The West Wing* was limited.

That was a structural thing. Mandy wasn't in the West Wing—she was literally *outside* of the West Wing.

This was the core issue. *The West Wing* was a physical space, and any time we left it, the magical quality of that environment disappeared.

Her role was reduced to a "will they or won't they" (have sex) with Josh, and that ended up playing like an add-on.

To everybody's credit, we got it quickly. The character, not Moira per se, wasn't a fit. I think Moira felt that way as well, as there was no possible integration for her character.

In addition to the main ensemble, the "trampoline"— those actors who brought the West Wing to life—was an essential part of the casting process. These are the people who bounced around, scene to scene, season to season, and several of them became beloved and award-winning recurring cast members playing staff, political operatives, reporters, military and family members. I'm including only those who came on board during Seasons One and Two when I was actively casting the show.

Like the trampoline list for *ER*, the following is in alphabetical order and is as inclusive as possible from my recollections and research. Also, I've indicated those performances that garnered Emmy nominations and wins.

THE WEST WING TRAMPOLINE

Actor	Character Name	Character Position	Years Appearance
John Amos	Admiral Percy Fitzwallace	Chairman of the Joint Chiefs of Staff	1999-2004
Timothy Busfield	Danny Concannon	Senior White House correspondent for *The Washington Post*	1999-2006
Timothy Davis-Reed	Mark O'Donnell	White House press corps reporter	2000-2006
William Duffy	Larry	Congressional liaison	1999-2006
Renée Estevez	Nancy	The President's confidential assistant	1999-2006
Melissa Fitzgerald	Carol Fitzpatrick	Assistant to the press secretary	1999-2006
Jorja Fox	Gina Toscano	Secret Service agent assigned to Zoey	2000

Clark Gregg	Mike Casper	FBI special agent	2001-2004
Kathryn Joosten	Mrs. Dolores Landingham	President Bartlet's executive secretary	1999-2002
Marlee Matlin	Joey Lucas	Democratic political consultant	2000-2006
Tim Matheson	John Hoynes	US Vice President (Emmy -nominated)	1999-2006
Glenn Morshower	Advisor to the President	Advisor to the President	2001-2002
Elisabeth Moss	Zoey Bartlet	President Bartlet's youngest daughter	1999-2006
Kris Murphy	Katarina "Katie" Witt	White House press corps reporter	1999-2005
Suzy Nakamura	Cathy	Sam Seaborn's assistant	1999

Charles Noland	Steve	White House press corps reporter	1999-2006
Bill O'Brien	Kenny Thurman	Joey Lucas's sign language interpreter	2000-2005
Michael O'Neill	Ron Butterfield	Secret Service agent	1999-2006
Devika Parikh	Bonnie	Communications aide for Toby Ziegler and Sam Seaborn	1999-2003
Oliver Platt	Oliver Babish	White House counsel (Emmy -nominated)	2001-2005
Emily Procter	Ainsley Hayes	Associate White House counsel	2000-2006
NiCole Robinson	Margaret Hooper	Assistant to Chief of Staff McGarry	1999-2006
Mindy Seeger	Chris	White House press corps reporter	1999-2005

Nina Siemaszko	Eleanor "Ellie" Bartlet	President Bartlet's middle daughter	2001-2006
Allison Smith	Mallory O'Brien	Leo McGarry's daughter	1999-2006
Anna Deavere Smith	Dr. Nancy McNally	National Security Advisor under President Bartlet	2000-2006
Peter James Smith	Ed	Congressional liaison	1999-2006
Kim Webster	Ginger	Communications aide	1999-2006
Kathleen York	Andrea "Andy" Wyatt	A Congresswoman from Maryland's 5th district and Toby's ex-wife	2000-2006

The end of filming the second season of *The West Wing* in April of 2001 was memorable for me for many reasons. But let's start with a Hollywood tradition: the wrap party.

I'm sure the tradition of the wrap party can seem like just another indulgence that show business people get as a perk.

We get together at a relatively fancy restaurant and eat and drink well.

Who pays for it?

Why is it necessary?

From my perspective, it's all about community.

The work of everyone from actors to art directors, best boys to builders, caterers to costumers, secretaries to studio executives and way more are brought together to celebrate the collaboration.

To share in the collective success.

To let our families and partners meet our co-workers.

To wear different clothes. (Although I personally usually go as myself to these events—rather casual.)

In any event, it's not a frivolous indulgence.

At the end of the second season of *The West Wing*, we gathered in a downtown restaurant. As I recall, the first floor was a big open space, and above was a full wrap-around balcony-like area.

Food and drink were everywhere.

I brought Karen Cease with me as my date. In a way, this made something that had been brewing more official. In what might be a scandalous move today, a warm and friendly work relationship turned romantic.

At the time, Karen was co-head of business affairs at Warner Bros. Television. She made many of the deals for *The West Wing* actors, writers and directors—most of whom she had never met.

We were downstairs talking with a guy from the Warner Bros. legal department and his wife.

When the "faces" of the show arrive—the actors, show creators/runners and directors—they bring the glamor and the party really can begin.

Brad Whitford and his then-wife, Jane Kaczmarek, arrived. She, of course, is a star in her own right.

They came up to us, and Brad (as always) was charming and lovely.

He introduced me to Jane by saying something along the lines of, "This is the guy who made this possible for me."

Before I could introduce Karen as "the one who made you rich," Jane burst into the conversation.

She had been among the women who, years earlier, had

competed for the role in *Just in Time* that Annette Bening won. (And, as you may recall, I ended up having to fire Annette.)

Jane had come very close.

She somehow blamed me for it going another way and was vehement, if not downright rude, to me about it.

Clearly, she had harbored this resentment and hostility for many years, despite her considerable success in the interim.

Brad smiled and shrugged his shoulders.

I always thought he had no idea that she would go there and was a bit nonplussed, if not embarrassed.

Apparently, I wasn't the only one who had a rough time at that wrap party. The next day the news broke that Aaron had been arrested at the Burbank Airport on his way to Vegas with a bag that had several illegal substances in it.

Maybe this was all a sign that it was time for a change for both of us.

I've described Aaron as a one-man band, and he is—perhaps now more than ever that he's a director. But I want to add that I don't mean this in a negative way. Control (in the workplace, at least) is what invigorates Aaron.

The more in control he is, the more alive in the moment he is.

This enhances his instincts and his judgment.

Judging from his track record, it all works out.

So, while we got great results those first couple of years of *The West Wing*, I never felt like I was allowed to be a real contributor or collaborator.

Now, I don't mind diminishing my own role in service to a project. But I'm not attracted to the idea of working with people whose process diminishes my role.

Over all of these years, I have asked John on maybe a dozen or so occasions to think about a casting decision that had stuck in my craw. He has always been fair and inclusive, allowing me to voice my opinion and honoring it—even if he didn't take action on it.

With Aaron, there simply wasn't room for that.

Now, that said, I read an article about him and his New York casting director, Francine Maisler, for his 2020 film, *The Trial of the Chicago 7*. In the interview, he lauded her for fighting with him.

"We argue all the time," admitted Sorkin. "She doesn't give in, ever, so there's no point in arguing with her, she's going to win, but it's a little bit entertaining that 10 minutes before I give up."[2]

So perhaps he might have been open to me fighting for a casting choice. And that says more about me than it does about Aaron.

In the end, our processes didn't mesh. To me, it felt like Aaron's process didn't allow anyone else to have a process. This might not be altogether fair—after all, I was in the room, and I deferred to him.

And it was clear this wasn't a democracy. Casting rarely is. So, I'm aware that it's fine for me to be passionate about what I do: I get to say "no" and "maybe," but it was ultimately Aaron and Tommy who got to say "yes."

So, ultimately, I became uncomfortable with my own deference. I felt diminished in my right to a role in the casting.

And that is never a comfortable or satisfying place to be.

I went to John not long after the Season Two wrap party and asked to be released. The timing of my request coincided with early plans for the 200th episode of *ER*. I felt it was time to direct my full attention back to my original baby: *ER*.

This felt especially right since I knew my dear friend Tony Sepulveda was eager to work on *The West Wing*. I knew his enthusiasm for the project would serve Aaron, Tommy and John well, which would be better all around.

Now, this might sound like a Mary Tyler Moore moment —leaving the show at its height before it went south—but as we all know, the show continued to be a powerhouse, winning awards and becoming an iconic series that defeated the odds and made politics sexy.

And, as it ultimately played out for a variety of reasons, including Aaron's busy schedule, budget overages and scheduling snafus, Warner Bros. asked John to encourage Aaron to leave the show in 2003, at the end of Season Four. Tommy also left at that point, leaving John at the helm.

Around the same time, John hired me to be vice president of talent and casting at John Wells Productions (JWP), so that brought me back, albeit tangentially, to *The West Wing* for Seasons Five, Six and Seven. I became a part of Laura Schiff's process as she beautifully and successfully cast those last three seasons.

My new role at JWP opened up a new world to me—casting-wise, anyway. From *Third Watch* to *Southland* and *Animal Kingdom*, I learned many valuable lessons about the good guys and the bad guys—and how often they're one and the same.

EIGHT

The Ensemble

THIRD WATCH, SMITH, SOUTHLAND, ANIMAL
KINGDOM, 1999-2021

As I mentioned, my official arrival at JWP was, of course, just a formality. I'd been working with John and his camp for around 15 years at that point, and my loyalty was more to him than anyone else then…and is to this day.

If I haven't said it enough, seeking community is a core driving force for me. When you're working on a series, you get that feeling—big time.

During that time, other opportunities arose to segue into features or take an executive role at a network, but I always turned them down. I was comfortable where I was.

I'm lucky in a million different ways, up to and including the fact that the group of creatives with whom I've long been associated has allowed me to enjoy both continuity and longevity. When a series ended, several of us would wind up working together on another project, which mitigated the sadness of seeing something we had put our hearts and souls into come to a close.

In a lot of ways, it was like being a part of a traveling circus. We each did our own act while playing off of one another, juggling the same projects simultaneously. It was always a wonderful mix of new and exciting, familiar and comfortable.

For example, there were several years of overlap between *ER*, *Third Watch* and *The West Wing*. During the 11-year *Shameless* run, we also had *Southland* and *Animal Kingdom* on the air.

The ringmaster of five decades of groundbreaking television is John Wells himself. We met sometime in 1986 when I joined Warner Bros., and John was doing a pilot about a family construction business that was loosely based on his relationship with his father and brother. My friend and colleague April Webster cast that show, but I know I met John at one point.

And then *China Beach* happened, and that was, of course, our first significant project together.

Now, this is not to say it was love at first sight. In the early days of our collaboration on *China Beach*, John thought I sometimes took shortcuts and admonished me a bit about that. (In my defense, I've told you how arduous casting using my antiquated manila folders systems was. Nowadays, AI does some casting presorting—now that's a shortcut!)

But eventually, during *China Beach*'s four-season run, we developed mutual respect and honestly enjoyed working together.

It was a no-brainer, then, when John reached out to me shortly after the end of *China Beach* to cast a pilot called *Angel Street*, which starred Robin Givens and Pamela Gidley. Written by John, it was directed by Rod Holcomb. Others of the *China Beach* alumni, like our editor, Jacque ("Jackie") Toberen, came along as well.

And then it was *ER*, *The West Wing* and so on.

It's not that John was the only creator I worked with during the first half of my casting career. But he was by far the best.

And I do have an interesting point of reference—a man whose behavior was both horrible and validating.

I credit Jerry Bruckheimer for solidifying my allegiance to and respect for John.

I was casting a pilot in late 2002 for Warner Bros. called *Skin* that Jerry was producing. It was a Romeo and Juliet plot set in the world of crime and punishment. The patriarch of the boy's family, Tom Roam, was a city district attorney played by Kevin Anderson, and his wife, Laura, was played by Rachel Ticotin. The patriarch of the girl's family, Larry Goldman, played by Ron Silver, was an entrepreneur who specialized in pornography, and his wife, Barbara, was played by Pamela Gidley. The girl's family was liberal and Jewish, and the boy's was conservative, Mexican-Irish, and Catholic.

The show was layered with conflict. And I'm not just talking about the script.

We were auditioning 16-year-old girls for the lead, and the viewing arrangement said it all. Jerry sat in front of a large L-shaped screening set up atop a riser.

The rest of us were down below, watching him view the audition reels.

It was all so transparent. Jerry was literally looking down on us.

After watching for a few minutes, he said, "None of them. I wouldn't fuck any of them."

Now, at that time, my daughter Joanna was about the same age as the girls Jerry so crudely critiqued. And all I could think was, "Well, you're about 100 years old yourself, and it's disgusting that you'd go there."

I left the room, walked straight over to the head of Warner Bros. TV casting, Mary Buck, and asked to be released from the project.

Interesting fact: Olivia Wilde was ultimately cast in her first TV role as Jewel Goldman, the "Juliet" character.

At any rate, it was the beginning of the end for me with Warner Bros. Not because of that incident, but because of a bigger shift in the studio's casting model, put into practice by Mary.

Until that time, Warner Bros. had casting executives that actually did the work of casting a project. But under Mary, the mandate was to change it to more of a network model, where executives would oversee independent casting directors who did the online work (as in hands-on, not related to the internet). This didn't interest me in the least. I enjoy being in the middle of the action, not on the outside looking in.

And I was furious because Mary had made promises that wouldn't happen—that I could stay at Warner Bros. and be an online casting director.

She had agreed to let me do what I do well. Now she was reneging.

To be fair, I'm sure she was pressured to make this change, and whatever she had told us when she first started, she had meant it sincerely.

Clearly, she had been overruled.

I was mad as hell and not going to take it anymore. I went upstairs in Building 140 to try to talk to Peter Roth, the head of Warner Bros. TV group.

Peter wasn't available.

I went on to the next highest-ranking executive, Craig Hunegs. Craig was EVP of business and strategy for Warner Bros. TV, so he wasn't involved with the creative processes. He was in charge of high-profile negotiations, including the renewal of *ER*, for example.

As I rambled on, it became abundantly clear that Craig had been among the decision-makers who strategically decided that an online casting department was no longer beneficial to the studio's bottom line. And that having a smaller group of people who supervised three or four or five shows was better than having a larger group of people who cast two or three shows.

Now, because my contract had lapsed and I was in an at-will period, I might have been in a precarious position. But because I was an "elder"—over 55 at the time—ageism might have been a concern for the studio.

Judging from the size of the exit package, I'm assuming they were trying to stave off a lawsuit.

It even included things I didn't have as a perk, like a car lease reimbursement. The sum covered a retroactive amount for all the years I'd been there. That alone was a small fortune by my modest standards.

Nice to be offered, but money, as we know, doesn't buy happiness.

And my happiness had everything to do with the work and the community and nothing to do with being put out to pasture well before my prime.

I walked straight from Craig's office over to John's at Building One on the Warner Bros. lot in a very emotional state.

Unlike a callous and crass Jerry Bruckheimer, John—a preacher's son—welcomed me with kindness, empathy and concern.

He told me, "Don't worry, John, we'll hire you here at JWP, and Warner Bros. will pay your salary."

This is John in a nutshell.

He's always generous. John is famous for saying we spend more time together as a group than we do with our families when we're in full production, so we must make it an environment of respect.

He also tells us repeatedly if there are problems, to bring them to him before they blossom into something horrible.

I'm also pretty sure that John was the one who suggested to Michael Crichton and Steven Spielberg that they do the *ER* profit-sharing I described earlier that had such an impact on so many of our lives economically.

Let me be clear: They didn't have to do that. That level of generosity is not "done" in our industry.

This is John's ethos, and that level of caring is in his DNA.

For example, during the onset of the COVID-19 pandemic, he demonstrated more leadership than our federal government. Even though nothing was in production, John hosted weekly Zoom catch-ups. And he always ended it by saying, "Look, I know you guys are having a hard time. If you need help, please get in touch with Joy Daffern."

Joy has the, well, joy of handling John's charitable and fun endeavors. She organizes all the wrap parties and corporate gifts. More importantly, she responds to all the requests for donations he receives.

During the pandemic, she and John made sure everyone was taken care of financially. John was also very actively involved, on behalf of the Writer's Guild, I believe, in negotiating with various unions about protocols and procedures.

Very few producers would make themselves available at no cost to do that kind of voluntary work.

John is one of them.

Workwise, John is prolific: an incredible writer, producer, director and leader. He's a unique and special person. I'm blessed to have had a very close relationship for all these decades—and it's all been almost exclusively professional.

I've never had a meal, just the two of us, for fun. John and I don't socialize outside of work, although the professional events he hosts are always warm and personal. I have many wonderful memories of spending time with the cast and crew of his productions at his various stunning homes.

I think some of my values around being professionally close but personally distant with actors come from the example John sets. You can't let your fondness for people you work with color the decisions you make for the good of your business.

That said, I genuinely feel so fortunate to have had this long and mutually productive relationship with John. It has allowed me to employ, train and guide numerous young people who have come through my office—and my life—and any accolade or award I've ever received, I share with them.

And always with John first.

This brings me to two people in the JWP world who have been close partners and colleagues. I know I'll continue to enjoy a genuine friendship that transcends our working relationship for the rest of my days with the first person I'd like to shine a spotlight on: Ned Haspel.

Ned served as JWP's vice president of operations from 1999 until 2021, when he became its chief operating officer. And it couldn't happen to a nicer and more skilled person.

For more than two decades, I've worked closely with Ned in negotiating deals with talent, among other tasks. We have a great rapport and fantastic relationship—again, mutual respect is at the core of how we operate.

Thanks to Ned's close working relationship with John, he's always been an impeccable representative of JWP. Together we have more than 60 years of television and deal-making experience. I particularly appreciate how naturally Ned balances the actors' needs and desires with fiscal responsibility.

I'm sure if you asked Ned, he'd be humble about his accomplishments. But he has been integral in negotiating all the rights deals (and beyond) on JWP's behalf in concert with Warner Bros. business affairs executives for the company's biggest hits and the shows that I am so proud to have helped cast. This includes *ER*, *The West Wing*, *Third Watch*, *Southland*, *Shameless* and *Animal Kingdom*.

If the name "Haspel" rings a bell, that's because it's Ned's family (grandfather and dad) who originated the Seersucker suit. I'm lucky enough to have been gifted a few Haspel jackets and shirts, mainly because, left to my own devices, a Dodgers sweatshirt and a pair of blue jeans would suffice.

As you can probably tell, I adore Ned. He's an example of the kind of community John fosters behind the scenes, and he's a rock-solid foundational part of the company—and, for more than two decades, of my day-to-day life.

The second, Chris Chulack, was my dear friend and close collaborator for more than two decades. Chris became John's go-to director and executive producer after Rod Holcomb began to scale back his workload—right around when my working relationship with John solidified. I helped Chris make the transition from post-production and line producing to a very successful career as a director.

Our work was always very close on many iconic JWP shows. We did *ER*, *Third Watch*, *Smith*, *Southland* and early seasons of *Shameless* and *Animal Kingdom* together.

Chris and I were friends. We were guests in each other's homes.

Then and now, Chris reminds me of someone else who made an indelible impression on my life.

My mom, Sylvia Frank.

She was a sensitive soul. However, her energy was aggressive.

Mom displayed a combination of power and vulnerability. She was also a cynic.

I don't know if her skepticism produced the experiences that reinforced it. Or if her experiences created and validated her cynicism.

Mom famously said, "Life is a series of disillusioning experiences."

She wasn't able to see that it also is a series of hopeful experiences.

Of collaborative experiences.

Of creative experiences.

But Mom was right.

Some events hurt.

Some discoveries disappoint.

So, we'll get to the disillusioning experience I had with Chris. But that wasn't until 2021, so let's step back and take a look at our long and fruitful association, beginning in the mid-late 1990s.

In terms of casting, John doesn't usually attend early sessions. He saves his eye for when we get down to making choices.

So, the process of casting many of the shows on the JWP roster was handled by Chris and me (plus my second chair, which has, over time, included Kevin Scott, Sara Isaacson, Cheryl Kloner, Melanie Burgess, and most recently, Kim Wong and Tawni Tamietti), along with whoever headed up John's television division. (These executives have included Kristin Harms on *The West Wing* and *Third Watch*; Andrew Stearn on *The West Wing*, *Third Watch*, *Southland* and *Shameless;* and Jinny Howe on *Animal Kingdom* and *Shameless*.)

Chris and I began working together on *ER* back in 1994. While we had a respectful and fruitful working relationship on that show, it was *Third Watch* that solidified our bond.

Now, *Third Watch* was filmed in New York, and I'm based in LA, so much of what I did beyond the pilot was done in a supervisory capacity. The show was a breakthrough for a few actors, notably Bobby Cannavale, who played Roberto "Bobby" Caffey.

Permit me a slight digression here—in those days, Bobby was such a pothead (and to be totally transparent, so was I) that you could get loaded just knocking on his dressing room door. Years earlier, I was casting a TV show called *Ohara*, starring Pat Morita. Everybody thought it was "O'Hara," potentially about a brawny, Irish-Catholic NYC cop, but it was about an LA-based Asian detective who used spirituality and intuition to solve crimes. Pat Morita played the title character, who my son had loved in the *Karate Kid* movies, so I took Oli to meet him in his trailer. When we opened the door, about a kilo of reefer smoke quickly engulfed us. All respect to those who knew then that legalizing it, not criticizing it, was good for creativity.

During the early 2000s, beyond *ER* and *Third Watch*, Chris and I worked on a handful of promising projects that didn't end up taking, including *Citizen Baines* (2001, starring James Cromwell), *Presidio Med* (2002–2003, starring Dana Delany and Paul Blackthorne) and *Smith* (2006–2007, starring Ray Liotta, Virginia Madsen, Simon Baker and Jonny Lee Miller).

Of all of those shows, I was most disappointed that *Smith* didn't work. It was about Bobby and Hope Stevens (played by Ray and Virginia), suburbanites who covered up Bobby's criminal life with his posse of high-end thieves.

It was brilliantly written and produced by John and directed with pace, energy and style by Chris.

The casting, if I do say so, was impeccable. I'd loved Ray since *Something Wild*. Our female lead, Virginia Madsen, was still hot from a 2004 surprise cinematic hit: the wine-themed *Sideways*. Our two younger leading men were Simon Baker, who went on immediately after our show was canceled to the critically acclaimed series, *The Mentalist,* and Jonny Lee Miller, who, along with Lucy Liu, later headlined another CBS hit, *Elementary.*

I visited the set and had a classic Ray Liotta moment. They were shooting in a gigantic auto warehouse, where there was a robbery. Ray's character worked for an insurance company, and it was a very tense scene.

All of a sudden, a cell phone rang. It was not part of the script.

It didn't matter. Ray went off: "This is my fucking office!" The entire cast and crew, in a panic, fished around their pockets to make sure it wasn't their cell phone disturbing Ray's concentration.

Finally, his assistant reached into Ray's backpack and pulled out the culprit.

Ray's phone.

I'd like to say everyone laughed, but there was stone silence. Years later, when I received the Hoyt Bowers Lifetime Achievement Award from the Casting Society of America (more on that in a minute), I followed Ray Liotta, who was seated by me at the lectern. I relayed that story and mused, "Is he coming after me?" That got a few (nervous) laughs.

Back to *Smith*'s fate. Anti-heroes were all the rage at the time, just not on CBS.

Smith lasted just three episodes on air.

It might have run for multiple seasons if it had been made for basic or pay cable a few short years later.

Ah well, you can't win them all. Although, the series Chris and I did next was a winner: *Southland*.

John and Chris wanted to develop a cop show. To prepare, Chris watched endless episodes of the show *Cops*—he wanted whatever they created to feel like a documentary. It would be handheld and as gritty, both visually and rhythmically, as possible.

Initially, they almost optioned one of famed police writer Joseph Wambaugh's books, but that didn't happen. Eventually, a writer named Ann Biderman emerged. She had had a long relationship with a high-ranking police official in New York and had gotten her start writing for *NYPD Blue*. The new series was to take place in South Los Angeles (hence, *Southland*) and cover stories from the perspective of detectives and patrol officers.

I enjoyed Ann. Shortly before the production of *Southland* commenced, when Karen and I were in New York, we met Ann for dinner. She was delightful, filled with a million great stories. Ann reminded me of a lot of the women I knew as a kid. She's a tough New Yorker, smart, independent and a feminist—strong as hell. Later, she butted heads with people on the show—notably Chris—which led to her leaving *Southland*.

After Ann left, a guy called Jonathan Lisco came in. He later went on to spearhead the development of *Animal Kingdom*.

We developed a tight bond on *Southland*, and to this day, when we email, we sign off as "JL1" (Jonathan) and "JL2" (me).

With John, the string of productions can be like a relay race with frequent handing-off of the baton. This is another example of how the loyalty thread plays out with those collaborators who work well with John (as in Jonathan's case, but Ann's, not so much).

Back to *Southland*. NBC picked up the pilot in 2009. Because it was network TV, it couldn't be quite as gritty as Chris wanted it to be.

That was the beginning of a conflict.

Here's the interesting thing about pilot casting: It really can be a harbinger of things to come. It's almost always the first sign that there's a significant difference of opinion about the show between the studio, the network and the creators.

Putting together the cast is when those cleaves are usually discovered and revealed.

A quick sidebar anecdote that illustrates just this:

We were working on a pilot in 2015 written by the woman who now owns an entire night on ABC: Krista Vernoff.

It was called *Studio City* after the San Fernando Valley neighborhood where Krista had grown up. The story was said to be quite autobiographical.

One of the leads was a teenage girl returning to her father's blended family from her life with her alcoholic, mentally ill mom.

Her dad was a part-time singer-songwriter and full-time drug dealer to the stars. The ambitious teen had musical aspirations. It was a potent cocktail of drama and trauma.

John had been in London shooting a movie starring Bradley Cooper called *Chef*. While he was there, he heard about a young actress named Florence Pugh.

My office arranged for Florence to send in a tape from her London home base. We had, of course, been seeing lots of people for the part in LA, New York and Chicago as well.

John liked Florence and authorized flying her in to compete for the role in person.

We kind of tortured her, making her stay well beyond the original schedule as we adjusted her look, hair and clothes to get her approved by a reluctant network.

They didn't get it.

John pushed, and they eventually relented.

It's never a good idea to force the network's hand because you end up wrong even when you are right. Creating and maintaining network enthusiasm is crucial to pilot pick-ups.

Studio City died despite the presence of Eric McCormack as the adult lead because, at least in large part, they never got on board with Florence.

Think about that now that Florence has survived, and quite nicely, I might add. Academy Award nominations and the world at her creative fingertips.

Okay, now back from the Valley to *Southland*.

While the network flattened the show a bit, they didn't take all of the life out of it, thankfully. That, in considerable measure, had to do with our casting, starting with Shawn Hatosy and Regina King.

Shawn I had long admired—he's a hell of an actor. We first hired him on *ER* to play a character with multiple personalities. He has a true gift in his ability to move seamlessly from meek and reserved to dangerous and scary. On *Southland*, he played Detective Sammy Bryant, a cop in a dissolving marriage.

After Shawn was in place, we met with Regina. Her long-time manager John Carrabino, who is both lovely and tough, took the position that she shouldn't have to read. So, instead, we had a meeting in my office.

At the time, Regina was moving, and most of her stuff was in storage. She showed up at my office for a meeting with Chris, Ann and me wearing a pink velour sweatsuit because she had no other clothes available.

I must confess: the warm rosy hue of her sweatsuit just made her remarkable eyes and electric smile pop, and her warmth, intelligence and strength shone through most stunningly.

I often say casting is falling in love—and then behaving yourself.

Well, I fell hard for Regina. From that first meeting, it was clear she is one of a kind, the way she exemplifies so many extraordinary qualities in abundance. It's no coincidence that she's gone on to become an award-winning actress and director. And clearly, she was Detective Lydia Adams.

And then, of course, we had Michael Cudlitz as Officer John Cooper, a brave cop, addict and gay man, closeted to most of his coworkers. I met Michael years earlier through his wife, Rachel, and knew he had what it took to play such an interesting, complex role.

Other notable actors in the pilot included Ben McKenzie (Officer Ben Sherman), playing an earnest character who was an enormous departure from the resident bad boy he played in the teen drama, *The OC*. Arija Bareikis then came on board as Officer Chickie Brown. I loved her in an award-winning off-Broadway play called *Intimate Apparel* and knew she would be able to play a tough yet appealing character.

Rounding out our cast were a handful of hunks: Tom Everett Scott (Detective Russell Clarke), who starred as drummer Guy Patterson in the hit Tom Hanks film *That Thing You Do!*; original Brat Pack member C. Thomas Howell (Officer Bill "Dewey" Dudek); and Kevin Alejandro (Detective Nate Moretta). As I recall, a female exec who had a crush on Kevin was in the room when he auditioned, much to his chagrin. Still, he was able to pop the clutch and get the job.

I'd say the *Southland* ensemble was one of the most successful collections of not just actors, but people, that we ever put together. I always do my best to employ the "no assholes" rule, because one bad seed in the company can cause irreparable damage to the community and its collaborative environment.

It also makes things much more pleasant, if not easier, to bring agreeable, reliable, professional people into the mix.

Now, this must make *Southland* sound like the ultimate kumbaya experience.

It wasn't.

The show got canceled twice, first by NBC and later by TNT. The second season was set to premiere on NBC in September of 2009. It then got pushed out to late October, and a couple of weeks before the air date, the network canceled altogether.

One thing Chris and I have in common is we both hate being told what to do. And, at the time, we certainly were riding high from *ER*'s success.

So, I think one of the things that hurt *Southland* at NBC was that Chris didn't respond diplomatically to network notes.

That said, there were many notes I vehemently disagreed with as well. For example, Regina's character, Detective Adams, had several partners in her unit. We wanted to pair her with a Latino actor, and our sights were set on the talented Laz Alonzo.

Laz, who is of Afro-Cuban descent, was nixed by NBC essentially because he was "too black to be brown." Apparently, the network's marketing team thought he wouldn't read diverse enough, or perhaps that too many Black cops in one car wouldn't appeal to viewers.

Whatever the thought, it seems that the decision was made out of fear of offending lobbying organizations, not out of an actual progressive ideology.

TNT picked up the show in November 2009, and it ran from January 2010 until May 2013. Laz joined the cast in 2010 as Detective Gil Puente.

And eventually, we added several more characters, notably Lucy Liu as Office Jessica Tang in Season Four—who had one of her earliest jobs on *ER* as a mother with an AIDS baby—and Lou Diamond Phillips as Officer Danny Ferguson. (Fun fact: Lou was also a star in a John Wells production that Chris produced and directed called *The Advocates*.)

Southland was a memorable show for me for a variety of reasons, but mainly because it was the series I was working on in 2009 when I received the most prestigious honor of my career: the Casting Society of America's (CSA) Hoyt Bowers Award.

I had received a number of their Artios awards at previous dinners for *ER* and *The West Wing*, but this was different and very special.

Since 1985, the Hoyt Bowers Award has been given to a casting director or executive for career achievement.

It is in memory of a man who was among the first casting directors.

As I am writing this memoir, our profession has lost two giants: first, Mike Fenton, the CSA's co-founder and iconic *Back to the Future* casting director (1989 Hoyt Bowers recipient) in December 2020. Then, in February 2021, Lynn Stalmaster passed on. He was perhaps the most famous casting director ever and the first to win an (honorary) Academy Award in 2016. Lynn received his Hoyt Bowers Award in 2003.

I knew Mike a little and met Lynn on one occasion, very briefly.

A few of my colleagues (well, bosses) had received this honor, including Barbara Miller (1996), Mary Buck (2004) and Marcia Ross (2005).

In 2006, an old friend from the Taper in the '80s, April Webster, also received a Hoyt Bowers Award (2006).

No one enters the casting profession to get attention.

At least no one in their right mind.

I've had way more than my share, and I'd be lying if I didn't admit that it's always fun and gratifying.

This was special. It is a highlight of my life and career—in part because, unlike other awards, you know in advance that you are getting it. That way you can make some plans and preparations.

My dear friend and longtime Warner Bros. colleague Tony Sepulveda had gifted me a shave from his barber. (Funny, the details you remember!)

I practiced my speech from a little balcony overlooking Beverly Hills.

I bought a table for the event and invited people to witness it.

My son Oliver and his wife Amanda were there.

My daughter Joanna and her then-partner were as well.

Of course, Karen was there.

Former and present valued staff were also present: Patricia Noland, Kevin Scott, Sara Isaacson, Cheryl Kloner, and my second chair at the time, Melanie Burgess.

The cast of *Southland* bought a table and cheered loudly. (We were also nominated for an Artios Award for casting the pilot.)

John, Chris and Ned were at another table with others from JWP.

Agents, managers, casting colleagues, actors and others made up the rest of the hundreds of people.

I had asked Allison Janney to introduce me, and we sat together on the dais.

We had a bottle of excellent California pinot with us that we promised each other that we wouldn't drink until after our speeches.

Didn't happen.

Allison was a riot.

She told a tall tale of walking barefoot in the rain on the streets of New York City, passing a ringing payphone (remember them?), picking it up…and it was me wondering if she would come to LA to read for *The West Wing*.

I was up next.

I spoke from the heart.

I got some laughs.

I probably cried a little.

Having my children there was the cherry on top.

An unforgettable night that I have forgotten many details of. I had spent the day in a hotel room at the venue, and Karen and I retreated there after a glorious evening filled with warm congratulations and great pride.

I believe it happened, although it seems a bit like a dream.

Once you win a lifetime achievement award, it might seem counterintuitive to keep going, but of course, that's what I did. And I'm not alone: many of my colleagues who have won Hoyt Bowers continue to work to this day. John won the CSA's Career Achievement Award in 2006—I'd say he's done a few significant things since then, too.

One, of course, was the show *Animal Kingdom*. (Don't worry, we'll get to *Shameless* in the next chapter.)

As mentioned, Jonathan Lisco was the driving force behind bringing the Australian film to US audiences on the small screen. He wrote the pilot, which follows the movie quite closely.

And what a show! The flip side of *Southland's* cops and the progenitor of the one that got away—*Smith*. And even though it's about a crime family headed by Janine "Smurf" Cody and including her sons and grandson, ultimately, the show is about sensuality.

Food, drink, drugs, sex and violence. Fast cars, faster motorcycles, surfing, skydiving, crane jumping.

Casting the show had a sense of that excitement and urgency. We knew right away that we wanted Shawn Hatosy for the brooding sociopath Andrew David Cody, aka "Pope."

After all, we knew Shawn so well from *Southland* and *ER*, professionally and personally. As I've mentioned, he is so capable of transforming from vulnerable and quiet to horrifyingly dangerous and powerfully intimidating.

The network, however, was initially a no-go on Shawn. They were looking for movie stars who played bad guys to be cast right out of the gate. (It shows you how *not* memorable any of them were because I can't remember one tape or audition.) However, the idea was first to solidify the commerciality of the series with big-name gets and then figure out the rest of the characters.

And so, the first character we cast was the Cody family matriarch, Smurf. We made a list of well-established actresses of a certain age. We were looking at women with a body of work that included roles with lethal sexuality and a contained kind of ferocity—Smurf's attributes that were so well drawn in the pilot script by Jonathan.

Who would you cast?

Susan Sarandon, I'd bet, would top your list. She topped ours, along with Debra Winger and, of course, Ellen Barkin.

These women are all around my age and are actors I've loved and appreciated most of my life.

Ultimately, the network fell in love with the idea of Ellen as Smurf. And so, we got the script to Ellen and she agreed to sign on.

This is so indicative of today's golden age of television. When I first started in the business, television made stars. And now, thanks to the increased competition between network, cable and streaming services, television success is often made by the talent involved: the bigger the name, the better.

Once Ellen was in place, we needed a known actor to play one of the sons. So, we had a general meeting with Scott Speedman, the heartthrob from the late 1990s/early aughts hit, *Felicity*. He was charming, handsome and smart—the perfect veneer for Baz, Smurf's adopted son, who's actually quite manipulative and dangerous.

Interestingly enough, the first two actors cast were also the first to go—and not because they weren't good—they were both excellent in their respective roles.

Both Scott and Ellen left, at least in part, because they are used to being number one on the call sheet versus being content to be a part of the ensemble. There was a reticence to collaborate, which is about personality, not creativity.

And look, their reputations speak to that. I believe Ellen is known to be complicated. She certainly reminded me of a much younger and more beautiful version of my mother: strong, difficult, a survivor. During the filming of *Animal Kingdom*, Ellen became a very vocal advocate in the #MeToo movement, from indignities she reported suffering at the hands of Terry Gilliam during the *Fear and Loathing in Las Vegas* film shoot. I have tremendous respect for her and all of the women in our industry who spoke out.

It's notable that intimacy coordinators weren't a thing in television until 2018. It's honestly unthinkable.

That said, you almost can't help but respond to Ellen as a sexual being. And a laser-sharp, hyper-intelligent woman. All of that came into play at table readings. I'd often end up reading the male authority parts opposite her. And it was always thrilling—and a touch terrifying.

At the last table reading for Smurf's final scene at the end of Season Four, I told Ellen how much I admired her, and I was flattered and shocked when she complimented my acting skills (which I have none, so she was clearly being exceptionally kind). She said lovely things to me, and that's a part of who she is.

And she can also be cruel and impossible—attributes that she played up so well as Smurf.

As for Scott, well, he put more weight on his own commercial value than he did on becoming part of the team. That said, even after his character officially exited at the beginning of Season Three, he ended up coming back to do a scene in Season Six where the character Pope is hallucinating. Scott was gracious and lovely, a real pro.

The other parts of the ensemble (besides Pope!) fell into

place beautifully. We had casting directors working with us from London, New York, Chicago and Sydney.

From London, we were sent Finn Cole, who was coming off a starring role (which he played opposite his real brother, Joe Cole) in the BBC's hit series, *Peaky Blinders*. We flew Finn across the pond, and he was clearly the answer. Naive and sweet, he can very easily and believably make the jump to jaded and dangerous. After all, his character Joshua "J" Cody has the biggest arc of the show, going from an innocent teen to a criminal mastermind. Also, it's through J's eyes that the Cody family comes into focus for the audience.

A tall order. And sublime acting talent was essential. Finn has "it."

Also, it was a happy coincidence that Finn has a close resemblance to Shawn (not cast yet, remember!), who would eventually play the twin brother of J's (unseen) mother, Julia, who overdosed in the pilot episode.

Now, to cast the other two brothers, Deran and Craig. It's fair to say that there's always at least one person from The Gersh Agency every year who will be one of the regulars in your pilot. Jake Weary read for Deran, the closeted surfer boy, and immediately we knew he was right for the role.

Interestingly enough, even though he's playing a gay character, women flip for Deran. For Jake, actually. He's sexy, adorable, and you can feel the parts where he's broken in a very real way.

At any rate, Jake was in Canada, shooting something after he did his initial reading, which, luckily, we had videotaped. It became a mad scramble to get the powers that be to see Jake's tape and then approve his availability.

Lucky for all of us, it worked out. And I've remained very fond of Jake throughout the series. He has told me that his audition was a game-changer for him, and he'll never forget it. Of course, what I remember most is the scramble, but that's how it goes.

As for Craig Cody, the network loved the actor Matt Barr, who has had a number of series on the CW. He's a great-looking, strapping guy with long blond hair (at the time, at least)—definitely a television leading man. But for our purposes, he lacked the three-dimensionality and the quixotic weirdness of the Cody family. And importantly, John felt he wasn't right.

And so, we found Ben Robson, a Brit who was on a show called *The Vikings*. He stands around 6'4" or so, and at the time, had messy hair and a crazy beard. He's beautiful in a real, not pretty, way. Before becoming an actor, I think he had a career in finance in London, and even today, he is an avid traveler who goes to strange places and does unusual things.

Aside from a not-so-great American accent (initially, that is), Ben was perfect. And most importantly, John loved him. Plus, we were late in the game, and our hand was forced—so we got him approved by the studio and network.

Once we had all of the Cody boys cast, we were able to go back to the network and appeal one last time for Shawn to play Pope. They said yes, and it was a done deal. To their credit, by the end of Season One, the formerly reluctant network enthusiastically affirmed and acknowledged how terrific he was.

And so, the Cody family mobile was complete. It was tricky in that everyone besides Baz had to look a bit like Ellen. They didn't have to look like each other, however, since they all had different fathers. Different shells and thus the delicate balancing act was achieved.

While Jonathan was *Animal Kingdom*'s showrunner, Chris executive produced the first couple of seasons and directed a handful of episodes. And I think it's fair to say that he and I both were excited about the series.

Like *Southland*, things came together amazingly well. Not to say it was without issues—clearly, there were lots of issues as discussed—but every time a piece landed, it fit just right. I'd say that the show benefited greatly from the working relationship Chris and Jonathan forged on *Southland*. Plus, Chris's muscular approach to, well, everything, thanks to his upbringing in East LA, helped fuel the early episodes' pace with raw power and breathless energy.

Another side note about Chris's visual rhythm: His background as an editor surely deserves full credit for that. I will say he didn't always have great communication skills with actors, and I feel that I helped him learn how to talk to performers so they could respond. I think it's fair to say I helped Chris see actors as something beyond just visual and rhythmic props, and prime them as a conduit to convey the story's emotional through-line.

That certainly worked with *Animal Kingdom*.

As it turns out, *Animal Kingdom* was the last JWP show I worked on with Chris: he left in 2017 to forge his own way. Because if you're in John's team, you have to be willing never to be number one.

And Chris had an enormous wish to prove that he wasn't just John's director, following in the footsteps of Rod Holcomb.

But it wasn't the last time I collaborated with Chris.

Chris had met a former Navy SEAL and developed a treatment about this elite force. CBS was interested, and Chris teamed up with writer Benjamin Cavell to create the series *SEAL Team*, which premiered in September of 2017, starring David Boreanaz.

The original casting director for *SEAL Team* was my colleague, Risa Bramon Garcia, who helped cast the pilot and the first two seasons. Then, the relationship soured, and I got a call in the fall of 2019 to have lunch with Chris and his then-head writer and showrunner, John Glenn. (I also know Glenn—again, too many Johns so, we'll call him "Glenn"—from a pilot we did together for Universal.)

We met at a fabulous Italian restaurant in the Valley. Over a bottle of wine and pasta, Chris and Glenn told me why they were unhappy with the casting director, and then they entreated me (that is, very forcefully requested) that I join them to cast the show.

Frankly, at that point, I wasn't terribly interested in network television. CBS was something of a mess at the time in the wake of the Les Moonves controversy.

A side story about Les, whom you may remember I worked for at Warner Bros. TV:

In November 2018, Karen and I landed in Washington, DC where we had a lovely Thanksgiving with my brother's family and then a warm and sunny week in the Dominican Republic.

We were in a town car heading toward our hotel for a one-night layover before heading back to LA and our homes.

I restarted my phone, and it practically exploded in my hand. A reporter from the *New York Times* had called me.

Gayle King from CBS had also left a voicemail.

Neither said what they wanted.

I will say, my receiving calls from significant people in the press is very unusual. I was afraid someone from one of the hit shows I'd worked on had died.

We had 30 more minutes to go until we got to the hotel, so I took a deep breath and dialed the print reporter from the *Times*.

She was on the business beat and explained the reason for her call: Les Moonves had been accused of serious misuse of his position during his Warner Bros tenure, and my name came up in the complaint.

Les had apparently told an actress that he would get me to meet with her and find her a role on *ER*.

This offer was part of what the actress alleged was an inducement for sexual favors.

Did that happen?

Absolutely not.

At least not the call he pretended to make to me or the return call he pretended I made to him. Barbara Miller was the head of the casting department then, and she and Les were tight. He would have called her to set up any meetings—not me.

In fact, the entire time that Les and I were both at Warner Bros., he never once called me directly.

I hated being drawn into this scandal. I told the reporter as much.

I never spoke to Ms. King.

When we got back to LA, my old college pal Steven Schwartz called. He knew that my dad had worked at the *New York Times* for many years and was damn proud of it.

Steven congratulated me and jokingly remarked how proud my father would have been to see my name in his beloved newspaper. The story had run on November 28th, 2018—days before she and I actually spoke. The reporter conveniently didn't mention that fact, as she was apparently looking for a follow-up story.

I laughed darkly. So much for journalistic integrity.

And I've said this before, and I'll say it again: The idea of the "casting couch" has always been producers, directors and executives—not casting directors!

It really should be called some other kind of couch.

Back to taking the job on *SEAL Team*: Although I was wary of the corporate BS at CBS, at the time, Meg Lieberman, whom I love, was the head of casting at CBS Television Studios. And there were many other Warner Bros. vets I would be happy to reunite with, too.

Plus, Chris and I went way back, and we had a comfortable routine. He liked the way I worked, which is to show five people for every part unless it's a big recurring role—and then I'd show ten. I'm very respectful of producers' and the directors' time, and I'm also confident that if I pick a handful of people, one of them will get the job.

As I've said a thousand times before, collaboration and community are my watchwords.

And even though Chris was no longer working exclusively with John, I knew they remained close friends. So there was no conflict around my loyalties.

I did, however, have some misgivings about the politics of the show. For heroes to triumph, there always has to be villains to beat. On *SEAL Team*, the bad guys were almost always Middle Eastern, which was difficult for me. That stereotyping is damaging to Muslim and Middle Eastern Americans. Plus, the pool of Afghani and Iraqi actors is notoriously shallow, so I had some trepidation about that as well.

But it was Chris. In times of change and pain, I tried to be there for him.

And so, out of an allegiance to Chris, I took over the casting of a show I honestly had no interest in.

I did two seasons.

Then one day in the spring of 2021, Chris fired me

No adequate reason was given, although I surmised it had something to do with a COVID-related conflict of an actor, but that seems like a flimsy excuse.

I guess loyalty only goes in one direction.

My mom was right, sadly.

Life has a strong element of disillusioning experiences.

I've been lucky enough to transcend most, but this one was especially painful.

This brings me to a word that, in my opinion, character-izes both Chris's actions and the series that I'm proud to have represented the penultimate chapter of my casting career: *Shameless.*

NINE

The Last Long Run

SHAMELESS, 2011-2021 (134 EPISODES)

[CASTING BY JOHN FRANK LEVEY, CSA]

(64 to 74 years old)

While others might see their career being flushed down the toilet by ageism and a host of other indignities, John is gearing up for an 11-season run casting Shameless, *a giant change from network television filled with moments of delight and disbelief. The anti-Frank, John has raised two responsible adults, more like friends now than children.*

Opening credits for *Shameless*

"I can't believe we get to do this!"

I think I said or at least thought that a million times during the 11 seasons of *Shameless*.

JWP's president of television, Andrew Stearn, championed the acclaimed British series *Shameless* for development in the US. And John wrote the pilot's teleplay.

From the first time I set my eyes on that script, I felt like a kid in a candy store. So many dirty, subversive ideas and swear-word-filled diatribes that came out of even the littlest Gallaghers' mouths!

Hell, even the credits were controversial. My sister-in-law could never get past the first two minutes because it's a succession of people urinating.

For millions of viewers and me, though, it's impossible not to fall in love with the Gallaghers—warts, piss, shit, bodily fluids and a whole host of gross-out moments aside. Of course, much of it is about an exemplary cast, but it's also about the writing.

One of the changes that I noticed from around 2010 on is the addition of playwrights in writers' rooms on television. Now, in some way, that transition is challenging because it's a different medium. But the richness of the stories and the uniqueness of the episodes has really been enhanced.

I think this was particularly true on *Shameless*.

For example, we had a writer named Sheila Callaghan, who came from the "RAT" (Regional Alternative Theater) movement of the 1990s. She wrote a lot of the episodes that delved into LGBTQ topics—all related to the kinds of things she had been writing about in the theatre. One of Ian's love interests and the first transgender character on the show, Trevor, was one of Sheila's creations.

Dominique Morisseau, a writer/story editor/producer on *Shameless*, is another perfect example. She's a fantastic playwright, and she also wrote the book for the musical, *Ain't Too Proud: The Life and Times of the Temptations*. Dominique also happens to be a wonderful actor, so when we did table readings, I would give her all of the hard female parts. And the episodes she wrote were, in my opinion, especially good, as her enthusiasm was always infectious and wonderful.

There are loads of other examples—for instance, writer and executive producer Daniele Nathanson has an MFA in playwriting from San Francisco State University and has had several plays produced.

My point is that none of these creatives were pulled from film school or writing programs for film and television.

Not having learned constraints allowed them to bring their unique styles and perspectives to the storytelling. Writers with a theatrical background bring a sort of American naturalism, which is so prevalent on the stage, to the small screen. Plus, they tend to use more dialogue than other writers do, ensuring that people talk like, well, how people talk.

Now, speaking of the people doing the talking, let's turn to how we cast each of the primary ensemble, most of whom lasted for all 11 seasons (with Emmy Rossum being the notable exception).

BREAKDOWN:

[FRANK] - The family patriarch, when he is sober enough to fulfill the role. (CAST - William H. Macy)

THE FOLLOWING ARE ALL SERIES REGULARS:

[FIONA] The eldest of Frank's children. She takes care of the rest of the brood with a strong and loving hand. She is sexy, attractive, fun, wild, responsible, smart, unpredictable and surprises herself when she is available for love. Some tasteful nudity and simulated sex required.

[LIP] This smart, handsome, athletic 16-year-old boy is a math genius and contributes to the household income by tutoring other students from the neighborhood with occasional side benefits. He has an acerbic wit and ready fists. His real name is Philip, but his nickname fits his smart mouth to a T.
This is a ragtag, rough and tumble, tough as nails, blue-collar, low income, working, poor family. Please do NOT submit pretty Hollywood actor types that you would see on network television.

[IAN] This slightly goofy and very likable 15-year-old is the third child of the brood. He feels his father hates him because he is most like his absent mother. Gay, he works at a neighborhood convenience store where he's having an affair with the closeted Pakistani owner. He is emotional, but when he and his brother Lip fight, he can give as good as he gets.
This is a ragtag, rough and tumble, tough as nails, blue-collar, low income, working, poor family. Please do NOT submit pretty Hollywood actor types that you would see on Network television.

[CARL] Caucasian, Frank's fourth child, this 11-year-old is still a kid, and except for the occasional amount of money he pinches from the church tithe box, he doesn't yet contribute to the family funds. Quieter than his older brothers with a droll sense of humor, he's a schemer and is always coming up with new ways of scamming to get what he needs...SERIES REGULAR

[DEBBIE] Caucasian, the fifth of the six children, this 10-year-old (going on 35) is a smart, competent, coffee-drinking girl charged with the responsibility of taking care of Liam, the baby. She's the apple of her father's eye, and just a little bit crazy...SERIES REGULAR

[VERONICA] This vivacious, sexy 34-year-old woman is the married neighbor. She's Fiona's mentor, friend and drinking buddy. She used to have a job at the hospital as a C.N.A, but lost it in the most recent layoffs. She's not a nurse, but takes care of everyone's medical needs in the neighborhood. Her marriage has a lively and very active sex life...SERIES REGULAR. Please submit actors of all races and ethnicities. Some tasteful nudity and simulated sex required (this will be an interracial couple).

[KEV] This handsome but none-too-bright 30-year-old is Veronica's working-class husband and bartender. She takes good care of him, and he takes good care of her. He can be a little jealous (wouldn't you be if Veronica was your wife?) and kind of macho but is a good guy at heart...SERIES REGU-LAR. Please submit actors of all races and ethnicities. Some tasteful nudity and simulated sex required (this will be an interracial couple).

[STEVE] This attractive, funny, daring, unpredictable and charming Caucasian man in his early to mid-20s seems like he comes from a privileged life, but he's actually a car thief. He's a romantic at heart and falls head over heels in love with Fiona—and eventually the whole family...SERIES REGU-LAR. Some tasteful nudity and simulated sex required.

And now, here are some of my favorite stories and recollections from casting the core ensemble of *Shameless*:

FRANK GALLAGHER:
WILLIAM H. MACY

Even though Bill was cast by the time the breakdowns came out, he wasn't the first actor approached for the role of Frank. I remember Woody Harrelson was pursued early on, but obviously he wasn't chosen for reasons I can't recall.

Bill was clearly right for the role.

Nearly 20 years earlier in 1992, John and I were in New York on a casting session. We saw Bill in a captivating and nuanced performance as a professor accused of sexual harassment by a student in an off-Broadway production of the David Mamet play, *Oleanna*. (Bill went on to play the same lead role in the 1994 film version, also written and directed by Mamet.)

We knew then that we'd want to work with Bill, and of course, we did shortly thereafter when we cast him as Dr. David Morgenstern on *ER*. We wanted him for a different role in the pilot, but Bill was already committed to a show called *Mystery Dance* (also a JWP production). By the time we were ready to cast Dr. Morgenstern, that show had been canceled, and John brought up Bill's name. We nabbed him as County General's chief of surgery and ER head.

I love Bill not only on a professional level but personally, too. He's such a generous actor, man, father and husband. Believe it or not, this had a significant bearing on Frank, who on the surface is the polar opposite: narcissistic, depraved and criminal.

It took a consummate pro to play the worst dad in the history of fatherhood and still maintain his likability. On some crazy level, Frank cares about his children. And then he does the most outrageous things of all time—the stuff that puts your jaw on the floor.

Bill made it all believable, relatable and even lovable.

FIONA GALLAGHER:
EMMY ROSSUM

Emmy was in New York when we were casting *Shameless*, and naturally her then-agent, Lorrie Bartlett (today, she's ICM's Head of Talent), got a hold of the script. Emmy read it, flipped out and desperately wanted to audition for Fiona.

At the time, Emmy had a bit of a reputation for being tough. Not that she was difficult, but she was known to be a bit demanding. So initially, there was a bit of friction around auditioning her, but quickly we relented.

She went into our New York counterpart's offices, Bowling/Miscia Casting, aka Kim Mischa and Beth Bowling, whom I've worked with for a long time and always enjoyed. They put Emmy on tape.

At the time, we were looking at other women for the role, but it was very difficult to find someone to convincingly play a 19-year-old who was wise beyond her years. I remember one woman, a junior in the USC acting program, was our top pick.

Until we received Emmy's tape.

Her performance was stunning, and in my mind, the choice was clear. Still, Showtime wanted options, so we brought her and two others in for a network test.

After her audition at Showtime's Westwood-based corporate headquarters, I remember sending Emmy to wait in the hallway outside the office of the then-president of Entertainment for Showtime, Bob Greenblatt. Also in the audition were Showtime's head of casting at the time, Beth Klein, John and me, among others.

Her in-person audition was a knock-out.

Emmy embodied the character perfectly—so many of Fiona's contradictory traits shined through in her performance: courage and fear; innocence and sexual forwardness and aggressiveness; nurturing and selfishness.

Like Bill, she made those contradictions believable, relatable and even lovable.

Emmy beautifully conveyed that despite how fucked up Fiona's personal life might be and how horrendous her relationships were, she could still take on mothering her siblings.

Inside the room, everyone instantly agreed she was it. I was sent to bring her back, and then either John or I (and I don't recall which one of us it was) said, "You've got the job. You're Fiona."

I do, however, clearly recall Emmy's reaction: she jumped up in the air, kicked her heels up behind her, and screamed something very Fiona-esque, like, *"Fuck yeah!"*

One final thing about casting Emmy that has stuck with me over the years: before we started shooting, John took her aside and said to her, "You know, your character shepherds all of these young children and rescues them from their problems, issues and difficulties. And you're gonna need to do that for the young actors who are playing your siblings. You're going to need to take on the role of Fiona."

And so, she did.

PHILIP "LIP" GALLAGHER:
JEREMY ALLEN WHITE

Like Emmy, our New York colleagues found Jeremy—fresh out of the Frank Sinatra Performing Arts High School in Queens—and put him on tape.

When we saw his audition, we were absolutely blown away.

We had our Lip.

I remember when he came out to LA after the pilot and before the series, he had a black eye, and he didn't really remember how he got it. Jeremy knew it happened on New Year's Eve and that it had something to do with a girl.

Just like Lip.

Cut to today, where Jeremy is now a grown man with a wife and two daughters. And I think it's safe to say his trajectory informed Lip's as well. While he's held on to all of the wonderful, risky, brave aspects of his personality, he's grown up and become a responsible adult. It's fantastic when you can combine your adolescent foolishness with your professional grown-up approach to your work.

And Jeremy is seriously gifted. There was a scene where his mom, Monica (played by Chloe Webb), tries to apologize to him for being a horrible mother, and an incredible array of emotions play out on his face. You see sadness, then all of a sudden, there's a flicker of him as a child.

It was a masterful performance by an incredible actor.

If I were casting a story about Bob Dylan arriving in Greenwich Village in 1961 or remaking *The Graduate*, Jeremy would top my list. At the very least, I'm thrilled to have cast him as Lip.

IAN GALLAGHER:
CAMERON MONAGHAN

Cameron was one of the first people we saw for Ian here in LA. He was wonderful right away, and we decided to start a test deal with him. (That's a deal you put in place for each of several actors for the same role in advance of their screen or live test. That way, when one of the actors is selected, the deal is done and the leverage doesn't switch to the actor.)

And then, his agent called and said that he was no longer interested in playing the part.

Cameron was still underage at the time, and although I don't know for sure, I speculate whether his mother influenced that decision. She was very involved in his career, and if she wasn't his manager, she was at least a quasi-manager. I'm thinking she perhaps worried that he might become stereotyped playing only gay characters.

At any rate, some weeks later, my phone rang at the office at Warner Bros., and it was Cameron. He said, "Hey John, is the part of Ian still available?"

I, of course, responded affirmatively, and he replied, "Well, I'd like to throw my hat back in the ring if it's not too late."

Hot damn! is what I thought, but out loud, I invited him to come back and see us. And of course, he kicked the shit out of the audition and became our Ian.

And the thing about Cameron and the role of Ian is that it allowed him so much latitude to bloom as an actor. He came in a delicate, frail, freckled, redheaded boy. By the end of the series, he became a strapping, ass-kicking young actor who plays a kind of utterly blue-collar neighborhood guy who just happens to enjoy having sex with men rather than women.

MICKEY MILKOVICH:
NOEL FISHER

While the character of Mickey wasn't in the pilot, it's worth mentioning him here because of the relationship that developed between Ian and him.

Ian and Mickey became fan favorites—everyone became invested in their bizarre relationship. The Gallaghers and the Milkoviches were like Romeo and Juliet's Montagues and Capulets with a bitter rivalry at the core. And Cameron and Noel were brilliant as the couple who falls in love in the midst of it all... in a storyline that was every bit as epic as the classic tale.

Our audience was ecstatic when, in Season Ten, their love finally culminated in their wedding.

Interestingly enough, in the whole history of *Shameless*, the only time the network pushed back on our casting choices was with Noel. The writing indicated that they wanted a big, tough, blue-collar street guy, and he is a small-ish, tough, blue-collar street guy.

So, at first, Noel was not approved, and we had to fight for him.

A worthy brawl, and fortunately for all of us, including the network, we won.

And in the end, love won.

CARL GALLAGHER:
ETHAN CUTKOSKY

Ethan came out of Chicago where the late, great casting director Jane Alderman put him on tape for us.

Mark Mylod, who directed both the pilot of the British series and our American version, took one look at Ethan's audition and said in his heavy accent, "Is it wrong to say that a 10-year-old looks stoned?"

Honestly, Mark was right. I'm sure Ethan wasn't stoned, but he had that perfect off-quality that made him a Gallagher through and through.

That was confirmed when Ethan came to LA to test for the pilot. He attached a paper tail to my untucked button-down shirt and followed me giggling across the Warner Bros. lot.

That innate mischievousness was very Carl.

And, boy, what a pleasure it was to watch him, along with Emma Kenney, who plays Debbie Gallagher, grow up. They've both become exceptionally talented actors, in part because they went to the Bill Macy School of Acting and the John Wells School of Performing.

It's not that they played themselves. The point is that in the scripts, the characters were so well conceived and realized that the actor really does have a leg up.

DEBBIE GALLAGHER:
EMMA KENNEY

Our New York casting directors, Kim and Beth, were responsible for finding Emma Kenney, who was, at the time, an adorable little 10-year-old, redheaded, freckle-faced urchin.

She had perhaps my favorite moment in the pilot. It's when Debbie comes downstairs and sees her dad, Frank, passed out on the floor. She quietly and simply puts the pillow behind his head to make him more comfortable.

As if Frank Gallagher really gives a shit where he falls down or sleeps.

VERONICA "V" FISHER:
SHANOLA HAMPTON

Melanie Burgess was my associate when we were casting *Shameless*, and when it came to the role of Veronica, I was so glad I had her at my side. In many ways, I felt like an OB-GYN who needed his nurse—particularly when Shanola came in to read.

She was so brave and willing to be Veronica in all her glory.

That frankly made me pretty damn uncomfortable. Shanola brought an openness to her audition that in another time, say, a decade later in the #MeToo era, might have compromised both her and me.

Later Shanola told me that she appreciates that we saw in her what we did, particularly since she was a UTA agent's "hip pocket" client at the time and didn't even have an agent of her own.

I don't even remember if anybody tested opposite Shanola. If they did, they were eliminated in the shadow of her vivaciousness. She's a delicious person, outrageous in all the best ways, a huge hugger and full of infectious energy.

I adore Shanola and know we couldn't have found a better person to embody Veronica.

KEVIN "KEV" BALL:
STEVE HOWEY

Like Shanola, Steve was the clear choice at the network.

He is quite simply one of the funniest people I have ever met. Truly, he is the king of understated comedy who can make a mere "Huh?" into the biggest laugh line ever.

While *Shameless* had a great deal of nudity, I think Steve was the only series regular who had a (brief) full-frontal shot.

At some point during the auditioning process, I recall John asking him if he was comfortable being naked, and Steve said, "Well, you know, for a guy my size, I'm only average." It was the first of thousands of times he made us laugh.

STEVE WILTON/JIMMY LISHMAN:
JUSTIN CHATWIN

Justin has a great innocence and sweetness, I believe partly because he's Canadian. That, juxtaposed with the character's deviousness and misrepresentation of almost everything to almost everyone is just genius.

The Steve/Jimmy character was so vital to the plot because it embodied all of Fiona's disastrous relationships.

The heat generated by Justin and Emmy was spectacular at the beginning of this series. For one thing, he happens to be undeniably beautiful, as is she. And so the two of them without their trousers on was a sight to behold.

It was a great combination.

While that is all of the cast members that were included in the pilot, here are a few standout memories of the other main characters we cast in Season One:

SHEILA JACKSON:
JOAN CUSACK

When we shot the pilot all those years ago, the role of the Gallagher's Southside neighbor with the surprising sexual life, Sheila, was played by our old friend and colleague Allison Janney.

It was a huge departure from C.J. Cragg on *The West Wing*, but Allison's range and talent are almost boundless, as we have learned since then.

I never saw the cut with her in it, but sadly for us, she became unavailable between the pilot and the first episode.

What to do?

Could we see anyone else in the role? And, perhaps more importantly, could our studio and network partners see anyone else as Sheila?

I phoned around to the major agencies, as clearly we were

going to need an established actress of some prestige. Any time you are casting a role opposite Bill, it needs to be someone who can push back with chops and equal force.

A name emerged that I really responded to: Joan Cusack.

I told John that she might be interested, pending material, and that her agent certainly was interested on her behalf.

John wasn't sure.

He said I could send her the pilot script and another script for her to read. Of course, we didn't want to send the cut of the pilot with Allison playing the part.

Joan responded, agreeing to meet. Not long after, she and I were seated in the second-floor lobby waiting for John's assistant to come and get us.

Joan seemed concerned about something.

We were just chatting casually when she asked if I had children. I replied that I did have a son and a daughter, almost 10 years apart.

In the pilot, while Sheila is busy in the kitchen, we see her daughter Karen getting a math tutoring lesson from Lip through an open archway.

To repay him for sharing his expertise, Karen slides to the floor to share her expertise with Lip—which happens to be fellatio.

Joan asked me if I would find it funny if I were in the kitchen a mere 15 feet away while my daughter was engaged in that activity.

"Of course not," I replied. "But it's funny to me in this context."

She nodded her head but not with much certainty.

The meeting was a smash. Joan is a native Chicagoan and one of the quirkiest and naturally funny people on the planet.

We made the deal, and Joan joined the cast.

She was fantastic.

She was brave.

She met Bill at least halfway, and she was a delight.

For all of those reasons and more, Joan as Sheila remains one of my favorite casting choices.

KAREN JACKSON:
LAURA SLADE WIGGINS

What was wonderful about Laura is how willing and appealing she is when it comes to doing brave and daring things. That came through in her audition, and, of course, she was shown in all sorts of compromising positions in the first couple of seasons.

One of my favorite stories is that she told her grandmother that we used a green screen when she had topless scenes, and it was somebody else's breasts.

So *Shameless*.

MONICA GALLAGHER:
CHLOE WEBB

When we knew we would be casting a mom for the Gallaghers, John and I spoke and immediately were like, "Chloe Effing Webb," because of course, we had all that history with her from *China Beach*.

She's the perfect opposite of Bill and the embodiment of erratic behavior. (At least the characters she's best known for, like Nancy Spungen from the film *Sid & Nancy*.)

Chloe, in reality, can be complex, but she's always a professional. And she brought an absolute honesty to that craziness in the same way Joan did for Sheila.

I think that's the hallmark of *Shameless*: people were willing to expose themselves, quite literally and figuratively, to embrace and allow into view their darkest and most bizarre traits.

And by "people," I mean everyone involved, not just the actors. John and Nancy Pimental and Mike O'Malley in the writer's room. Mark and, later on, Chris Chulack as directors. Iain MacDonald and Silver Tree, our producing directors.

When all of these creative forces involved in *Shameless* let their freak flags fly, it allowed everyone not to censor themselves—or each other.

The show was *Shameless*, not shameful.

It's not about being embarrassed.

It's about saying *fuck yeah*.

Chloe certainly did that.

MANDY MILKOVICH:
JANE LEVY
(Season One only)

I fell in love (professionally) with a very young and very new-on-the-LA-scene Jane Levy.

Her manager at the time was a man whose taste I had long appreciated. I agreed to see her for what was then a guest shot in the pilot of *Shameless*.

Mandy Milkovich.

The role was a member of the rival Southside family.

The racist, homophobic, violent patriarch Terry (played by Dennis Cockrum) would go on to play a big part over many seasons, and Mandy's brother Mickey would become a huge fan favorite in a relationship with Ian.

In a sense, she was kind of Juliet to Ian's Romeo (until her brother Mickey stole that honor).

They were best friends.

She was the first to know that Ian was gay.

She protected his secret.

We had a session with several young and talented women, including Jane.

After they all had read, we sat around and talked about it —Mark, John, Andrew (the JWP executive) and me.

A decision was reached, and it wasn't Jane.

Later that evening, I felt disturbed. I thought the wrong actress had been selected.

I agonized for a bit, and then said to myself, "Speak up. What do you have to lose?"

I called John at home, which was something that I very rarely did.

I asked him to please see Jane again for the role.

He agreed.

After her next reading, he changed his mind. Jane got the part.

And then, after Season One, Jane left to star in the network show *Suburgatory* and was replaced by the lovely and talented Emma Greenwell. It's worth noting Jane's post-*Shameless* career has included a Golden Globe nomination for *Zoey's Extraordinary Playlist*.

I'm glad I went to bat for her, even if her run on *Shameless* was short-lived.

LIAM GALLAGHER: CHRISTIAN ISAIAH

One of the things I loved most about working on *Shameless* was watching the kids grow from children to young adults both on-screen and off. The role of the baby of the family, Liam Gallagher, was an especially interesting and gratifying evolution.

As with most young children's roles, twins originally portrayed Liam: initially, he was played by Blake Johnson and Brennan Johnson. Starting in Season Three, Liam was portrayed by Brendan Sims and Brandon Sims.

In Season Eight, we cast Christian as our final Liam. As he told *Vulture*, John wanted to raise the stakes and expand Liam's story by sending him to a school with latent racism flowing as a thick undercurrent.

I'll never forget Christian at just 10 years old attending an early table reading. This is *Shameless*, so, of course, the language was shocking to him. Christian kept looking over his shoulder at his mom, Anita, asking with his eyes if it was okay to hear what he was hearing.

It must have been because Christian went on to have so many great moments with Bill on screen. And behind the scenes, I saw how encouraging Bill was, empowering the young man to become the excellent actor he is now.

When a series wraps, I often get emails from the cast, and I always cherish them. I received one such note from Christian and Anita, thanking me for the opportunity and trust that he would fulfill my vision. She went on to note how wonderful it was to be a part of a loving group of people who treated them like family.

How lucky we all were to have Christian and his mom in our *Shameless* family. I'm pretty sure it's safe to say he, like me, couldn't believe he got to do (and say) the things he did.

We also added a few main characters to the core ensemble over the years, notably Isidora Goreshter and Kate Miner.

SVETLANA YEVGENIVNA: ISIDORA ("IZZY") GORESHTER
(Guest Season Three; recurring Seasons Four through Eight)

Izzy joined as a guest star in Season Three, and right off the bat, it was a bold and daring role. I think we first saw her topless. Izzy is from Long Beach, California, but you'd never know it—she has a fabulous accent that she picked up from her Russian grandmother, for whom she's named.

Much like Bill, she's a lovely person in real life, while her character is someone who's not so nice (putting it mildly) and deeply troubled. Izzy had an amazing ability to capture the dichotomy of the character—someone who experienced horrible things as a sex worker in Russia and coming to the United States in a crate but still has a strong desire to survive.

Ultimately, because Izzy is so winning and lovely, she was able to do all of those dreadful things and redeem herself, which is the hallmark of *Shameless*.

TAMI TAMIETTI:
KATE MINER
(Recurring Seasons Nine through 11)

I met Kate at a general audition sometime before we were casting the role of Tami, Lip's love interest, and later, the mother of his child. At the time, she confessed that she had grown up at least part-time in a nudist colony with her parents.

Once we had Tami, who had a tradition of always having sex at weddings with her counterpart (in this case, she was the maid of honor and Lip, the best man), I knew she'd be right for the role.

And, of course, their coupling was iconic in the series, from the first time when Tami and Lip screwed standing up at the wedding (from her towering over him to vomiting on his shoes and insulting his sexual prowess) to the hopeful ending for the pair that implies they might not screw everything up.

It's a hope that seems feasible against all odds, thanks to Kate and Jeremy's palpable chemistry and excellent acting.

This brings us to *Shameless*'s trampoline—that revolving cast of characters who formed the background or had recurring supportive roles (like fan favorites and Alibi Room barflies, Kermit played by Jim Hoffmaster and Tommy played by Michael Patrick McGill).

Now, this being *Shameless*, I have to say that some of the auditions were absolutely priceless. For example, we had a part for a quasi-prostitute who had to perform oral sex on Frank because he had trouble getting an erection. It involved her doing her damnedest, including reaching her hand up inside his behind to sort of grab hold of his prostate.

The woman who won the role was, shall we say, inventive. In the audition, she was miming the whole thing—nobody was standing in front of her. It was a remarkable sight to behold.

Later, she sent the casting department a bunch of Blow Pops, which we passed out to the children who came to read.

So *Shameless*.

Like the trampoline list for all the other shows, the following is in alphabetical order and is as inclusive as possible from my recollections and research. (Please note it includes actors that appeared in at least two episodes, so it's not an exhaustive list—although it's long, as it spans 11 seasons!)

SHAMELESS'S TRAMPOLINE

Actor	Character Name	Character Description	Years Appearance
Joe Adler	Colin Milkovich	Mandy and Mickey Milkovich's brother	2012-2014
Keiko Agena	Brittany Sturgess	Childcare worker	2013
Patrick Davis Alarcón	Jason	Lip's AA sponsee	2018-2019
Chelsea Alden	Tish	One of Carl's love interests (sort of)	2021
Sasha Alexander	Helené Runyon	Lip's college professor who has sex with him	2015-2016

Juliette Angelo	Geneva	Friend of Ian who once had Trevor as a social worker	2017-2020
Shel Bailey	Kenyatta	Mandy's abusive ex-boyfriend	2014-2015
Diora Baird	Meg	The club manager where Fiona waitressed and promoted a night	2012-2013
Alessandra Ford Balazs	›Jackie Scabello	Fiona's Pasty Pie's co-worker who OD's on heroin and derails Fiona's engagement	2014-2015
Peter Banifaz	Farhad	Debbie's co-worker when she was a welder	2017-2019

Shakira Barrera	Heidi Cronch	Ex-con and one of Debbie's hook-ups	2020-2021
Jaylen Barron	Dominique	One of Carl's love interests	2016
Jenica Bergere	Lisa	Part of a gay couple who want to buy rundown houses to remodel in the Gallagher's Southside neighborhood	2015-2016
Emily Bergl	Samantha "Sammi" Slott	Frank's oldest daughter	2014-2015
Becca Blackwell	Father Murphy	The priest who introduces Ian to the girl who draws "Gay Jesus"	2018
Neal Bledsoe	Max Whitford	The predatory real estate guy Fiona deals with	2018-2019

Alex Borstein	Lou Deckner	Frank's lawyer (and also a member of the *Shameless* writing staff)	2011-2015
Dennis Boutsikaris	Professor Hearst	Lip's professor who catches him taking another kid's exam	2011-2012
David Bowe	Bob Tamietti	Tami's dad	2019-2020
Andy Buckley	Randy	Ingrid Jones's ex-husband	2018-2019
Carlease Burke	Roberta "Bob"	Monica's partner (Season One)	2011-2012
Michael Reilly Burke	Theo Wallace	A theology professor of theology who catches his wife, also a college professor, in an apparently delicate situation	2015-2016

Adam Cagley	Ron Kuzner	Lip's college roommate	2014-2015
Vanessa Bell Calloway	Carol Fisher	Veronica (and Marty's) mom	2011-2021
Scott Michael Campbell	Brad	A potential AA sponsor for Lip, ultimately friend and mentor	2016-2021
Ever Carradine	Erika	One of Frank's love interests who dies of breast cancer	2016
Jack Carter	Stan	The Alibi's landlord who lived over the bar	2012-2014
Laura Cerón	Celia Delgado	A woman who comes to the Gallagher house to discuss an important matter concerning Derek and Debbie	2015 (two episodes), 2016 (two episodes)

Dennis Cockrum	Terry Milkovich	The abusive Milkovich patriarch	2011-2021
Sarah Colonna	Lori	The assistant manager at the fast food place Carl works at	2019
Alicia Coppola	Sue	Ian's EMT boss	2016-2018
Madison Davenport	Ethel	An Amish girl fostered by Kev and Veronica	2011-2012
Bernardo De Paula	Beto	Nando's menacing henchman	2013
Rachel Dratch	Paula Bitterman	Ian's parole officer	2019
Julia Duffy	Candace Lishman	Steve/Jimmy's mother	2011-2013
Elise Eberle	Sandy Milkovich	Mickey and Mandy's cousin and Debbie's love interest	2019-2021

Eric Edelstein	Bobby Mallison	Lecherous manager of the grocery store Fiona works at	2013
Tate Ellington	Chad	Tries to get Fiona to stay on as the manager of Patsy's Pies	2016
Nadine Ellis	Dr. Brenda Williams	V's friend who invites her to a barbecue	2019-2020
Stephanie Fantauzzi	Estefania	Jimmy's wife and a drug lord's daughter	2012-2013
Sherilyn Fenn	Queenie Slott	Frank's ex and Sammi's mother	2016
Elliot Fletcher	Trevor	Ian's transgender love interest	2016-2018
Louise Fletcher	Peg Gallagher	Frank's mother and the Gallagher family matriarch	2011-2012

Richard Flood	Ford Kellogg	Fiona's love interest and an Irish carpenter	2017-2019
Jess Gabor	Kelly Keefe	Carl's love interest and daughter of an army officer	2018-2019
Thierre Di Castro Garrito	Marco	Estefania's lover	2012-2013
Nick Gehlfuss	Robbie Pratt	Mike's brother who seduces Fiona	2014
Dylan Gelula	Megan	An old friend of Debbie's who encourages her to seek child support from Derek	2019-2020
Luis Guzmán	Mikey O'Shea	Frank's friend who met him when they vied to be the face of Hobo Loco	2019

Harry Hamlin	Lloyd "Ned" Lishman	Jimmy's dad and Ian's booty call	2012-2014
Chet Hanks	Charlie	Sierra's ex-boyfriend and father of her child	2016-2018
Samantha Hanratty	Kassidi	Carl's love interest	2017-2018
Danube Hermosillo	Pepa	Derek's ex-wife	2019
Jim Hoffmaster	Kermit	Alibi Room barfly	2011-2021
Alison Jaye	Julia Nicolo	The petulant teenage daughter of Claudia, Debbie's ultra-wealthy girlfriend, who develops feelings for Debbie	2020

Amirah Johnson Scarlet Spencer	Xan	Eddie's niece who Lip "adopts" when her mother leaves	2018 (three episodes), 2019
José Julián	Joaquin	Lip's friend in college who injures himself on an acid trip	2015-2016
Steve Kazee	Gus Pfender	Fiona's ex-husband, a musician	2015-2016
Regina King	Gayle Johnson	Fiona's probation officer	2014
Jeff Kober	Jupiter	Founder of the commune and poppy farm where Debbie goes into labor	2016
Dichen Lachman	Angela	Jimmy's mysterious business partner	2014-2015

Dan Lauria	Mo White	Disgraced ex-congressman who Frank helps run for office again	2018
Ed Lauter	Dick Healey	A guidance counselor at the public school where the Gallagher kids are enrolled – he's strongly invested in Lip's future	2012-2013
Sharon Lawrence	Margo	Owner of Patsy's Pies and Fiona's business mentor	2016-2019
Morgan Lily	Bonnie	Carl's friend and partner in no-good who he meets in detention	2014
Pasha D. Lychnikoff	Yvon	Russian man	2016

Peter Macon	Dominique's Father	Chicago police officer and Dominique's father	2016
Joshua Malina	Arthur Tipping	Carl's police partner	2020-2021
Perry Mattfeld	Mel	Part of lesbian couple that lives in the building Fiona owns	2017-2018
James Allen McCune	Matty Baker	Debbie Gallagher's friend (and crush)	2014-2015
Jake McDorman	Mike Pratt	Fiona's boss and boyfriend at Worldwide Cup	2013-2014
Michael Patrick McGill	Tommy	Alibi Room barfly	2011-2021
Zach McGowan	Jody Silverman	Karen Jackson's husband and Sheila's former lover	2012-2013

Rebecca Metz	Melinda	A waitress and ex-addict at Patsy's Pies	2015-2016
Ruby Modine	Sierra	A waitress at Patsy's Pie and Lip's ex-girlfriend	2016-2018
Tyler Jacob Moore	Tony Markovich	A cop and the Gallagher's neighbor who has a crush on Fiona	2011-2016
Marguerite Moreau	Linda	Kash's wife and co-owner of Kash and Grab	2011-2012
Dermot Mulroney (replaced Jeffrey Dean Morgan, who played Charlie Peters, the original owner)	Sean Pierce	Former owner of Patsy's Pies and Fiona's junkie love interest	2015-2017

Joel Murray	Eddie Jackson	Sheila's husband and Karen's dad	2011
Arden Myrin	Dollface Dolores	A homeless woman who hooks up with Frank	2016
Paris Newton Presley Schrader	Franny Gallagher-Delgado	Debbie's daughter	2016-2021
Bojana Novakovic	Bianca Samson	Frank's doctor who is dying of cancer and has an affair with him	2015-2016
Toks Olagundoye	Leesie Janes	One of Carl's police partners	2020-2021
William O'Leary	Sgt. Rucker	A police liaison to the youth explorer program who confronts Carl with some problems	2020

Kerry O'Malley	Kate	A bartender at the Alibi	2011-2014
Victor Onuigbo	Nick	An intimidating kid who has been in prison for at least half of his young life and barely speaks	2016
Luca Oriel Damien Diaz	Derek Delgado	Debbie's baby daddy/Franny's dad	Season Five and Six (2015-2016) Season Eight (2017)
Melissa Paladino	Cami	Brad's partner then later, wife	2017-2020
Zack Pearlman	Neil	A wheelchair -bound guy	2016-2017
Jeff Pierre	Caleb	Ian's boyfriend	2016
Mary Kay Place	Aunt Oopie	The nurturing Republican aunt of Tami Tamietti	2019-2020

Lotus Plummer London Regans	Amy	Kevin and Veronica's twin daughter	2016-2019 2020-2021
Brooklyn Regans	Gemma	Kevin and Veronica's twin daughter	2020-2021
Chelsea Rendon	Anne Gonzalez	Carl's co-worker at Captain Bob's Shrimp Shack; they have a contentious relationship	2019
Stephen Rider	G-Dogg	Carl's drug boss	2015-2016
Elizabeth Rodriguez	Faye Donahue	An down-and-out, barfly who Frank takes a liking to almost immediately, but she is secretly out to get revenge	2019-2020
Ashley Romans	Alex	One of Debbie's lovers	2018

Alan Rosenberg	Professor Youens	Engineering professor and Lip's supervisor and mentor	2016-2017
Katey Sagal	Dr. Ingrid Jones	Frank's therapist and love interest	2018-2019
Nichole Sakura	Amanda	Lip's girlfriend (formerly his roommate's girlfriend) who sabotages his college career	2014-2016
Will Sasso	Yanis	A neighborhood guys who deliberately spends most of the day revving his motorcycle and making sexual threats to fight gentrification	2016

Amy Smart	Jasmine Hollander	Fiona's wild friend	2011-2012
June Squibb	Etta	An older woman who has "owned" the neighborhood laundromat forever	2016
Jessica Szohr	Nessa	Part of lesbian couple that lives in the building Fiona owns	2017-2018
Jennifer Taylor	Anne Seery	The headmistress of a private school that Frank is trying to get Liam admitted to	2016-2018
London Thor	Olivia	A waitress at Patsy's Pies	2016-2018
Levy Tran	Eddie	Lip's co-worker who leaves her niece with him when she leaves the country	2017-2018

J. Michael Trautmann	Iggy Milkovich	Mickey and Mandy's brother	2012-2015
Pej Vahdat	Kash	Ian's boss at the Kash and Grab and (married) lover	2011-2012
Idara Victor	Sarah	Lip's lifeboat friend while Tami is in the hospital.	2019
Gabrielle Walsh	Tanya	Derek's sister-in-law	2015-2016
David Wells	Father Pete	The predatory priest who delivers hospice patients to Sheila	2011-2013
Bradley Whitford	Abraham Paige	A gay man and political activist	2013
James Wolk	Adam	Fiona's Steve-like love interest	2012

Danika Yarosh Dove Cameron	Holly Herkimer	Debbie's former friend	2013-2014 (11 episodes) 2012 (two episodes)
Constance Zimmer	Claudia Nicolo	Julie's mother and Debbie's wealthy girlfriend	2019-2020

While there were so many memorable moments from the 11 seasons of *Shameless*, there are a couple that stand out from opposite ends of the spectrum.

First, a *Shameless* performance behind the scenes about an actor you might have heard of: Gary Busey.

Gary was a movie star, and then along came life, and he found himself auditioning for guest shots on television.

He came into our office for a guest-starring role, and I think he was used to his audition lasting as long as he felt it should.

And the part he was auditioning for had multiple scenes.

After maybe three or four go-rounds with the first scene, I knew there were 40 people in the waiting room, and we had to get rolling.

So, I politely said, "Hey, Mr. Busey, let's move on to the second scene."

Gary turned toward me, and other people in the room were genuinely afraid that he was going to deck me.

He said gruffly, "Don't rush me."

For the record, Gary is a big guy.

And I'm not.

It was a little frightening.

We didn't hire him that time.

Cut to the last season of *Shameless* where we were casting Frank's dad for some interstitial, bonus-type pieces.

Gary's name was on a list. And I wasn't available when there was a phone call to discuss the role, but John, writer/producer Nancy Pimental and my second chairs, Kim and Tawni, were on the call.

Nancy sparked to the idea, but Kim and Tawni tried to discourage it as Gary had a reputation for being difficult—which I could have reinforced had I been on the call.

Gary was hired.

The one time in all 134 episodes of *Shameless* that I ever got a complaint email from Bill was after shooting with Gary. He told me that he was unprepared, rude to the cast and crew and refused to comply with COVID protocols.

He added that the only way that scene would make it into the final cut is because of the miraculous work the people in the editing room do.

I apologized profusely to Bill because we knew better. Moreover, I knew Bill as someone who rolls with pretty much everything—except people who refuse to be part of the team.

For all the raunchiness and debauchery *Shameless* represented, in reality, we avoided shameful behavior.

On the other hand, there are the topics we put out to the world about real human experiences that at one time were thought of as "shameful," whereas today we know are quite the opposite.

Here's a great example:

Karen and I were on our way to a long Labor Day weekend on Cape Cod with old college buddies of mine.

We flew into Boston and got to our hotel very near the harbor, where we would take the ferry to Provincetown.

We walked in the summer breeze a few blocks to a seafood joint—oysters and clams for me, fish and chips for Karen. And as usual, a great bottle of Italian red to share.

The following day, we packed up our small suitcases and

walked to the dock from where we thought the ferry would depart.

Our information was wrong, and we were lost.

A kind person sent us in the right direction, and because we were relaxed and really looking forward to the trip, we didn't get too uptight.

We made the launch nearly the last to board.

There weren't two seats together on the outdoor deck, so Karen took the first available seat.

I found one by the door to the inside cabin.

If you're not familiar with Provincetown, or "P-town," as it is affectionately called, it's an East Coast mecca for the LGBTQ community. The boat's passengers reflected that.

The sea got rough as hell—with beers and cocktails in hand, everyone was swaying and stumbling.

Right next to the door between inside and outside was a young teen helping people in and out.

They were diligent about their self-appointed job.

On my other side was a nicely dressed woman who was clearly traveling with the young person.

The teen was dismissive of the woman the way kids sometimes are with their parents.

The woman and I got to talking. The teenager was listening.

The mom told me they were going to P-town so her child could immerse themselves in gay culture. The teen was beginning the transition process.

I had recently had my first interaction with the transgender community casting the role of Trevor on *Shameless*.

The person who got the job was Elliott Fletcher.

He had done several episodes of a show that was popular with teens and was now doing our show.

When I mentioned this, the distant and dismissive young person suddenly joined the conversation.

They became animated and excited.

Elliott was their idol and role model.

They grabbed Mom's phone and called Dad to share the amazing news.

Mom gave me an email address, and when I got back to LA, I was able to share this with Elliott, who was delighted to hear, as he takes being a role model very seriously.

What's a shame is that people are only now realizing that we are all just ourselves, doing the best we can with what we've got.

Some people's behavior is shameless—even more so than was found on the pages of any given *Shameless* script.

That said, I've had my fair share of seeing the good, the bad and the ugly of human nature throughout the 35-plus years I've been casting television shows. Now's the perfect time to share some audition stories that transcend a particular series and can be filed under "life lessons."

TEN

The Outtakes

Some audition stories transcend a given show or period of time. It's about the people and the authenticity they bring to a performance: sometimes it works, and other times, not so much.

In no particular order and loosely grouped, here are a few of my favorites.

Good for Laughs

A clown came very late to her audition in full makeup.

I told her as gently as possible that the session was long over.

She began to cry.

Her makeup was a mess.

She was inconsolable.

Later that evening, my dear friend Tony Sepulveda was in some chat room of actors who were demolishing me for making a clown cry.

✛

We had a role for a male in drag.

As always, we wanted it to be authentic, so we gathered a group of men who regularly dressed in drag.

One plus-sized fellow in a red velvet dress with white faux fur trim at the hem and cuffs called herself "Big Mama" and concluded her reading with a seductive wink. She then proclaimed, "If you're good to Big Mama, Big Mama will be good to you."

Despite that charming come on, she did not get the part.

We were casting the president's daughter, Zoe Bartlet, in *The West Wing* (the role that ultimately went to Elizabeth Moss).

The scene involved the president sharing a family recipe for chili. One of the ingredients was the spice cumin.

An actress who clearly wasn't a cook pronounced it "come-in" and then switched to "see-men."

As she was leaving, Aaron whispered, "Not in my chili!"

We couldn't help laughing out loud.

(And just so you know, I can laugh at myself...)

While casting a pilot called *The Big Time* written by my dear friend Carol Flint, about the early days of television, a variety show depicted in the pilot featured a ventriloquist act.

As usual, I was reading the role opposite the actor and his dummy.

I began to read the scene and became confused.

I wasn't sure who to look at—the doll or the man.

Suddenly, I felt the blood rush out of my face and became dizzy to the point of almost passing out.

It turns out I'm kind of terrified of ventriloquism. Yikes.

Celebrity Moments

The following stories are about some now well-established actors I spotted in their nascent days during the spring show-case season. It's always an exciting time as it ushers in a huge crop of new and well-trained talent every year.

We also get to see other casting directors, agents and managers who we usually don't see in person.

The biggest knockout actor I've ever seen in a university or college acting program was Jessica Chastain from Julliard.

Her charisma, fierceness, softness, sense of humor, stature and relatability were all off the charts.

The timing was right as well. We were in the heyday of *ER*'s remarkable success. That meant money was available.

I introduced Jessica to John, and he sparked to her immediately.

We made a holding deal for a lot of dough for a recent graduate in exchange for one year of exclusivity.

Jessica did a guest shot on *ER* and became a series regular on an awful pilot for the WB based on the hit from bygone days: *Dark Shadows*. Lucky for her, the year ended there. And, of course, Jessica went on to become an award-winning film star we have all come to love.

Josh Gad from Carnegie Mellon (John's alma mater) wowed everyone by doing all the characters from *The Wizard of Oz* in three minutes or so.

We hired him for his first role on television in a dramatic part on *ER*.

His remarkable career to date includes the lead in *The Book of Mormon* on Broadway, voice work on *Frozen* and a whole lot of other successful projects.

Samira Wiley was in the annual and very energetic showcase from Juilliard's prestigious program in 2010.

Lithe and beautiful, she combined intensity and vulnerability in an intoxicating mix. I had a general meeting with her after the showcase, but she was so red hot from her performance that I was never able to cast her. Not that I didn't try—a half-dozen years later, we were casting the fifth lead on a show called *Miranda's Rights* for Universal and NBC. Samira naturally read well, we invited her to the callback, and at that point, she declined.

While I don't know for sure, I'd imagine that coming off of her incredible work as Poussey Washington in *Orange Is the New Black*, she knew she was right for a bigger role than just the fifth lead of a series. It's a good thing she held out: Samira went on to co-star as Moira Strand in *The Handmaid's Tale* starting in 2017, a role for which she won an Emmy for Outstanding Guest Actress in a Drama Series in 2020.

Angel Lakata Moore was in the UC San Diego class. She read for a small role as a nurse on *ER*.

She struck me with her easy manner and simple, honest approach to the characters she portrayed.

If I write "simple and real," it means I loved the actor's work.

It was a perfect fit, and Angel went on to do 34 episodes as Nurse Dawn Archer (2006–2009).

I have used her several other times with excellent results.

❖

Megan Hilty from Carnegie Mellon sang for her showcase.

Enough said.

Megan has gone on to Broadway with starring roles in *Wicked*, *9 to 5* and more. And she had a spectacular turn as an actress vying for the part of Marilyn Monroe on the innovative television series *Smash*.

Plus, she has a fantastic nightclub act—I was blessed with her singing "Happy Birthday" to me from the stage of the Carlyle Hotel.

What a thrill.

And now for some household names whom I had the pleasure of reading:

Saturday Night Live star Molly Shannon came in to read for the classic female best friend and sidekick in a rare comedy pilot that I had been assigned.

It was based on the stand-up of a woman named Andrea Walker.

Molly had some business planned with stuff in her purse that was loosely scripted.

All kinds of things were dumped on my office floor: Tampons, lipsticks, cigarette lighters, chewing gum and so on.

It was physical comedy extraordinaire.

After she got everything back in the bag, she rose and headed for the door.

She missed it by several feet and crashed into the wall.

I've never known for sure whether she did that on purpose or not.

She didn't get the job, although she was fabulous.

In Season Five of *ER*, George had fulfilled his original contract and was moving on. It would certainly create a hole in the fabric of the cast.

How to fill it?

Jon Stewart came in to meet. He was everything advertised.

Whip-smart. Maybe the brightest person I had ever met besides John and later Aaron.

Naturally, Jon was funny. He's among the very few who can talk about important stuff and have a take that was at once thoughtful, serious and bent in a hilarious way.

What a delight and a privilege.

Despite all of that, Jon wasn't the answer.

On September 12, 2001, I met with a woman on whom I had/have a huge crush.

Padma Lakshmi.

I (along with millions of other fans) had watched her on the Food Network doing a show about Indian food and travel called *Padma's Passport.*

I was taken by her realness exemplified by her scar and her delight in sharing her culture, country and cuisine.

Padma arrived a bit discombobulated.

Security was newly tightened, and everyone was worried that a storied film and television studio would make a symbolic target for America's terrorist enemies.

Almost nobody was on the lot that day.

The guard at the gate had very thoroughly searched her vehicle and especially her gym bag.

I wondered whether his enthusiasm was a kind of racist suspicion of people who look like Padma.

Padma seemed to imply that she thought it was more misogynistic. "He had an inordinate interest in my gym bag," she said with a knowing and wry smile. Was he in search of her underwear?

We laughed and chatted about food, irony, travel, my work and hers. It was more damn fun.

I have since watched every episode of her show, *Top Chef.*

Padma, if you're reading this, I'm a bit of a foodie and always available to be a guest at one of your tastings.

Right around the time my marriage fell apart, I had the awesome honor of meeting with Smokey Robinson for a general role.

The Tracks of My Tears by Smokey Robinson and the Miracles is in my top 10 songs of all time.

The lyrics.

The music.

The emotional connection.

The phrasing.

All perfect.

And after Blaine and I split, I could relate to the song even more than ever before.

Still, it was an honor and a privilege to meet Smokey.

Nothing ever came of it in the practical world.

However, it was remarkable for me on a personal level.

While casting the first season of *ER*, I had a brush with true greatness with the famous and very influential acting teacher Sanford "Sandy" Meisner.

I had great respect for him and always responded when I saw on an actor's resume that they'd studied with him.

Sandy had a laryngectomy in 1970 for throat cancer, and he spoke through a hole in his throat. The sound was otherworldly.

And, of course, his charisma and intelligence were evident.

John and others answered Sandy's questions about his character, Joseph Klein, an elderly gentleman with a DNR whom the doctors save in the episode "Sleepless in Chicago." They discussed the relevant matters of the role and the way production was handled.

Eventually, Sanford asked what he would be paid. I told him the figure—it was something like $6,479.

He winked at me and said, "What's the $79 for?"

It made me laugh, and he laughed as well.

Later, Noah Wyle, who had several scenes with Sandy, remarked that it was the highlight of his career.

Sandy's scene played in a loop at his memorial service when he passed away a couple of years later. This rare television appearance on *ER* was also his last.

Sometimes, It's Personal and It's Business

A woman I knew from Priscilla's Coffee House in Burbank came in and read for a very pregnant woman who had leaped off the wagon and was plastered, defiant and abusive. The woman was in AA and still had all the residual effects of her drinking days: a rough boozy voice, a booming laugh as jolting as an earthquake and a dark sense of humor.

She told me in the hallway that she wanted to leap right in —no small talk—until the scene was over.

She committed fully, and her performance was frightening, deep, revealing and honest.

When she finished, she said, "Hello, my name is Georgine, and I'm an alcoholic. I've been sober for more than a decade, and I'm a reliable adult who can access my past."

She got the part.

We had cast a young transgender person, Elliot Fletcher, for the role of Trevor on *Shameless*.

While reading with a man around 50 years old, Elliot's performance somehow came up.

The man revealed that his daughter had been friends with the actor at an all-girls Catholic school they both attended.

He made no secret that he was disgusted by his transition and the school's tolerance of it.

We were flabbergasted by his lack of compassion.

He didn't get the job.

In a rare comedy pilot that I worked on (the same one that Molly Shannon auditioned for), another actress came in for the same role.

She sat down in the chair in the center of the room.

I greeted her and asked how she was doing.

She burst into tears.

As it turns out, she had just left a coffee place around the corner where her fiancé had broken off their engagement and asked for the ring back.

I certainly felt for her, although it would have been better for her to reschedule.

She didn't get the part.

After my mom moved to Burbank and became my neighbor, I got the crazy idea that she'd be good as a patient on *ER*. So I asked permission to hire her without an audition—after all, she was a big star in my life ("offer only"). And in an act of excess, I paid her nearly double what anyone else would have gotten.

When the day came, she was so intimidated by everything on the set, that she didn't know she could ask permission to go to the toilet. So she sat in character in a wheelchair for hours. Finally, she was up. I don't remember the dialog, but I do remember in the scene, Anthony Edwards was walking by, and she put out her cane out to stop him, saying something like, "Can you help me? I've been sitting here for hours."

A prime example of art imitating life.

Don't Have a Good Idea (At Least Not When You're Auditioning)

If there's one piece of advice I have for auditioning actors, it's to mind your manners. And, while you're at it, be sure you have made an accurate assessment of the nature of your relationship with the people you are interacting with (aka the casting director).

An actress who later became quite famous was in my office reading for a TV movie.

It seemed every made-for-television movie that year had the word "stranger" in its title.

I think this one was called *A Stranger Waits*.

She was auditioning for a "bad girl" who pulls a knife on another character in the scene.

She actually pulled a butter knife out from somewhere.

It wasn't sharp, but when she moved it toward me, I reacted.

I grabbed her wrist and knocked it to the ground.

She did not get the part.

A gentleman who trained at one of America's great acting programs and has gone on to a big presence in the movie world came into my office to audition for *Shameless*.

At the end of the scene, he hurled a chair hard behind him.

It smashed into the wall we had painted blue so that people's faces popped in taped auditions.

It left many dents and scratches.

The actor acted as if nothing had happened—even casually placing the chair in front of the damage.

Similarly, in another bizarre moment in my office, an actor forcibly threw a shoe in the direction of my associate who was reading with them.

Fortunately, it sailed over her head.

Neither got the part.

A well-known character actress in her early 60s tried to insist that my casting associate, Melanie Burgess, who was reading with her be "fully available, *physically and emotionally*," while they played the scene.

We do have intimacy coordinators, but being present during auditions is not part of their job.

She didn't get the part.

A very well-known actress brought her dog into the room. It was part of the scene, but it went to hell in a handbasket.

The dog couldn't wait for its cue and became the focus of the scene.

Neither the actress nor the dog got the job.

A young woman reading for a sexy role wore a very short skirt to her audition.

As a result, she spent the entire time pulling on the hem to keep us from seeing her unmentionables.

She maintained her privacy but didn't get the part.

While working for Marsha Kleinman, I helped cast a film called *Burglar.*

There was the role of a bad guy who had a physical altercation. On the third or fourth callback, an actor I had read with all the previous times took me aside and asked if he could grab my shoulders with both hands and give me a shake.

I was game—what the hell?

When the time came, his adrenalin was pumping so completely that he violently grabbed me by the front of my shirt and shook me so hard that it ripped down the front.

Then, adding insult to injury, he slammed me against the wall.

I had had enough. I bounced back at him and swung my best right-hand punch.

The director was a big southern guy and normally very mellow. He stepped between us.

My favorite linen green-checkered shirt was in tatters.

He didn't get the job.

Now, let's talk about what it takes to be right for the role, from my 35 years (and counting) of experience as a casting director (and maybe my 74 years and counting experience as a human being).

Epilogue

It's been quite a journey since the first page when I told you my dad's formula for successful storytelling:

Tell them what you're gonna tell them.

Tell them.

Tell them what you told them.

So, now is the time for me to tell you what I've told you.

On the surface, I've filled you in on a bit about me, personally and professionally. And, of course, much of what I shared is about casting iconic television shows, including *China Beach, Growing Pains, The Adventures of Brisco County, Jr., ER, The West Wing, Third Watch, Southland, Animal Kingdom* and *Shameless,* among others.

Thanks to hindsight, I've learned that when you embrace a collaborative spirit, you naturally evolve. Central to collaboration is communication. And that holds the ticket to success in any field, and certainly in entertainment.

For example, at the Taper, I frequently worked on new plays. So, I developed the habit of asking questions to understand the writer's perspective. Also, as I had been a director in the theatre, I had no problem comprehending the television director's perspective. And because I'd started it all thinking I might be an actor (along with scoring a date with my crush, Betsy Swift), and later taught and directed actors, I get the actor's viewpoint.

All of this led to a long and fruitful career in casting. So, even though I often see my career as a series of happy accidents, the truth is being "right for the role" is about the life you cast yourself in.

In my case, I often joke that I've been successful in two major roles: as an artist and a whore. I understand both the commercial aspects and the artistic sensibility, and I've always been somehow able to bring them together.

If I had to bottle my taste, here are the ingredients that I seek in an actor: Charisma, electricity, attractiveness, sexuality, intelligence, humor, humanity—a life force. Also, good manners.

Almost nobody will have all of that, although I have worked with several who have come close if not gone all the way: George Clooney, Jessica Chastain, Lucy Liu, Regina King, Allison Janney, Rob Lowe, Bradley Whitford, Eriq La Salle, Bill Macy and Emmy Rossum, to name a few.

When it comes to auditions, my opinion is that a long monologue is almost always useless. If you've prepped for six months or you're Meryl Streep, perhaps, it might work. But really, I'm interested in seeing how the person does with immediacy, intensity and the right-now-ness of working on a piece of material in the moment.

More generally speaking, I believe that you'll go further in life if you recognize the importance of playing a productive role in a group no matter what you're doing. As Father Boyle, the founder of Homeboy Industries, with whom we consulted during the casting of *Southland,* said, "What unifies us as revolutionaries of tenderness is the longing to find our true selves in loving…in community."

And having fun with our compadres while also doing excellent work.

It's also about being truthful to yourself and those you are surrounded by. That's the best way to roll with inevitable change and see it as an opportunity, not an obstacle.

Over my long career, a lot has evolved, from how we do the business to the business itself. The world and how people show up have transformed, and I consider myself very lucky to help usher in an era in casting that better reflects society the way it is—diverse, inclusive, quirky and raw.

The irony of writing my memoir during the strangest time in my life—the COVID-19 pandemic—is not lost on me.

To be honest, as casting became a "brave Zoom world," I was hyper-aware of a sense of loss.

After all, people and their stories have been my life's preoccupation and occupation. In-person interaction tells a much more complete story, and we learn so much more about the actors in the process. Doing things more virtually than not is a loss I think we'll all feel, even though some might argue seeing actors on screens in tiny boxes helps approximate how the audience will watch the show on their cell phones.

To give you a sense of the shift, here are some notes I jotted down while working on the first two episodes of the sixth and final season of *Animal Kingdom*, which aired in August 2022.

We are continuing to explore the earlier lives of our characters. So, we are meeting three of them at 16 and 17: Julia and her twin brother Andrew (later "Pope") at 16, and her adopted brother Baz at 17.

Julia:

We never saw Julia as an adult, although we did meet her in Season Five when she was around ten. As a result, some elements of her look are established, although people change a bit after puberty sets in.

Now Julia is 16 and in full rebellion against her mother, Janine "Smurf" Cody. She loves her brother Andrew and doggedly protects him.

Baz is a year older than the twins, hot, and in pursuit of Julia sexually.

She is drinking, smoking weed and taking acid.

We received 45 or so self-tapes for Julia. All the actors had to go on were descriptions in the breakdown and the scenes we sent them. It's also always helpful if the actor is a viewer with some knowledge of the back-story to guide them.

That isn't different from the old days. (And by "old days," I mean 2019 and before...not so old.)

Then it changes.

I would react to an actor's work in those bygone days if the look were in the ballpark.

We would then talk a bunch and go again. I'd see if the actor made the appropriate adjustments.

(Remember, adjustments aren't necessary if the actor is clearly wrong or right for a role. So, if I give adjustments, it's following a hunch that may be proved or disproved depending on how they respond. It's about the process—not the results.)

We whittled the Julia contenders down to 25 to send to the producers. They loved them.

They sent us nine for a Zoom callback session. We got the producers to reduce it to seven possibilities.

Those ladies will meet in the morning for a Zoom call back in the hopes of getting down to two or three at the most for a final mix and match.

Baz:

Both Andrew (later Pope) and Baz have been established as adults by Shawn Hatosy and Scott Speedman, respectively.

This both narrows the field and makes it harder at the same time.

Today we sent a whole bunch of young guys for Baz at 17. They all fell into the trap of wanting to be likable.

The character is a sexual predator and opportunist. He wants to and will succeed at bedding his adoptive mother and his sort-of sister.

The producers agreed on 10 to go forward.

After a tussle that I generated, they agreed to eliminate three or four by the morning.

We will then set up the remaining six or seven for a Zoom callback.

Andrew (Pope):

We also sent about 20 young actors tonight for Andrew at 16. It's by far the hardest role to get right.

We have such a clear vision and idea of who he becomes because Shawn's performance is so vivid, and his look is so specific that we are reeling a bit.

My Little League baseball coach used to clap his hands when I was at bat and holler, "It only takes one, Johnny, only one."

I'm hoping like hell that there is one that fits the bill.

This is tricky because we can only send what we have recorded on Zoom and encourage the producers to watch with greater openness. More falls on their imagination than the actors'.

Zoom Callbacks:

The producing director Nick Copus was on the Zoom call, as was the head writer, Daniele Nathanson.

My second chairs, Tawni and Kim, divided responsibilities: Tawni read with the actors while Kim took care of the technical aspects.

I was the host introducing everybody and welcoming the actors trying to ease the weirdness of a Zoom callback.

I also briefly discuss the nudity and simulated sex that is a part of each role.

Then Nick, Daniele, Kim and I muted and disappeared so the acting could begin.

It went well. We quickly selected two options for each male character.

An FYI for actors: In this case, our ultimate decisions boiled down to whether the actors looked like the older male characters. This doesn't mean you don't need talent—you do—but decisions are sometimes made in great part on your appearance in addition to your performance.

For Julia, we trimmed the seven talented young contenders down to four. (We agreed on the Julia options, but I think we had them in a slightly different order.)

The discussion was short, and we eliminated the people who didn't feel as right to get down to the two actors we felt were best as Julia.

Partly for economic reasons, many of the actors still in the running were not in Los Angeles. Because of that and COVID protocols, we decided to do the upcoming mix-and-match chemistry reading via Zoom as well.

The two remaining actors for each role will be there, along with Leila George, the woman who plays the young Smurf (a role we established in Season Five). John Wells will attend that session and make the final decisions.

This will be a first for me.

I am an old dog, so transitioning to new tricks is hard.

Anxious to see if we can really see chemistry via Zoom. It's cumbersome and incomplete, but in the COVID world, it's the best we can do.

Sometimes it seems to me that any talented actors will have some kind of organic chemistry by nature. But we are looking for a specific dynamic and hoping it springs to life as the creative members of our team imagined.

Clearly, technology has taken over the world. But that said, it's not a replacement for human beings. As I see it, the casting director's primary job is to help storytellers tell stories.

And those stories are about people.

Their nature, flaws, conflicts, triumphs, pleasures, passions, fears, friendships, failures, families, loves and losses. All of those things are as old as humankind. They are the same stories that have always been told around campfires in every culture.

We may be clothed differently and use new tools, but we're after the same things we've always been after.

When you're casting series regular roles on hit television shows, you have to have fabulous talent. You have to have a great, winning likability and relatability. They have to fit into the balance of making an ensemble and re-making an ensemble. This you may recognize as my mobile analogy.

If you hang a beautiful piece of turquoise here, but you don't have anything to balance it on the other side that's contrasting in color with the right weight and size, then the whole thing tips over. And so you just keep plugging away and trying to keep your cast fresh, exciting, smart, winning, likable, charismatic and sexy.

Now, that mobile analogy can extend to life itself. For me, the balance of experiences has helped me grow into the role I was born to play. My friends, family, classmates and co-workers all have provided balance and counterbalances to my lived experiences.

And the stories, which I've been lucky enough to help bring to life, have also shaped my worldview in profound ways. Casting people who are HIV-positive, transgender, deaf, and/or marginalized for any other reason has been the highlight of my career. Each unique and sensitive pocket of humankind allowed me to get to know that world and grow and change as a person.

The eternal quest to find community and, along with it, a better version of myself.

Now, please note that work is ongoing. As I joked with John Wells first on the occasion of my receiving the Hoyt Bowers lifetime achievement award in 2009, and again in 2017 at my 70th birthday party, maybe it's best for your boss to not be at such milestone occasions.

Then again, when you are part of a community, you grow together. This is the secret to both longevity and staying vital for much longer than you might as a lone wolf. So, for example, during a tiny lull in my career around 2012, I took on an interesting casting job for a fun video game project: *Grand Theft Auto 5*. (My work on *Southland* and intimate knowledge of the diverse communities of Southern California made me a natural fit. The project was so top secret, I didn't even know what I was doing. Note to self and to you, dear reader— always ask for a piece of the profits!)

This should help disabuse a popular Hollywood myth: You don't become irrelevant because you've aged. You age when you allow yourself to become irrelevant.

And so, I keep showing up, doing my part.

That's the role I chose in life. It's always been right for me —and I've grown into being right for it.

Other People's Memories

I've always wanted to advance art and artists. The idea that I have accomplished this is astounding and gratifying beyond my ability to express.

Being in connection with these great artists and lovely men and women of such talent is the gift that keeps on giving. And working on this project with Trudi has given me the gift of perspective

I just read every script with an openness bringing my intelligence and sensitivity to the work. I never thought about the collective accumulated value of my contributions.

Now I see that I had a small part in the enormous success of these iconic television shows, and the people associated with them (and me), and I am proud, humbled and grateful.

▭

"When you're starting off in this industry, the people who you interact with in the beginning are so important. John Frank Levey saw something in me and gave me the chance early in my career to succeed. Myself and so many others in Holly-

wood appreciate John and celebrate his accomplishments
throughout the years."
-Jessica Chastain, Academy Award-winning actor (first professional job, *ER*)

"To be blunt, the audition is the worst part of acting. For
every great audition which results in getting the job, there are
dozens that were disappointing, disastrous, debilitating,
depressing experiences. And perhaps the worst audition is
when you walk into the room and nail the scene, wow the
director and have complete confidence that you are perfect for
the role. And you still don't get the job. Greater minds than
mine have searched for a better way to get the right actor for
the role, and no one has come up with a solution. We can only
thank the Lord for wonderful casting directors like John Frank
Levey.

During the run of *Shameless*, I got to watch John in action, and
what is immediately apparent is his great empathy for what
actors are going through. He genuinely wants each actor to
shine. He is gentle, soft-spoken and has a knack for making the
room a safe place. He's horrified when things fall behind
schedule and the actors have to wait. He's gracious with his
appreciation for their preparation and time. And when the
actor leaves the room, he is right there to sing their praises
when deserved and to remind us where we might have seen
the actor before. He is amazingly perceptive about what any
given actor will bring to a role, so the writer and director feel
good about relying on his taste and advice. And he's astound-
ingly generous about seeing new actors.

But the proof of the pudding is the final product, and for 11
years I watched in amazement at the magnificent actors who

were a part of *Shameless*. Not only did John make it look easy, but he always appeared to be having the time of his life."
-William H. Macy, Emmy and SAG Award-winning actor (*ER*, *Shameless*)

———

"John Frank Levey not only had an eye for talent, he loved talent. Not everyone has both, and most people have neither. The list of people he discovered or cast speaks for itself. He has seen it all."
-Rob Lowe, Emmy-nominated and SAG Award-winning actor (*The West Wing*)

———

"*ER*'s success was an incredibly diverse ensemble—offering proof of concept for inclusive casting every Thursday night. John Frank Levey was largely responsible for that. He certainly changed my life."
-Noah Wyle, Emmy-nominated and SAG Award-winning actor (*ER*)

———

"First and foremost, I think John has great taste in actors. One of the things that made me feel so comfortable on *The West Wing* was the fact that all of my castmates had come from very strong NY theatre backgrounds. We had shared experiences that allowed us to bond very quickly. Acting is a team sport and John stacked the bench deep! We were surrounded by seasoned actors."
-Allison Janney, Emmy, SAG and Academy Award-winning actor (*The West Wing*)

━━━

"It's rare and invaluable to walk into an audition in LA and know, without a shred of doubt, that casting is one hundred percent on your side. It makes you a better actor. That's what John Frank Levey brings and I couldn't be more grateful for it. Hard to put into words how grateful I am to John Frank Levey. His belief in me and ongoing support transformed my career and changed my life. John Frank Levey is a good kid. Lots of potential. I think he's gonna have a great career."
-Noel Fisher, actor (*Shameless*)

━━━

"The auditioning process is unlike any other job interview, it's also unlike the actual work of an actor. The actor needs to instantly trust the process and feel at ease enough to be vulnerable, enraged, sexy, funny...the list goes on and on, but most importantly they need to feel comfortable in the moment, so they can take risks. I have auditioned for John on three separate occasions (*ER*, *Southland* and *Animal Kingdom*) and they were all emotionally complex roles. The environment he creates in the room is an actor's dream. It never felt like I was in an audition with John; instead, it was as though I was already right there on set tearing into the scenes without any inhibitions. It's a rare achievement in the perplexing casting process.

Now that I've been on the other side of the camera as a director, I'm even more impressed with John's respect and understanding of the actor's craft. He places every single artist in a position to succeed. We have worked together on over a hundred table reads and part of what makes John so incredible is the fact that he is a talented actor in his own right. When he cold reads COP #2, I can hear his fundamental and innate understanding of the character. The moment I discuss casting with him, I realize he's a step ahead of me, and COP #2 already has a backstory. It helps me discover something deeper, unexpected and spontaneous in the choices. Put simply, my collaborations with John have made me a better artist."

-Shawn Hatosy, actor (*ER, Southland, Animal Kingdom*)

"Collaborating with John Frank Levey is a writer's dream. Episode after episode, John "gets" the script and each character's purpose. His acquaintance with good actors—whether established or brand new—is vast. John's casting sessions offer an abundance of choices, and he keeps the often hair-splitting deliberations that follow auditions focused, sensitive and fun."

-Carol Flint, Emmy-winning writer and producer (*China Beach, ER, The West Wing*)

"Working with John was a master class in the craft of casting, and in the creative joy and passion one can find in collaborating with artists."

-Jinny Howe, former EVP and Head of Television, John Wells Productions (*ER, Southland, Animal Kingdom, Shameless*)

"A true craftsman in this industry, John has always handled his career with such an earnest passion that is truly palpable, whether in the casting room or at a table read on set. I feel so incredibly honored to have had the opportunity to kickstart my career working alongside John as a mentor, colleague and

friend, and I can't wait to continue working with him in the future."
-Jacob Weary, actor (*Animal Kingdom*)

"When you work with someone who loves their job, they tend to be relentless in the best possible way. They leave no stone unturned. They're not afraid to say, 'We need to see a few more people.' Or 'I know what you're thinking, but look at this before you make a final decision.' That's John. The voice of reason, not doom. A goldmine when it comes to casting, because not only is he going to present you with the best choices, he's not afraid to go back to the well if your gut is telling you there's more. But you usually don't second guess him. He's right. John becomes that gut instinct which is why John Wells, Chris Chulack and Ann Biderman love him so. And as someone working my way up the ranks, John someone I loved working with and learning from."
-Cheo Hodari Coker, NAACP Image Award-winning writer and producer (*Southland*)

"From 1987–1991, I had the great fortune of being a part of the ensemble of actors on the ABC television drama *China Beach*. Set in Vietnam during the war, the series featured a cast of characters that included American army nurses and doctors, frontline soldiers, 'rear and upper echelon mother fuckers,' Red Cross volunteers (aka Donut Dollies), mysterious entrepreneurs (me!), as well as a host of Vietnamese characters. All of these characters were written with great depth and emotional reserve, which in turn required actors capable of illuminating all of those complexities.

Thinking back all these years later about the *China Beach* cast, leads as well as guest actors, I marvel at the extreme care, discernment and taste that John Frank Levey brought to the series in all of his casting decisions. John's innate under-standing of script analysis and character description, and then matching that with the right actor is John's singular talent."
-Marg Helgenberger, SAG and Emmy Award-winning actor (*China Beach*)

"I met John Frank Levey early in my career when everything in the entertainment business was new to me, most especially the treacherous audition landscape. For my initial audition for the television series *ER*, there was plenty to be nervous about —most especially the creatives, John Wells and Steven Spiel-berg! John welcomed me into his office and instantly, I felt at ease and capable of showing my best.

Years later, I joined the cast of *Southland*, an ensemble of incredible talent orchestrated by—once again—John. His kindness has always made me feel welcomed and encouraged, as it has for so many decades to the benefit of countless actors. The real stars of our industry are casting directors like John who not only launch careers but more importantly, set us up to be a part of beautiful stories unfolding."
-Lucy Liu, Emmy-nominated SAG Award-winning actor (*ER, Southland*)

"One of the things that stood out to me right away about John was that he was the type of casting director that truly rooted for actors. When you walked into a room with him, you really felt how much he wanted you to win.

My fondest memory was the day that I tested for ER. After the audition, I was down in the parking lot at NBC talking to the other two actors that had also tested. I saw John exiting the building about 20 yards away and when the other two actors had their backs to him, he gave me a thumbs-up. Of course, I just took it as a good luck gesture, so I just smiled and waved politely. Sensing my denseness, he then gave an even more enthusiastic thumbs up.

It still took me five minutes after he was gone to realize he was secretly telling me the role was mine. Ten minutes after that, my agent called me to confirm. Even after the huge success of the show, it was always great to see how John always treated actors with respect and care."
-Eriq La Salle, Emmy-nominated, SAG Award-winning and NAACP Image Award-winning actor (*ER*)

"My relationship with John has spanned over 10 years. He has played a pivotal role, both personally and creatively, in my career. When he knew you were right for something, he moved mountains…to think of how he went through his encyclopedic knowledge of actors to arrive at the right fit…I can't tell you how fortunate I feel to have him be an advocate of my work and also the opportunity to get to know him over the years.

He always makes an effort to get to know who you are as a person and an artist. John has a relaxation to his approach… At the same time, I feel he sees past all the barriers you might try and put up. A wonderful artist himself, he will go to the mattresses (maybe 'go to war,' don't want anyone taking this literally) for someone he really believes in.

If you were lucky enough to have him in your corner, then you know what I mean. I really feel like my relationship with him is sewn into the fabric of my journey in a structural way. I know I'm not the only one."
-Dichen Lachman, actor (*Shameless, Animal Kingdom*)

"*Right for the Role* is fantastic. Thoughtful, illuminating and just plain fun."
-Lydia Woodward, Emmy-winning writer and producer (*China Beach, ER*)

"John Frank Levey is one of the most admired casting directors in our business. I will be forever grateful as he was instrumental in allowing me to take the reins from him in Season Three of *The West Wing*. I am in awe of his talent, his taste, his generosity and his friendship."
-Anthony "Tony" Sepulveda, Senior VP, Casting at Warner Bros. TV

"I am loving this so much. I love your words—unusual, thoughtful and brilliantly descriptive. I had to whip open my dictionary, and I feel a little smarter today (on page 157 ironically, haha).

Your stories are captivating and your history is so compelling. Gosh, I don't think I knew a lot of who/what/where you were 'from' both emotionally and mentally. There were snapshots of your life revealed in your stories—but they are executed so well. They plop us smack dab into your office, your car, your home, your dinner parties, theatre rehearsals, your heart.

It's a laser-sharp insight into how you all masterfully came together once you decided to be unapologetic and embraced every wonderful and different characteristic about yourself—wowie! An explosion from a lovely, charming, witty and astute man and so much more. What a lesson."
-Mindy Kanaskie, associate producer (*The West Wing*)

"I worked with John Frank Levey from the first days of *China Beach* back in 1986. We were casting great young actors, from Dana Delany and Marg Helgenburger and Robert Picardo to Chloe Webb, Michael Boatman and Brian Wimmer. So many others—Ricki Lake, Concetta Tomei and on and on—remarkable artists who blessed us with their talents.

John is a true artist himself, and his genuine love of actors and the filmmaking process made him a vital creative partner. John Sacret Young and I could never have realized our original vision without him or sustained it through its remarkable run. He always had a great story or an anecdote to lighten up and enlighten endless casting sessions, and this book of a special life spent in film is full of those stories.

I can't think of a better insight into the magic behind the truth of filmmaking, which is casting is destiny. We live and die by it. Our visions would never come to life without the right actor for each part. We would have gone to war with John any day, and we did."
-William Broyles, Jr., Academy Award-nominated screenwriter and co-creator of *China Beach*

"I have had the honor to know John Frank Levey for almost
25 years now. He is an incredible person and I have learned so
much from him throughout the years. Not just how to make a
good cast deal, but how to be an honorable human being
while doing your best to live life to the fullest.

I've had the ups and downs like us all, but I've had Levey to
help prop me up during the downs, and cheer me on for the
ups and for that, I'm a better man and truly grateful to call
John Frank Levey a dear friend."
-Ned Haspel, COO, John Wells Productions

"John Frank Levey had that thing where you could tell he
really loved actors. He'd bring me in on everything that I was
right for, and I'd always get callbacks. After one callback, he
said to me, 'Can I talk to you for a second?' and I said 'Um,
yeah.' And he said, 'Hey Marish, I notice that every time you
come in here, you kill it on your first audition, but when you
come back, it's never as good. Why is it that you're so good on
the first one, but not on the second? It's a pattern like you're
sabotaging your callback. You need to figure out what that is
and deal with it.'

It was a painful thing to hear. And doubly painful because I
knew he was right. I left there with a lot to think about, but
one of the things that struck me the most was that here was
this casting director who doesn't owe me anything, who I've
now known for a while but not in a friendship kind of way,
and he goes the extra mile—beyond the extra mile—with this
tough love moment. Here was John Frank Levey making an
investment in me.

Years after that, it could be as many as 10, I went in to audition for *ER*. I killed it, and I knew I killed it. The day after, I had another audition for something I didn't like at all, and John said afterward, 'Oh my god, you tanked that!' And I said, 'Yeah, I know I tanked it because I hate it.' Then I asked him, 'What happened yesterday with *ER*?' And he told me he didn't know what was happening with the role but that I'd done a great job.

So I said, 'I want to go talk to John Wells.'" I expected him to laugh, but he said, 'All right.' 'Seriously?' I asked him. And he said, 'Yeah, let's go'—like it was the most normal thing in the world.

So we walked together across the Warner Brothers lot to John Wells's office. The assistant was sitting there, and I said, 'I'd like to talk to John Wells.' She looked at me, then at her calendar. Then she raised her eyebrows and looked back up at me and asked, 'Do you have an appointment?' Of course I had to say I didn't, but from behind me, I heard John Frank Levey say, 'She only wants to talk to him for a minute.'

I thought to myself, *Wow, this guy literally has my back. This is John Frank Levey, and he believes in me, and here he is, this wonderful, generous spirit, on my team, backing me up.* His support meant everything to me. Everything. And I honestly don't know if I would have had the courage to have the conversation that came next with John Wells if John Frank Levey hadn't been standing right behind me.

John Wells came out and said, 'Mariska, hi.' He was friendly, but he had that tone where someone is trying to figure out what you're doing in their office. 'Do we have an appointment?'

I said, 'No. I just want to talk to you about my audition yesterday.' He said 'You did great. But I usually cast it a little closer to type.' Then I asked him, 'Did anyone do better in the audition than I did?'

He took a moment, then answered honestly, which I appreciated. He said 'No. But you're very strong. And you're striking, with your dark hair. You're a force.'

I took a beat, and then I said 'So, no one did better than me, but I didn't get the part because I'm strong?' And John Frank Levey and I left. By the time I got home, I had the part.

You can feel John's love for actors, and how deeply he appreciates what they're up against. He takes an interest in the best way, the way a great teacher takes an interest. He's such a soulful human that he just falls in love with the human spirit. You can feel his love for the art form. For bravery. For the nobility. For the trying. His love, support, encouragement—his beautiful heart—truly shaped the course of my trajectory, and I am forever grateful."
-Mariska Hargitay, Emmy-winning actor (*ER*)

◻━━

"I was but a smaller version of my larger self when I first met John Frank Levey one breezy May morning in 2003. I was performing in my school (Carnegie Mellon University's) Drama Showcase, a performance that consisted of me playing multiple characters from *The Wizard of Oz*.

Unlike everyone else in the room who didn't quite know what to make of me, John decided to call me into his office. He sat me down and said to me that I was a riot and that he would be on the lookout for something that could be the right fit for me.

Usually, when someone promises you something like that in Hollywood, it's met with a steady diet of silence and broken dreams. John, however, always a man of his word, did just that, and less than one year later, I got my first paid gig in Hollywood.

It was a gig befitting any actor showcasing his range by playing Dorothy Gale and The Cowardly Lion…the NBC medical drama *ER*. If that doesn't speak to John Frank Levey being a visionary, frankly, I don't know what would.

Because of John, I got my SAG card and my big break, and am in the second decade of a dream career built on the foundation of his passion, belief and guidance. He is truly one of the greats."
-Josh Gad, actor (first professional job, *ER*)

━━━

"I met John Frank Levey in 1996 when I directed my first *ER* episode. 1996 was a year where *ER* was the biggest show on television with ratings coming in at 34 million views per episode. I was rather early in my career and had enormous respect for the series, so you can believe I was nervous as hell when I got the job.

Before I got to set, I watched every single episode of *ER*. There were many facets of *ER* that I admired and was moved by. Most notable of all elements was its unique guest cast. Of course, I revered the cast regulars that the world came to know and love, but I had a special spot for the guest cast: from buzzworthy guest stars to small parts with one line.

Never in my career have I worked with a casting director that was so dedicated to finding great characters as well as unique and undiscovered talent. The actors John finds are always real, honest and true to the story at hand.

John consistently brings in people I have never heard of but are so uniquely right for the part. He finds actors from every walk of life—actors I have never seen or heard of before, all of whom are consistently seasoned and prepared. John's gift of finding actors who are specifically right for any part has been uncanny. Any actor knows that if they are lucky enough to get a John Frank Levey audition, they have to do their best. John—more than anyone I know—has turned so many actors into household names. Have you heard of anyone from *Shameless*? What about *The West Wing*?

There are many stories I could tell concerning our casting sessions together, but each job with John has left me confident that whether first, second or third choice, he always knows who will best serve the story.

There is something special about John's casting choices. The actors John chooses make you care for the character's journey or their plight. You feel for their malady or laugh at their portrayal. Whatever is called for, John has the answer to. He puts his heart into what he does and that makes my job— any director's job—so much easier.

John and his team are by far the best casting team I have ever worked with, and I will look forward to every opportunity to work with him again."
-David Nutter, Emmy Award-winning director (*ER, The West Wing, Shameless*)

"John Frank Levey loves actors and does everything he can to make us feel safe and empowered. What makes him an extraordinary casting director is that he has never relied on casting me in a role I've played before.

As an actor, I am often called upon to play the same type of character over and over. Every time John has called me in to audition, it begins with him imagining me in a role that nobody has seen me play, something outside of my comfort zone. His belief in me as an actor gives me the confidence to explore that uncharted part of myself.

Whether it's a mentally ill man having an anxiety attack, an intelligent assistant to a Supreme Court Justice or a lonely man exposing himself to an undercover female police officer, John always challenges me to step into a character I've never played before, which is absolutely thrilling."
-Tim Bagley, actor (*ER, Southland, Shameless*)

"I wouldn't have a career if it weren't for John. John gave me my first job. I wasn't quite right for the role in my first audition according to the producers. But John saw something and he knew how to get it from me. His creativity, generosity, specificity and persistence I remember so clearly many years later. I am forever grateful!"
-Jane Levy, actor (*Shameless*)

"John Frank Levey rises in the pantheon of casting directors as truly one of a kind. His exceptional eye for extraordinary talent is like no other. I've always felt very lucky to have collaborated together with John.

You can have the greatest script, the greatest director, beautiful sets and gorgeous cinematography, but if you do not cast the *right* actors that fully embody the characters to tell your story, none of it will matter. John Frank Levey always gets it right!"
-Mimi Leder, Emmy-winning director and producer (*China Beach, ER, The West Wing, Shameless*)

———

"Two words come to mind when I think of John Frank Levey: life changer! When he believes in you, he fights for you and opens doors to change your life. That's what he did for me, and I'm forever grateful."
-Shanola Hampton, actor (*Shameless*)

Endnotes

3. The Breakthrough

1. Janice Arkatov, "The Siege of Troy Evans, Montana Storyteller and Ex-Con," *Los Angeles Times*, June 30, 1989, www.latimes.com/archives/la-xpm-1989-06-30-ca-3017-story.html.
2. Gerald Goodwin, "Opinion | Black and White in Vietnam," *New York Times*, July 18, 2017, www.nytimes.com/2017/07/18/opinion/racism-vietnam-war.html.

4. The Interlude

1. Brian Lowery, "Two Dozen out in WB Merger," *Variety*, Sept. 2, 1993, variety.com/1993/tv/news/two-dozen-out-in-wb-merger-110219/. Accessed 30 Dec. 2021.

6. The Star-Maker

1. "AmfAR, Thirty Years of HIV/AIDS: Snapshots of an Epidemic: The Foundation for AIDS Research: HIV / AIDS Research," *Amfar.org*, 2010, www.amfar.org/thirty-years-of-hiv/aids-snapshots-of-an-epidemic/.
2. David Marchese, "Amy Poehler Is into What Gen Z Is Selling." *New York Times*, February 22, 2021, www.nytimes.com/interactive/2021/02/22/magazine/amy-poehler-interview.html.
3. Anne Kelly-Saxenmeyer, "Official Guide to Actorfest 2004—Giving Actors Shots," *Backstage*, May 4, 2004, www.backstage.com/magazine/article/official-guide-actorfest-giving-actors-shots-35817/. Accessed 30 Dec. 2021.

7. The Media Darling

1. "0.17: Casting the Pilot (with John Levey)," *The West Wing Weekly*, November 12, 2019, thewestwingweekly.com/episodes/017 (accessed December 30, 2021).
2. Chris O'Falt, "Aaron Sorkin and Casting Director Francine Maisler," IndieWire 25, January 2021, https://www.indiewire.com/influencers/aaron-sorkin-francine-maisler/.

About the Author

John Frank Levey is a four-time Emmy Award-winning casting director. He has cast such iconic television shows as *China Beach*, *ER*, *The West Wing* and *Shameless*, as well as dozens of other television series, miniseries, TV movies, digital series, video games and feature films. Levey is also a five-time winner of the Casting Society of America's Artios Award and the recipient of its prestigious Hoyt Bowers Award, given for excellence in casting and outstanding contributions to the casting profession. *Right for the Role* is his first book.

After decades at Warner Bros., Levey became Vice President of Casting for John Wells Productions before launching his own casting company. Throughout his career, he has been a proud collaborator with many great writers, actors, producers and directors—he is most gratified for the friendships he's forged and the talent he has helped foster. Personally, Levey is most proud of his children, Oliver Leo and Joanna Claire.